W0254281

The Plight of the Stateless Rohingyas

The Plight of the Stateless Rohingyas

Responses of the State, Society & the International Community

Edited by
Imtiaz Ahmed

 The University Press Limited

The University Press Limited
Red Crescent House, Level 6
61 Motijheel C/A, Dhaka 1000, Bangladesh
Phone: (88 02) 9565441, 9565443, 9565444
e-mail: info@uplbooks.com.bd
Website: www.uplbooks.com.bd

Second impression, 2014
First published, 2010

Cover design by Masud Al Mamun
Cover photograph by Jim Worrall/UNHCR 2008

ISBN 978 984 506 015 8

Published by Mohiuddin Ahmed, The University Press Limited, Dhaka. Book design by Ashim K. Biswas, produced by Abarton and printed at the Akota Offset Press, 119 Fakirapool, Dhaka, Bangladesh.

Contents

List of Tables, Figure, Boxes and Maps

Tables

Figure

Boxes

Maps

Contributors

Imtiaz Ahmed, Professor of International Relations, University of Dhaka, Dhaka-1000, Bangladesh. Team Leader of the Project and Editor of the Book.

Delwar Hossain, Professor of International Relations, University of Dhaka, Dhaka-1000, Bangladesh. Consultant of the Project and contributing author of Chapters 2, 3, 4 and 5.

Shahab Enam Khan, Assistant Professor, Department of International Relations, Jahangirnagar University, Savar, Bangladesh. Consultant of the Project and contributing author of Chapters 6, 7 and 8.

Md. Faridul Alam, Assistant Professor, Department of International Relations, Chittagong University, Chittagong, Bangladesh. Consultant of the Project and contributing adjunct author of Chapters 5 and 7.

Acknowledgements

We are greatly indebted to all the government agencies, NGOs with experiences in public and private sectors, academics, civil society and private sector representatives who lent their time and knowledge to this study. This work could not have been accomplished without the splendid support and cooperation of Ms. Barbara Richardson, the former High Commissioner of Canada, Ms. Pia Prytz Phiri, the former Representative, United Nations High Commissioner for Refugees (UNHCR), Mr. Shabbir Ahmad Chowdhury, Director General (South East Asia & Counter Terrorism), Ministry of Foreign Affairs, GoB, Brigadier General A.T.M Amin, former Director, Counter-terrorism Bureau, DGFI, Dr Zafrullah Chowdhury, Chairman, Gonoshasthaya Kendra, Mr. Uttam Kumar Deb, IOM, Mr. Gulam Maula Khan, Director, Technical Assistance Inc. Mr. Arjun Jain, Senior Protection Officer, UNHCR, Bangladesh, Mr. Jim Warell, UNHCR Representative, Cox's Bazaar Office, and Ms. Marina Aksakalova, UNHCR Representative, Cox's Bazaar Office.

We duly acknowledge the contribution of the following research students from the University of Dhaka, Jahangirnagar University and Chittagong University in completing the work: Sheikh Shams Morsalin, Shama Jahan, Jolly Nur Haque, Mohd. Amirul Islam, Humayra Morsheda, Md. Abu Daud Biswas, Md. Hasnaine Aftab, A.S.M Tarek Hassan Semul, Md. Imtiaz Chowdhury, Meherunnesa, Ashraful Azad, Shaon Shyla, Md. Atiqur Rahman, S.M. Mobassherul Alam Chowdhury, Shagufta Mahjabin, Najmus Saqib, Md. Jannatul Habib, Sumaiya Nour, Muhammad Imtiaz Hassan, Kazi Lakiya Hassan, Md. Zafar Imam, Umme Nabilatus Sayema, Fatema Hossain Urmi, Fariha Jasmin, Rubab Ferdousi Siddiqua, Natasha Ishrat Kabir, Istiaque Alam Russel, and Raihan Akhtar Zarna.

We also deeply appreciate the support of Professor Amena Mohsin, University of Dhaka for her candid feedback and critical comments, which proved helpful in preparing this work. Invaluable assistance was provided by the Canadian International Development

Agency (CIDA), UNHCR, University of Dhaka, Jahangirnagar University, University of Chittagong, Bangladesh Riffles (BDR) and Arakan Historical Society, Chittagong. We also like to appreciate the contributions and support of Mahbubul Haque, Founder Trustee and Director, Neeti Gobeshona Kendro, Al-haj M.A. Kalam, President, Arakan Historical Society, Al-haj Rais Ahmed, Vice President, Arakan Historical Society, Al-haj MD. Ali, General Secretary, Arakan Historical Society, Al-haj MD. Amin, Treasurer, Arakan Historical Society, Mr. Mohammad Ali, Secretary, Arakan Historical Society, Mohd. Shahidul Islam, Programme Officer, Young Power in Social action (YPSA), Md. Mokhlasur Rahman, Project Manager, PHALS, supported by Handicap International, Bangladesh PRM Programme, Dr Mohd. Yunus, President of Arakan League for Justice and Freedom (ALJF), and Md. Shahjahan, Teacher, Cox's Bazar High School, Cox's Bazaar. Finally, we would also like to acknowledge the assistance given to the team by BDR Cox's Bazar range, Banoj Kumar Majumder, Superintendant of Police, Cox's Bazar, Major Atiq, DGFI, Teknaf area, Mr.Md. Jashim Uddin, OC, Teknaf Police Station and Members of the Cox's Bazaar Press Club, particularly in conducting the field activities of this study.

Preface

The year 2009 marks the 17th year for the Rohingya refugees in Bangladesh. Despite various initiatives for their repatriation, notably by the UNCHR, the problem has not been resolved. The Rohingya refugees continue to experience violence and coercion over the years which have inevitably fostered a climate of fear and distress among them. The issue of Rohingya refugee crisis has long been ignored in the development discourse in Bangladesh. The subject remains one of the least researched areas to the academic community both in Bangladesh and beyond. Critical research on this protracted refugee situation is necessary to assist the Government of Bangladesh and other stakeholders to resolve the crisis, and that again, effectively and efficiently.

This study, carried out under the auspices of *Centre for Alternatives* involving students and faculty members of three public universities—Dhaka, Chittagong and Jahangirnagar, has examined the experiences of two groups of refugees: those residing as *documented* refugees, individuals who had requested official asylum in Bangladesh and were subsequently granted refugee status, and the *undocumented* refugees, individuals who are not entitled to the services of Bangladesh government or the UNHCR. As such, this study provides a comprehensive overview of refugee experience in Bangladesh. It may be noted that there is a lack of credible data on the exact number of undocumented refugees residing in Bangladesh.

In tracing the plight of the Rohingya refugees, the study shows that the Rohingya refugee problem was created in the course of several historical trajectories. It has been demonstrated that the Rohingyas are both stateless and refugees. First, they became stateless in their homeland and then eventually they had to embrace the status of refugeehood under conditions of persecution, discrimination and torture. The Rohingya refugees in Bangladesh have continued to remain stateless amid their refugeehood. The causes to their refugeehood can be categorised as primary factors (as enumerated in the 1951 Convention), secondary factors (as identified in the 1969 OAU Convention) and auxiliary factors (such as economic, ecological and demographic change). The denial of citizenship rights, denial of freedom of movement, eviction campaigns, forced labour, expulsion from their lands and property, violence and physical torture contributed to the making of the Rohingyas stateless and refugees.

There are two critical points in understanding the Rohingya refugee problem. First, the causes and conditions of their refugeehood are becoming almost identical. The Rohingyas who fled to Bangladesh as a remedy to their sorrows and sufferings in Myanmar have been witnessing almost the same extent of miserable conditions of their life here. The Rohingyas are living in a state of impoverishment as refugees in camp and non-camp areas of Bangladesh. Second, the dynamics of current conditions of the Rohingyas are creating new questions about their identity. The narratives of the Rohingya refugees clearly demonstrate that they dream a future where hope is the driving force. A democratic Myanmar or resettlement in a third country preferably a developed one or living in Bangladesh marrying a Bangladeshi girl capture some of their dreams, but certainly not all. This can be regarded as the greatest force in their lives. However, it does not mask their traumas they experienced in Myanmar and subsequently in the refugee camps in Bangladesh. Trauma and their traumatic memories will continue to influence their lives and shape their identity.

As borne out in this research, refugees face multi-pronged psycho-social and human security threats. Four major dimensions of security have been identified in this study—politico-military, economic, social and environmental. While primary responsibility for refugee security clearly rests with the host government, it has been repeatedly stressed that the problem of security should be an issue for which a multiplicity of actors share responsibility - refugees themselves, local populations, country of origin, host country, donor states, regional organisations, the UNHCR and its operational partners. The refugees interviewed expressed their deep concern regarding the treatment they receive in the camps and in their country of origin. The research notes that the quality of services to the Rohingya refugees in the areas of housing, food, health, education, legal aid and skill development needs to be improved. Addressing these issues is a complex task, and the government cannot do it on its own.

This study has identified that the relationship between internal security of Bangladesh and the life and living of the refugees is a complex subject and needs further probing. On the one hand, the refugees are the victims of insecurity, and on the other, they are often involved in criminal activities. It has been observed during this research that the refugees are often politically used for electoral motives, engaged in criminal activities, and manipulated by ideological extremist groups and insurgent groups from the Northeastern regions of India and Myanmar. Due to physical resemblances between Rohingyas and Bengalis, and influx of unmanageable size of Rohingya refugee population into Bangladesh, it has become virtually impossible to distinguish between the legitimate and illicit political dissents.

While coming to the question of response of the Bangladesh state, the study observes that generally the Rohingya refugees are portrayed as a burden to Bangladesh. The GOB often argues that there has been no tangible benefit from hosting them, only a drain of its limited resources. Despite this general perception, over the years the GOB has been involved in short-term and long term measures to address this problem. Apart from the management of the two refugee camps located in Cox's Bazar, Bangladesh has been active in bilateral and multilateral processes. Bangladesh has been closely working with Myanmar and the international community for its permanent and durable solution. Bangladesh shows strong support for multilateral initiatives in resolving the Rohingya refugee problem on the long term basis. Bangladesh faces an acute economic challenge disproportionate to its resources for hosting a large number of undocumented refugees. However, to provide a framework to address repatriation and to lessen the influx of refugees, such as those mentioned in this study, the Government of Bangladesh should adopt a national policy or strategy on refugees. Besides, government has no effective mechanism to identify a refugee, monitor and provide services to the refugees coming from Myanmar. Moreover, government lacks concrete policy to provide strategic guidance to various stakeholders dealing with the refugee issue. Therefore, adoption of such policy will enhance the government's ability in mitigating the problem and strengthen inter-agency coordination, collaboration and cooperation in this regard.

The study argues that CSOs could be an important actor in finding solutions for the Rohingya refugees and in contributing to peaceful and safe repatriation of the refugees. However, civil society does not act in a vacuum. In particular, the role of government in encouraging and providing security to the civil society actors is essential. Working with refugees during their migration can enable them to play important roles in the bilateral relations between Bangladesh and Myanmar. It is important to recognise that due to absence of a democratic government in Myanmar, any civil society response from Myanmar may not be possible. The CSOs, along with the international community and National Human Rights Commission in Bangladesh should undertake a formal role to monitor the protection of the human rights of the refugees. This would allow a structured platform, apart from governmental initiatives, to provide solutions to the difficulties faced by the refugees to either return to their country of origin or in settling to a third country. This would pave the ways for bilateral negotiations and will contribute to the peaceful repatriation process.

The study observes that the response of international community to the Rohingya refugee issue is positive and proactive. The support from the IC is reflected in three areas—humanitarian assistance, diplomatic pressure and resettlement programme. While the humanitarian assistance in the form of financial and technical support is contributing to the survival of the Rohingyas in the refugee camps, the diplomatic support remains vital for its long term solution. The resettlement programme which is most liked by the Rohingyas is also contributing to mitigate their sufferings in the refugee camps. Among the actors in international community, the UNHCR is playing the key role in addressing this problem. The major challenge for the international community is the large number of unregistered Rohingya refugees in Bangladesh who cannot live in the camps. Besides, there has been rising number of Rohingyas who cross the Bangladesh-Myanmar border every day. Critics also argue that humanitarian support will not bring an end to the Rohingya refugee problem. It is evident from the field visits that most of the Rohingya refugees are unwilling to go back to their own country. On the other hand, the allure of resettlement in the third countries mainly in the developed world has created tensions and instability in the camps. The Rohingyas are often cheated by the false information regarding resettlement. The bottom line is that the international community has a lot to do regarding the Rohingya refugee problem.

Finally, it is important to materialise a collaborative effort between the government and civil society to contain the social and economic impact of protracted refugee situation. The international community needs to approach the refugee issue in the context of broader development agenda. The commitment of all stakeholders, including the government, humanitarian agencies, local communities and donors, is required. Cooperative and combined effort can assist in alleviating problems and assist refugees to participate to the fullest extent possible in their life in Bangladesh and following their return in Myanmar.

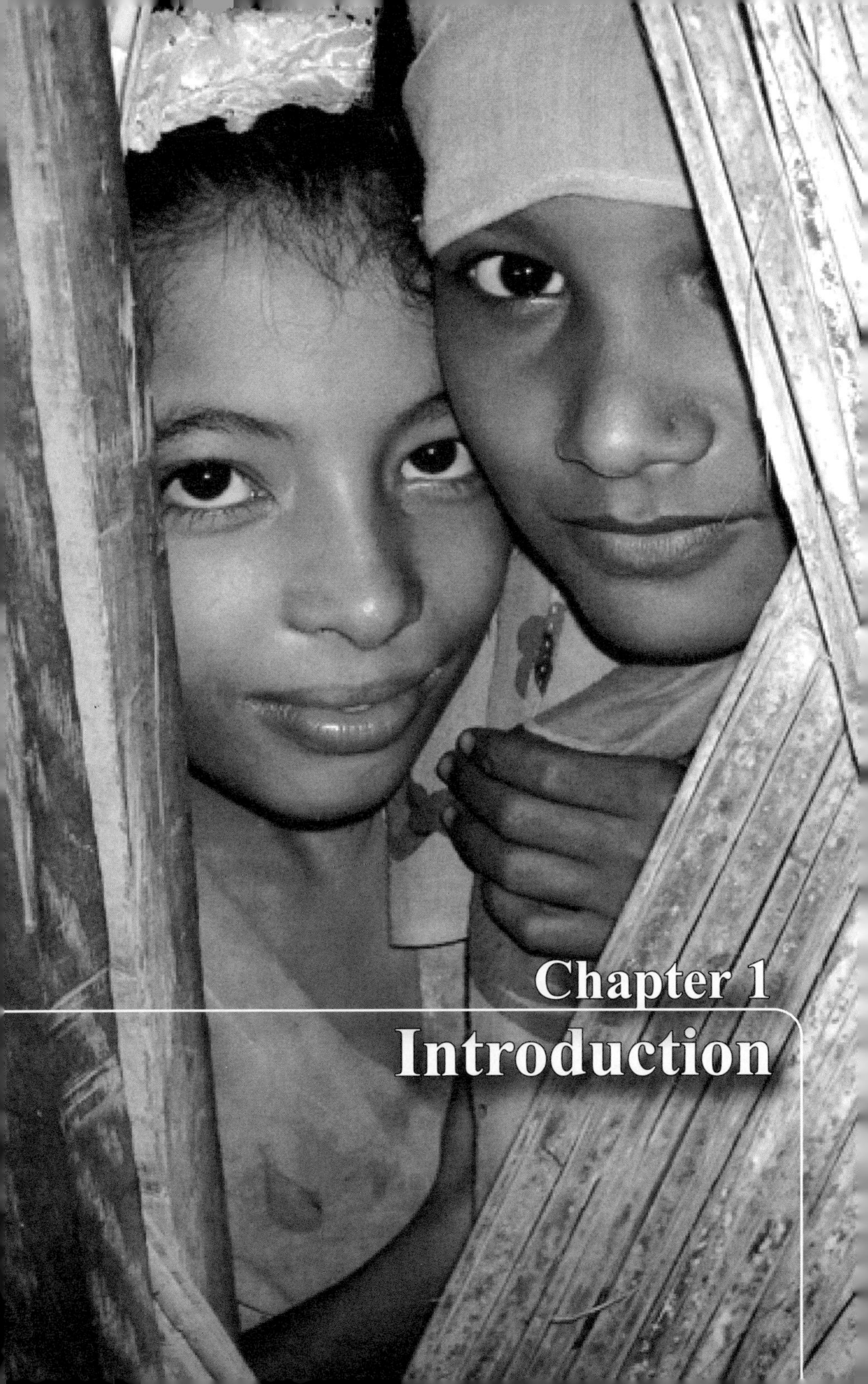

Chapter 1
Introduction

Photograph by Jolly Nur Haque/IR/DU 2008

Bangladesh is one of the major countries facing the problems of refugees, migration and displacement. The emergence of Bangladesh as an independent country bears testimony of critical significance of refugee issues and concerns. Besides, the uneven project of development and nation-building has exposed the people of this country to different forms of migration and displacement. In the early 1990s Bangladesh witnessed a wave of a quarter of a million who fled to Bangladesh due to brutal persecution by the Myanmar authorities. A series of global and national efforts were made to resolve the Rohingya refugee crisis in Bangladesh. Nevertheless, these initiatives have not been able to resolve the problem entirely.

Today Bangladesh hosts 27,150[1] officially documented Rohingya refugees in the two camps of Kutupalong and Nayapara in its southern Cox's Bazaar district. Although all the officially registered Rohingyas were taken back by the government of Myanmar except 27,150, it is known to all that still more than 200,000 Rohingyas are living outside the official camps and staying here and there around the country. Local people claim that almost all the repatriated Rohingyas later came back and started living in and around Chittagong. Some estimates suggest that there are about 300,000 nationals of Myanmar outside the official camps who are illegally staying mostly in areas of Cox's Bazaar, Bandarban, Chittagong and Dhaka city. However, accurate statistics for undocumented refugees living in Bangladesh do not exist.

The Rohingya refugee problem is a long standing issue in Bangladesh. More than a decade and a half has passed and yet there is

1 Based on UNHCR, *UNHCR Global Appeal 2008-2009*, p. 229. http://www.unhcr.org/home/PUBL/474ac8da11.pdf

no solution. It has multi-dimensional negative effects on the host country starting from the economy to security concerns. One of the critical dimensions of this problem is that over the years it has remained an isolated and a local issue in Bangladesh which can be considered a major reason behind its persistence. Against this backdrop it can be argued that the Rohingya refugees issue remains a major challenge for Bangladesh in terms of economy, security and international relations. This study has critically examined key issues and concerns behind the continuing problem of hosting the Rohingya refugees.

The principle aim of this study, however, is to generate fresh thoughts and ideas on different aspects of this problem. For the purpose of this study, a refugee would mean, *'a person who flees to a foreign country or power to escape danger or persecution owing to a well-founded fear of being persecuted for reasons of race, religion, nationality, membership of a particular social group, or political opinion, is outside the country of their nationality, and is unable to or, owing to such fear, is unwilling to avail him/herself of the protection of that country'.*[2]

It may be noted that the word 'Rohingya' is not officially recognised in Myanmar. Imtiaz Ahmed identified two theories for such denial of the state. One theory suggests that the Rohingyas are descendents of Moorish, Arab and Persian traders, including Moghul, Turk, Pathan and Bengali soldiers cum migrants, who arrived between the 9th and 15th centuries, married local women, and settled in the region. Rohingyas are therefore a mixed group of people with many ethnic and racial connections.[3]

The second theory suggests that the Muslim population of the Rakhine State is mostly Bengali migrants from the erstwhile East Pakistan and now Bangladesh, with some Indians coming during the British period. This reason is further premised on the fact that since most of them speak Bengali with a strong 'Chittagonian dialect', they cannot but be illegal immigrants from Bangladesh. The government of

---

[2] Convention relating to the Status of Refugees, adopted on 28 July 1951 by the United Nations Conference of Plenipotentiaries on the Status of Refugees and Stateless Persons convened under General Assembly resolution 429 (V) of 14 December 1950.

[3] Ahmed, Imtiaz. 2002. 'State and Statelessness in South Asia: Reaping Benefits from a Reconstructed Discourse on State and Nationality'. *Theoretical Perspectives*. Vol. 9 and 10. 2002-2003. Pp. 3 -4. See also, Razzaq, Abdur and Haque, Mahfuzul. 1995. *A Tale of Refugees: Rohingyas in Bangladesh*. Dhaka: Centre for Human Rights. See also, Muang, Shwe Lu. 1989. *Burma: Nationalism and Ideology*. Dhaka: UPL.

Myanmar, including the majority of Burman-Buddhist population of the country believes this to be the case.[4]

With the possible exception of the pre-military days of early 1960s, the government of Myanmar at every stage of governance and national development has systematically denied providing the Rohingyas any kind of recognition, including the right to acquire citizenship. It may be mentioned that at one point of post-independent history of Myanmar, the Rohingyas claim of separate ethnic identity was *recognised* by the government of Premier U Nu (1948-1958). The chapters in this study have highlighted that the current regime in Myanmar would not give in and change the nationality or citizenship laws in favour of the Rohingyas without collective effort from international community. In fact, with the possible exception of some exile groups, none of the recognised ethnic groups in Myanmar have supported the cause of the Rohingyas. Even Aung San Suu Kyi is surprisingly silent on this issue.[5]

Therefore, considering the above background, this study strives to find a balance between being prescriptive enough to ensure change will occur and allow enough flexibility to enable the stakeholders to formulate a comprehensive strategy and action plan in the ways that the latter feel best to meet local need and resource availability and fit those within local structures. The study has also attempted to identify the needs and gaps within services for the Rohingya refugees which are provided by various stakeholders, i.e. governments of Bangladesh and Myanmar, international donors, civil society organisations, NGOs, INGOs, private sector and media. In this context, the study proposes a set of recommendations which has been formulated after thoroughly investigating the magnitude of the problem and analysing the sufferings and plights of the Rohingya refugees.

In line with the aforementioned perspectives, the study is organised into eight chapters. Chapter 2 traces the historical origins of the Rohingya refugee migration in Bangladesh. This chapter introduces the notion that the patterns of refugee migration are a product of interrelationship among the oppressive regimes in Myanmar, crisis in identity—ethnic, political and religious, and lack of attention from the international community. This chapter also raises two timely questions. First, what is the identity of the second generation of refugees

4 Ibid.

5 Ibid.

in Bangladesh? Second, can states realistically and successfully respond to the challenges posed by the Rohingya refugees? The chapter concludes by exploring the root causes of refugee migration and analysing the making of *statelessness* through different periods of Burmese history—pre-colonial, colonial and post-colonial.

Chapter 3 portrays the psychosocial dimensions of the refugees and their perception of identity and reality. This chapter provides a framework for examining, from different perspectives, the issues associated with the reality and experience of being a refugee. Therefore, the main emphasis has been to understand the psychosocial dimensions of refugeehood.

Chapter 4 considers the security dynamics of the refugee problem in Bangladesh. The chapter argues that there is a close and critical link between the Rohingya refugees issue and security of Bangladesh. It becomes more apparent if security is understood from a holistic sense by including four major dimensions of security—politico-military, economic, social and environmental. The relationships between security, internal or external, and the refugees are a complex subject to comprehend. On one hand, the refugees are victims of insecurity, and on the other, they are often involved in criminal activities. The security dynamics become more critical when inter-state relations between Bangladesh and Myanmar are considered.

Chapter 5 critically examines the role of Bangladesh in settling the refugee issue. Initiatives and responsibilities assumed by the state agencies has been discussed which systematically identifies the principle achievements and remaining impediments in resolving the Rohingya refugee issue between Bangladesh and Myanmar. It has been argued that the government of Bangladesh should carry out proactive multilateral diplomacy and the refugee issue should be seen from a broader development approach. The chapter identified that Bangladesh government has undertaken lenient and persevering outlook to resolve the Rohingya refugee issue while the government of Myanmar gives mixed signal about their seriousness regarding repatriation of the Rohingya refugees. There is a need for active involvement of international donor community and civil society organisations in advancing the initiatives of the government of Bangladesh.

Chapter 6 highlights the accomplishments and derelictions of international agencies and donor community in improving the livelihood of the refugees. In order to strengthen the role of international community, international and regional level donor conferences could be organised. In such platforms possible means and ways to resolve the Rohingya refugee crisis could be discussed. The chapter highlights that international community, in particular, may consider providing more funds for reconstruction of accommodation and educational infrastructure, strengthen health services, and efforts to develop skilled labours. While some international donors are helping in these areas, the funding is still too low and the donor community in general has not stepped up to the plate. Finally, the chapter stressed that all the stakeholders involved in the refugee regime should broaden their support to include the refugees who are without documentation and living outside the refugee camps.

Chapter 7 focuses on the involvement of non-state actors including civil society, NGOs and media in shaping the Rohingya refugee discourse. It could be argued that for peaceful and meaningful settlement of the refugee issue civil society organisations (CSOs) could actively participate. In Bangladesh, despite a vibrant and dynamic civil society, its role in the Rohingya refugee discourse has tended to remain confined within offering urban-based pedantical supports while some national and international NGOs are offering operational assistance. Advocacy on formulating refugee or migration policies has been limited, particularly when compared to other fields such as environment or human rights where the civil society has had a significant impact on policy development. Such dichotomy between cognition and activities has been critically reviewed in this chapter.

Finally, Chapter 8 concludes with the issue of what is to be done. It proposes a list of recommendations for the stakeholders involved in the refugee discourse. To this end, timescales in implementing the recommendations have not been specified; instead the level of involvement has been stated. This chapter recommends practical and tangible issues to deal with the persistent problems to eventually facilitate and create favourable conditions for return. It has been observed that the repatriation of the Rohingya refugees is a complex undertaking that places an enormous burden on Bangladesh and state institutions, the UN and other entities involved. Successful repatriation of the refugee population and protection of their rights in Bangladesh largely depends on the Government of Bangladesh, active involvements of the international community, support from the civil society organisations and political consensus.

Stories collected from the documented and undocumented Rohingya refugees have been annexed in this study. As the stories will attest, the exodus of refugees from Myanmar springs from varied circumstances. The stories are the narratives of continued plight of displacement and psychological traumas suffered by the Rohingya refugees. The stories also identify the principle impediments to their return.

Whatever the nature of refugee influx, debates over hosting the refugees or to push them back inevitably needs to be discussed in public. There is a need to generate popular consensus to accommodate multiple perspectives and contexts in resolving the refugee issue. This study indicates that the refugee issue needs to be brought into the centre of development discourse in Bangladesh. Burden of hosting refugees has pressing impact on society and economy of Chittagong Hill Tracts region, and on sustainable development of overall Bangladesh. Lack of attention from the policy makers, gap between programs for documented and undocumented refugees and lack of donor assistance is the central hurdle in the way of both sustainable repatriation and promotion of third country resettlement. In this study a blend between economics, security, politics and policy has been created. This would allow one to explore the refugee dynamics from the perspective of the multiple actors that are especially central to the rehabilitation and repatriation process.

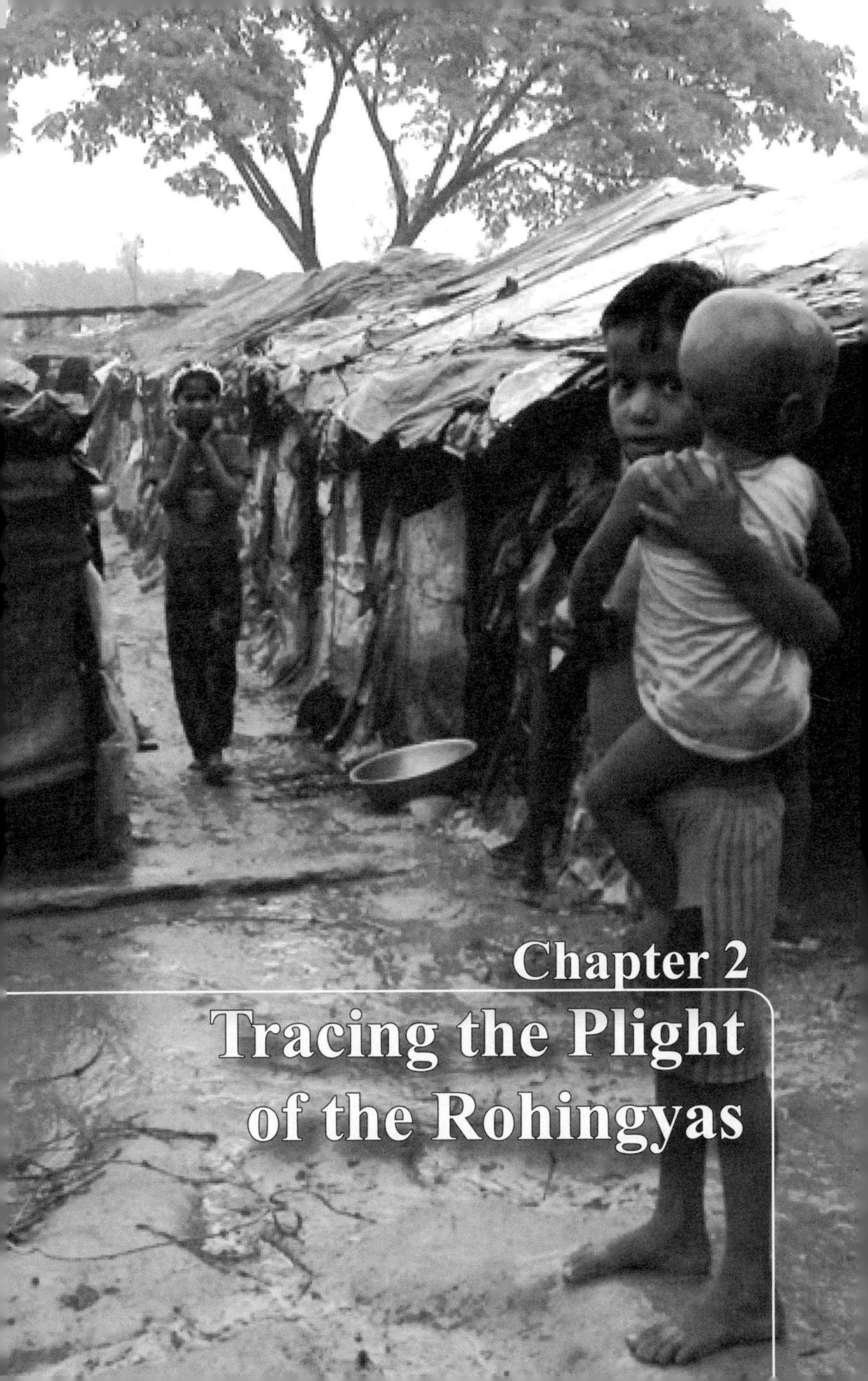

Chapter 2
Tracing the Plight of the Rohingyas

Photograph by Md. Faridul Alam/IR/CU 2008

The Rohingya refugees problem is a major issue directly affecting Bangladesh, Myanmar and the Rohingya people. The problem of the Rohingya refugees was triggered by the fact that according to the Myanmar (Burma) military government, the Rohingyas were only Bengalis and they did not deserve to be Burmese citizens. The government prefers to call them 'residents of Rakhine state'. The military regime even refuses to call them 'residents of Myanmar' in order to deny them the right to live anywhere in the country. It may be mentioned that Muslims make up 76 percent of the population of northern Rakhine state. In June 1978 a total of 167,000 Rohingya refugees entered Bangladesh; since then it is known as a refugee-receiving nation, indeed, for the first time in its short history as an independent state.[1] Some regard the Rohingyas as one of the world's most persecuted people while others believe that they are one of the most forgotten in the world. Medicine Sans Frontiers (MSF), which was involved in providing humanitarian assistances to the Rohingya refugees in Bangladesh, describes them as "one of the ten world's population in danger of extinction."[2] Facing severe human rights abuses and massive ill treatments by the military junta, the Rohingyas have become one of the most persecuted communities of Burma. Historically speaking, the Rohingya people have been driven out of Arakan in large numbers on four major occasions: 1784, 1942, 1978, and 1992.

1 Bhumitra Chakma, "Bangladesh State and the Refugee Phenomenon," http://www.safhr.org/refugee_watch18_4.htm accessed on 12 June 2008.

2 Haque, Mahbubul, *Ethnic Conflict in Burma and Rohingya Issue*, Paper presented in Seminar organised by Neeti Gobeshona Kendro, 2008.

Today over a million people, approximately 200,000 live in Bangladesh, 20,000 in Malaysia and about 700,000 in different Arab countries and smaller numbers in Western countries and Japan. There are still another one and a half million Rohingyas living in Arakan under serious hardship and repression.[3] The Rohingya refugees issue has been increasingly globalised through the involvement of several state and non-state actors. Besides, the dispersion of the Rohingyas to different countries of the world brings about a new dimension to this problem. In this context, identification of the Rohingyas as "Asia's new Palestinians" deserves much significance.[4] Imtiaz Ahmed rightly captures the underlying issues behind the Rohingya refugee problem as he argues that the problem is a demonstration of protracted statelessness as well as protracted refugeehood.[5] However, in order to understand the Rohingya refugee problem there is a need to focus on its historical context, the root causes behind the exodus of the Rohingyas. Here three key areas have been identified. The first section examines the historical process of how the Rohingya people became stateless in their own state. The second section identifies how the Rohingya people became 'refugees' from their 'stateless' condition. Finally, how the Rohingya people are surviving as refugees in Bangladesh in various camps and non-camp areas has been explored.

2.1 THE BIRTH OF THE STATELESS ROHINGYAS

The reproduction of statelessness of the Rohingyas is a defining feature of the Rohingya community which shows their state of alienation from the rest of the society.[6] Looking back at history, it is clear that in the aftermath of the Burma's War of Independence from the British colonial rule in 1942-1948, ethnic minorities of Burma were being repressed and harassed and from that time the relations between

3 Abid Bahar, "Rohingya Nation: Contemporary Problems and Making Certain of the Uncertain Future," http://www.kaladanpress.org//index.php?option=com_content&task=view&id=1468&Itemid=27 accessed on 12 August 2008.

4 Cited in Imtiaz Ahmed, "Globalization, Low-Intensity Conflict and Protracted Statelessness/ Refugee hood: The Plight of the Rohingyas," Available Online. http://programs.ssrc.org/ gsc/publications/quarterly13/ahmed.pdf, accessed on 26th July, 2008.

5 Ibid.

6 Imtiaz Ahmed deals with this issue extensively in his paper titled "Bangladesh-Myanmar Relations: The Stateless Rohingyas," available online. http://www.burmalibrary.org/docs/ Imtiaz-Ahmed.html accessed on 15 September 2008.

the Muslims and the Buddhists of Arakan began to deteriorate. The military regime of Burma labelled Muslims as residence foreigners and effectively reduced them to the status of stateless. However, prior to that, the Rakhines and the Rohingyas lived in harmony.[7] Historically, three phases of the birth of the stateless Rohingyas can be identified—pre-colonial, colonial and post-colonial.

2.1.1 Pre-colonial Era

The Rohingyas have been living in Arakan[8] (now East Rakhine) for about thousand years. They have their own language, culture, and heritage. Prior to its becoming part of Myanmar in 1785, Arakan had been an independent Kingdom for 2000 years. For the first few hundred years, Arakan was divided into two Kingdoms, South Arakan of Sandoway and North Arakan of Arakan proper. The two parts were united into one in the last part of the 13th century and this status of Arakan lasted till 1785 A.D when the Kingdom was merged with Burma (Myanmar).[9] In the fifteenth century they had established a great Arakanese Empire known as Maruk-U Empire. At that time, Mrohaung was the capital city of Arakan for about 400 hundred years. In 1784, Burmese King Badaw Paya invaded and annexed Arakan. Then Arakan was annexed to the British India in 1825 after the First Anglo-Burmese war.

The pre-colonial phase of the history of the Rohingyas is marked by the infiltration of the Muslims in Arakan. The first Muslim infiltration into Arakan took place during the reign of Mahatoing Tsandaya (788-810 AD), when several Arab ships wrecked off the coast of Rambi (Rambee) Island. The Muslim sailors somehow escaped and started to live in Rambi Island of Arakan by taking permission of the King.[10] They are called *kulas* or foreigners in the Arakanese history. The

---

7 Jarlath D'Souza, *Rohingyas: A Case for Human Rights Violation* (Dhaka: SHETU, October, 1992) pp. 14-29.

8 According to the 1997 statistical yearbook, published by the Government of Myanmar, the 'Official' population of the Arakan or Rakhaine State, where most Rohingyas reside, numbered around 2.6 million. See, for details, Imtiaz Ahmed, "Globalization, Low Intensity Conflcit and Protracted Statelessness/Refugeehood: The Plight of the Rohingyas," in John Tirman, ed. *The Maze of Fear,* New York: The Newpress, 2004, p. 183. See also the map of Arakan in appendix 2.1.

9 Karim, Abdul, *The Rohingyas: A Short Account of their History and Culture,* Arakan Historical Society, 2000, p.1.

10 Siddiqui, Md. Muhibullah, *Arakaner Musalman,* (Chittagong: Arakan Historical Society, undated) p. 252.

Second Muslim infiltration into Arakan took place in the fifteenth country. This century is very important for the history of Arakan, because most of the Muslims who entered Arakan during this time were the Bengalis and these Bengalis went there by invitation of the ruling princes for a political cause. In 1406 the Arakanese King Min-Saw-Mun attacked some areas of Burma but failed. When the Burmese King expelled Min-Saw-Man from his Kingdom, the latter came to Gaure, the capital of Bengal and took asylum in the Kingdom of Sultan Gias Uddin Azam Shah.

The third infiltration of Muslims from Bengal into Arakan took place in the middle of the 17th century. There is evidence of the presence of Bengali Muslim poets and authors in this period. Bengali poets like Daulat Kazi, Alaol, and Magon Thagore created the Golden era of Bengali culture and literature in Rosang.[11] The last Muslim infiltration into Arakan took place in 1660, when the Mughal Emperor Shah Shuza took shelter in Arakan although he was later murdered along with his family by the order of the King of Arakan.[12]

After the conquest of Arakan, the Rakhines began to call the subjugated people of the newly conquered Arakan comprised of Hindus and Muslims as the 'kulas' meaning the dark skinned aboriginals. Even today Moghs call the Rohingyas as 'kulas'. After the fall of the Hindu Chandras, chaos continued for a while. As in India where due to the Aryan invasion from the north, the racially dark skinned Dravadian population moved to the south, the same happened to the Rohingyas. But in Arakan, Mongolian invasion from the south led Rohingyas to migrate towards the north to what is known today as 'Northern Arakan'. The dark skinned aboriginal Hindu Chandras and Muslims began to flee toward north and the Moghs remained largely in the south, joined by the invaders from Burma. Thus started the history of Arakan with two people—the Rakhines and the Rohingyas. The Arakan history shows that the Rakhines and the Rohingyas lived in peace for centuries.

2.1.2 Colonial Era

The pre-colonial peace and harmony between the Rakhines and the Rohingyas in Arakan turned into ethnic hatred and suppression in the

11 Karim, Abdul, op. cit., p.35.

12 Karim, Abdul, ibid., p.40.

colonial era. In 1784, Burmese King Badow Paya invaded and annexed Arakan. Badaw Paya was not a successful ruler, although he ruled the country for about 40 years. In fact, his period was marked by anarchy and degeneration of the Arakanese.[13] The Burmese rule came to an end when Arakan was annexed by the British in 1825 after the First Anglo-Burmese War. The relation between Rohingyas and Rakhines began to grow bitter at the instigation of the third party, the British colonialists, followed by the Burmese. During the Second World War Japan occupied Burma and British troops withdrew from Arakan, which created a serious administrative vacuum. The Rakhine communalist in connivance with Burma Independence Army (BIA) killed 100,000 Rohingyas and drove out 50,000 across the border to East Bengal in order to depopulate the area of Muslims.[14] Relations between the two communities deteriorated. Rohingyas were kept away from all negotiations with the British during independence of Burma in 1948. Aung San and leaders of other nationalities signed the historic Union Treaty on 12 February, 1947, by which the Union of Burma was formed consisting of individual nation state with the right to secede after ten years if the nationality so wished.[15] The agreement was adopted and included in the Union's constitution under the heading 'Right of Secession'. No Rohingya representative from Arakan was invited to attend the convention. The Rohingyas had been left out of the Union treaty; they had no constitutional guarantee of their rights and freedom from the independence of Burma. During this time, it appears that Rohingyas are victims of Burmese extremist nationalism based on race and religion, and the rise of Buddhist fundamentalist extremism during 1940 and 1947 in Arakan.

2.1.3 Post-colonial Era

The post-colonial history of the Rohingyas started with a political tragedy in Burma. In July 1947, Aung San and six cabinet ministers were assassinated in Rangoon and U Nu became the new leader and Chief of the cabinet. This new government ruled the country for nearly ten years. As the Rohingya Muslims were not recognised as a separate

---

13 Razzak, Abdur & Haque Mahfuzul, *A Tale of Refugees: Rohingyas in Bangladesh*, The Centre for Human Rights, Dhaka, 1995. pp.15-18.

14 Ibid.

15 Ibid, p.20.

group which not only devoid them of identity but also made them stateless, the movement for a separate Muslim State in Burma became a reality. Some Rohingyas took up arms to establish their rights. Later on, on the pretext of granting them political rights and giving them similar treatment along with other nationalities, they were persuaded to lay down their arms.[16] In reality, the Rohingyas came under a systematic process of oppression by the military regime of General Ne Win.

Since 1962 Burmese Army General Ne Win ruled the country until 1988. He and his Revolutionary Council and Burma Socialist Program Party made it a policy to suppress and oust the Rohingya Muslims out of the country by banning all Rohingya socio-cultural organisation and activity. Burmese Army General Ne Win's rule from 1962 to 1988 was a reign of great misery and terror for the Rohingya Muslims of Arakan. During Ne Win's regime, Burmese Authorities undertook different tactics to oppress the Rohingyas. In 1978 the 'Dragon Operation' launched by General Ne Win forced at least 300,000 Rohingyas to enter into Bangladesh causing tremendous political and economic problems on her.[17] Most of the Rohingyas went back to Myanmar in 1979 under an agreement between the two countries.

In 1982 the Government of General Ne Win declared Rohingyas as stateless people through promulgation of an Act, the 1982 Burma Citizenship Law.[18] Ironically, the whole Rohingya community of Burma was denied their nationality and was systematically deprived of their rights to citizenship and effectively reduced to the status of statelessness by this act. The new citizenship law is a very complex and highly restricted one. It was promulgated after the Rohingya refugees return from 1978 exodus to Bangladesh. It may be argued that this discriminatory law was specially designed to exclude the Rohingyas from acquiring the legal citizenship of Burma. In fact, there are certain sections in that law directly prohibit the Rohingyas to be eligible to apply for any kind of citizenship status of Burma.

According to this law there are three categories of citizenship status: (1) full citizenship, (2) associated citizenship, and (3) naturalised

16 Maung Shew Lu, *Burma (Nationalism and Ideology): An Analysis of Society Culture and Politics*, University Press Limited, p.21.

17 *Myanmar Refugees in Bangladesh*, 23rd April, 2001.

18 Ibid.

citizenship. A person is issued colour coded citizenship security card in consistent with his/her citizenship status: Pink, Blue, and Green respectively. A large number of Rohingyas do not fall under any of these three categories of citizenship status. They are not eligible to have Burmese nationality because of Section (2) and Section (3) of the 1982 Burma Citizenship Law.[19] To prepare the voter list for 1989 general elections, the authority initiated scrutiny through issuing the National Registration Certificate (NRC) and Foreigner's Registration Certificate (FRC) in Rakhaine state. The Rohingya Muslims were then put through harassment as the Myanmar immigration authorities insisted on categorising the Muslim inhabitants as 'Bengali Burmese'.[20] The immigration authorities refused to accept the citizenship application from the Muslim population which resulted in the exclusion of a large number of Rohingya Muslims from the voter list.[21]

The State Law and Order Restoration Council (SLORC) after the 1988 military take over decided to set up a number of new military cantonments in Rakhaine State, particularly in the North, where the Muslims were a majority. The authorities took the lands belonging to the Muslims without any compensation; rather they were told to be rehabilitated in unsuitable mountainous region. The Muslims saw themselves becoming homeless from their stateless conditions. The SLORC started to build cantonments and roads and forced the local inhabitants to work in the construction project with little or no wages at all. After occupation of the Muslim lands the SLORC gave surplus lands to Rakhine convicts and retired Army personnel on attractive terms, an attempt to change the ethno-demographic pattern of the area.[22] The Myanmar military authorities have destroyed many Muslim places of worship, looted their properties, killed the inhabitants and raped their women.

---

19 Section (2) of the 1982 Burma citizenship law has defined a national. "National" mean persons belonging to the Burmese race such as Kachine, Karen. Kayah, Chin, Mon, Rakhine, Shan of the state and persons belonging to such racial groups who have settled in any territories now included within the state as their permanent home from a period anterior to 1824 AD. The Rohingyas do not belong to any ethnic race as described by the Section (2).

20 Razzak, Abdur, op.cit., p.20.

21 Ibid.

22 Ibid.

2.2 THE BIRTH OF THE ROHINGYA REFUGEES

The Rohingya people witnessed a painful transformation of their status from 'statelessness' to 'refugeehood' in modern times. As the idea of refugee was not prevalent earlier, the Rohingyas simply took shelter in different places mainly in Bangladesh. A systematic oppression and annihilation began through ethnic cleansing of the Rohingyas community. Terrified by the eviction campaigns and due to the uncertainty and insecurity regarding their life, property, honour and dignity, a large number Rohingya Muslims fled from their ancestral homes in Burma and took refuge in Bangladesh. The Rohingya majority areas of Burma are adjacent to the border with Bangladesh. That is why it offers them an easier escape route.[23] Arakan, separated from mainland Myanmar with mountains, thick forest, rivers and creeks, finds its northwest boundary Naaf river line with Bangladesh most convenient for communication with outside world. As indicated elsewhere, the emergence of the oppressive military regime in Burma immediately after the end of the Second World War had been the prime force behind creating an atmosphere of persecution leading to the exodus of the Rohingya people. Violence against civilians appears to be a fundamental component of the overall military strategy of the Myanmar army. US Committee for Refugees (USCR) states that, "the Myanmar military actions were the part of a deliberate campaign of terror aimed at driving the Rohingyas out of the country.[24] At this point one needs to ask what factors caused the massive influx of the Rohingya refugees? What are the objectives or hidden agenda of the military regimes to resort to oppression and torture against the Rohingyas?[25]

Critics like D' Souza and Shwe Lu Maung refer to military's 'racism' as the prime cause of the unrest among the Rohingyas.[26] As part of its 'National Reconsolidation' policy, the Burmese Government is fully committed to the project of Burmanisation, the assimilation into mainstream Burman culture of all the diverse ethnic cultures and

23 Wipperman, Tom and Haque, Mahbubul, *Between a Rock and Hard Place: The Rohingya of Bangladesh and Burma* (Dhaka: Neeti Gobeshona Kedro, October 2007) p. 6.

24 *Burma: Information on Situation of the Rohingyas,* (INS Resource Information Centre).

25 Brother Jarlath D'Souza, *Rohingyas: A Case for Human Rights Violation* (Dhaka: SHETU, October, 1992) pp. 14-29. See also, Shwe Lu Maung, *Burma: Nationalism and Ideology,* (Dhaka: UPL, 1989) p. 95.

26 D'Souza, 1992, op. cit. p. 24.

Table 2.1 Number of Rohingyas in Camp and Non-Camp Areas as of April 2008[27]

Serial	Name of Camp/Area	Number of Rohingyas				Remark
		1992	2000	2008		
				Legal	Illegal	
1.				13,575	13,632*	*accroding to official record it was 2,50,877 and 90% of these were repatriated
2.	Nayapara Camp			9,532	5,245†	†3000 unregistered, 1000 relieved from jail and rest was mistakenly excluded during registration
3.	Domdomia Camp			–	14,000	
4.	Illegal Rohingyas living in our Area of responsibility			–	77,085♠	♠Approximately
Total				23,107	1,09,962	

Source: ATM Amin, *"Security and the Rohingya Refugees"*, Paper presented in Methodology Workshop on 10-11 May 2008, Dhaka, organised by Centre for Alternatives.

peoples of Burma.[28] Jarlath also focuses on the religious dimension of oppression against the Rohingyas. Although Burma is known to be a secular country with no official state religion since independence, both civil and military rulers have associated the state with 'Theravada Buddhism'. Shwe Lu Maung suggests that the ideology of the Burmese Regime is the complex fusion of three cultures—military-religio culture, mythical and political—to which militarism is the backbone. The army builds the inner core[29] of the regime. At the same time, it follows the religio mythical culture including spiritual astrology, numerology and mystical fortune telling. All these are tied up to the mythology of Burmese-ness.[30]

D'Souza brings forth the issue of geo-economic importance of the Arakan. The coast belt of Arakan is rich with natural resources like petroleum, possible uranium, iron, and coal. The soil of Arakan is very fertile. There are a number of rivers in Arakan which are rich in fish. It

27 The estimate has gone up since then.

28 Cgris Lewa, 'IDP's In Burma' in C. R. Abrar and M P Lama, eds. *Displacement within Borders: The IDP's of Bangladesh and the Region* (Dhaka: RMMRU, 2003) pp. 169-175.

29 Shwe Lu Maung, *Burma: Nationalism and Ideology*, (Dhaka: UPL, 1989) p. 95.

30 Ibid, p. 102.

has a coastal water line of 300 miles long. Arakan is a place of military interest to the regime. It can be used as a buffer zone in case of any war or confrontation on South Asia.[31] However, the specific factors that have been the driving forces behind the exodus of the Rohingyas include: denial of citizenship rights, denial of religious freedom, denial of free movement, forced labour, forced relocation, arbitrary taxation, expulsion and other form of human rights abuses.[32]

The first and foremost cause behind the exodus of the Rohingyas is the denial of citizenship rights in their homeland. Nationality determines the ultimate relationship between the state and the individual because it is important for the protection of the basic human rights. Section (2) of the 1982 Burma citizenship law has defined a national as a person belonging to the Burmese race such as Kachine, Karen, Kayah, Chin, Mon, Rakhine, and Shan of the state and persons belonging to such racial groups who have settled in territories now included the state as their permanent home from a period anterior to 1824 AD. The Rohingyas do not belong to any ethnic race as described by Section (2). Through its 1982 Burma Citizenship Law, the State Peace and Development Council (SPDC) have recognised 135 national races of Burma and the Rohingyas are not one of them. They were identified and declared as the 'Resident Foreigners' of Burma by the SPDC. The SPDC does not accept the existence of the Rohingya as an ethnic group of Burma.

Box 2.1: Driving Forces behind the Rohingya Exodus
• Deprivation of citizenship
• Forced labour
• Forced eviction and relocation
• Deprivation of right to education
• Massive killing
• Sexual harassment
• Looting of properties
• Breaking mosques and
• Lack of religious freedom

31 Brother Jarlath D'Souza, *Rohingyas: A Case for Human Rights Violation* (Dhaka: SHETU, October, 1992) p. 24

32 Cgris Lewa, 'IDP's In Burma' in C. R. Abrar and M .P. Lama eds. *Displacement within Borders: The IDP's of Bangladesh and the Region* (Dhaka: RMMRU, 2003) pp. 169-175.

The whole process to secure citizenship is overburdened with complicated requirements and has practically denied the Rohingyas of their rights to be citizens. The question of granting citizenship and to decide whether any race is a national or not solely depends upon the council ministers.[33] Even the right that the associated and naturalised citizens may or may not enjoy are also determined by the Council of Ministers.[34] Besides, to acquire the Burmese citizenship for a new born baby, at least one parent of the baby must hold one of the three categories of the Burmese citizenship. So there are stateless children in Burma.[35] By denying their citizenship, the Burmese Government has deprived the Rohingyas from all of their national rights, prevented them from owning land and property title and left them vulnerable to forced labour and land grabbing and other forms of human rights abuses. It has also denied their rights to take recourse to the law.[36]

The second major cause that forced the Rohingyas to leave Burma is the lack of freedom of movement.[37] Myanmar is a country where travel and other restrictions are a part of common experience and the Rohingyas are suspected to be the most severely restricted group of Burma by the Amnesty International.[38] The GOM restricted the Rohingyas from travelling within Arakan as well as to the other parts of the country. They are not allowed anywhere beyond their village boundaries without getting permission from the local Peace and Development Council Chairman. They can obtain the necessary travel documents under restrictive regulations and pay official and non official fee (bribe) at various check points of the destination. The Rohingyas have to request the Village Peace and Development Council (VPDC) for a pass to move around their township. They have to apply to the Township Peace and Development (TPDC) to go beyond their township and to go outside their district they need to apply to the

33 Razzak, Abdur and Haque, Mahfuzul, '*A Tale of Refugees Rohingyas inBangladesh*' (Dhaka: The Centre for Human Rights, 1995) p. 30.

34 Ibid, p. 8.

35 Zaw Min Htut, 'Human Rights Abuses and Discrimination on Rohingyas', (Japan: BRAJ), p. 57.

36 Ibid, p. 55.

37 'The Role of UNHCR', Human Rights Watch, (available at http://www.hrw.org/reports, 2000/Malaysia/maybr008.htm).

38 Ibid, p. 12.

District Peace and Development Council (DPDC).[39] The pass needs the consent of the NaSaKa, IPD (Immigration Department), Military Intelligence, Police, Riot Police and Customs. All has to agree to the request and only after then the permit has to be purchased by the respective travellers. Restrictions on movement have not only limited their economic opportunities, it has also divided their social relationship. Many of the Rohingya families have been divided and separated. Unless they are allowed to visit, the members of the family cannot join their relatives working and living in a distance or outside the Arakan. The high restrictions on movement give Rohingyas the feeling of living life in a virtual concentration camp.[40]

Third, the Rohingyas have been victims of rape and sexual violence. The interviews with the documented and uncommented Rohingyas confirm that Rohingya women often fall victim to rape and sexual violence. In some cases Rohingya women have been raped by NaSaKa soldiers, and in other cases by Rakhine civilians. Fourth, the Rohingya people had been subjected to systematic eviction campaigns in Myanmar for decades. Some analysts term it as 'demographic engineering' and 'strategic hamleting'. The most brutal methods, strategic hamleting and removal of people by terror or economic sabotage are carried out by the Burmese army on the civilian population as part of their counter insurgency programme.[41] People were resettled in designated areas chosen by the government officials. People were evicted from urban areas to slums like ghettos. It has resulted in creating thousands of internally displaced persons (IDPs) in Myanmar. D'Souza estimates that there have been no less than twelve major 'operation' or eviction campaigns against the Rohingyas carried out between 1948-1984.[42]

Fifth, Myanmar was described as the 20th century model of slavery practice by an inquiry Commission Report of the ILO.[43] It is a country where forced labour is widely used. As the government thinks that it has the right to extract labour, it is an obligation of all persons in

39 Essentially controlled by the military.

40 Ibid, p. 111.

41 Lewa, op.cit., 2003, p. 170.

42 Jarlath D'Souza, "Rohingyas: A Case for Human Rights Violation", ShetuReport 1, 1992 edited by Philip Gain. Dhaka: Shetu, 1992.

43 Afk Jilani, '*Human Rights Violation in Arakan*', p.155.

Box 2.2: Forced Labour in Burmese History
The Military junta of Burma is practicing the primitive conscription of forced labor of some ancient Burmese kings. As they are the autocratic kings of Burma, Burmese king Bodaw, after conquering Arakan in 1784, forced 20,000 Rakhines to carry the huge booty from Arakan and the heavy Buddhist statue of Mahamayat Muni across the Arakan hills to Mandalay. Thousands died on the way due to fatigue and hunger. In the words of historian Harvey, "Quite apart from extortionate revenue, there were continued extractions of human cattle. Three thousands were called to work on the Meiktila Lake and none ever returned. 6,000 were dragged away serve against Chienmai in Thailand, where they died of diseases in numbers. When in 1797, more than 2,000 were required to work on the Mingun Pagoda; the people beat the war drum and rose wholesale.
Source: AFK Jilani, *Human Rights Violation*.

Myanmar to provide such labour.[44] Civilians of both sexes, of all ages and various fitness levels are forcibly and arbitrarily seized by local police and military units to provide such labour.[45] Even the children become the victims of forced labour. In his report, the UN Special Rapporteur Rajsoomer Lallah claimed that children as young as eight years old are used as unpaid forced labour to help build temples and pagodas. According to his report, forced labour is used as a part of the campaign to repress the ethnic minorities of the country. During forced labour, a large number of incidents of human rights violations occur including summary execution, rape, torture and ill treatment.[46] Reports of the Human Rights Watch say that those who refuse to work are tortured, which often leads to death.

According to the report of Amnesty International 2004, people are forced to maintain camps, build and repair roads, build the gas pipe line, work on plantations belonging to NaSaKa, provide firewood in the military camps, fetch water, bake bricks and perform sentry duties at night in their own village.[47] The use of forced labour badly impacts people's ability to sustain their livelihood activities. Most of the Rohingyas are unskilled labourers. A day without pay means a day

44 Syeda Rozana Rashid, *'A Comparative Study on Vulnerability and Coping Mechanism Between Rohingya Refugee and Chakma IDP Women'* (Dhaka: BFF, 2005), p. 39.

45 Ibid.

46 Ibid, p. 154.

47 Ibid, p. 13.

without food for the whole family. They have to build the houses of model villages, pagodas and monasteries, work on infrastructure projects and military camps free of charges. They also have to plough the land allotted to the new Rakhine settlers after grabbing the land from the Rohingya themselves.[48] Even if they are paid, the payment of their labour is very low from the usual market rate. In Arakan the non Rohingyas are not usually drafted into forced labour.[49] ILO and UN accused the government of Burma for the massive human rights violations during forced labour but the projects of various UN bodies like UNDP, UNHCR, WHO, UNICEF, WFP, FAO are carried out by the same forced labour.[50] Another major concern is the prison labour. The SPDC has established a number of large and small prison labour camps all over Arakan. The Rohingyas convicted for crimes or fabricated cases are taken to these forced labour camps where they are subjected to heavy and exhaustive works.

Fifth, the Rohingyas have been subject to expulsion and arbitrary confiscation of land and property. The Government of Myanmar (GOM) is the owner of all the lands of the country. Tenants may acquire land use rights which can be inherited by the children. The Rohingyas cannot own any land or property because only the full citizens are given the right to a title of land. Still some Rohingyas have been able to acquire tenancy of land over the years because of customary law that are practiced in most of the villages of Arakan.[51] A large portion of lands in the Rohingya villages were confiscated by the government. Many of the Rohingya families were uprooted and relocated to new areas from places they have been living for decades.

The rapid expansion of the Burmese Army has necessitated the building of new camps and facilities including the army food supplies as well as for commercial profit projects such as power generation hydroelectric plants or prawn farms etc. Hundreds of acres of land were confiscated for these purposes.[52] The affected villagers have never received any compensation for such confiscation. Confiscated lands were distributed to the government sponsored Buddhist settlers.

48 Ibid, p. 157.

49 Ibid, p. 13.

50 Ibid, p. 157.

51 Ibid.

52 Ibid.

Box 2.3: Model Villages
To implement its Human Barrier policy the government of Burma has taken a plan to establish 'Model Villages' to populate the Rohingya majority areas of Arakan by the Rakhaine and Buddhists people. Model villages have been established in the confiscated lands of the Rohingya communities. The government has replaced Rohingya Holy places, historical monuments and relics by building monasteries, pagodas and other Buddhist structures. Under the border area development program the junta has provided each of the habitant families of such model villages with providing 3 acres of Rohingya lands for cultivation, 0.2 acres of land for housing. They distributed each of the new settler families with kyat 40,000 as lump sum monetary help, Kg 40 per head free of cost per month, one pair of bullocks and one bullock cart. Each of such model villages has been provided fifteen 5 Hp Honda Tractors.
Source: AFK Jilani, *Human Rights Violation*.

The SPDC has a policy of relocating Burmans or Rakhine families into new 'Model Villages' comprising the land that have been seized from the Rohingyas. There are 26 such model villages in Rohingya Township with 100 families in each.

The settlers of these so-called model villages are NaSaKa members and their families, former insurgents, non Rohingyas and people from plain localities. Thus the Rohingyas become landless, shelterless with no means of livelihood. They ultimately end up by taking refuge in Bangladesh.

Seventh, the Rohingyas who are predominantly Muslims did not have religious freedom. Historically, they could not practice their religion with dignity and honour after the military take over of the country. Everything started to degenerate as the military took the power with the ideology of Burmese way of Socialism.[53] Since the day of independence, the government has been keeping the Muslim population of Arakan as a balancing force against the Arakanese Buddhist. But after General Ne Win and his junta took over state power, he put a wedge of disunity between them. The military government has closely associated itself with the 'Theravada Buddhism' in practice and thus the Government has identified itself with Buddhism and Buddhist doctrine. The military imposed a great deal of restriction upon non-Buddhist religious activities. In Arakan

53 Ibid, pp. 59-67.

the Rohingyas are warned not to grow beard, not to dress in Islamic outfits.[54] The military authorities have banned and locked up many mosques and religious schools. They are not allowing the Muslims to build permanent structures of mosques or anything related to Islam. They have restricted the renovation, repairing and maintaining of the existing Islamic structures including historical mosques, religious schools, and Muslim relics. Islamic structures of historical importance are deteriorating in absence of proper maintenance. The authorities have imposed restriction on even carrying out funeral rites to the graveyards.[55] As the Rohingyas are not full citizens of Burma, they do not have access to the state run schools beyond the primary education. They cannot attain any position in the civil services. The regime does not allow any person from Muslim faith to obtain a government employment. Authorities have restricted the number of Qurans and Bibles into the country. Without prior approval by the government, the Holy Quran cannot be translated into indigenous languages.

Finally, government of Myanmar imposed a financial coercion in the forms of extortion, arbitrary taxation and unfair penalties. Extortion, looting and theft of money, livestock and property by local military, police and NaSaKa is a daily occurrence for the Rohingya.[56] "Extortion is so serious that if we travel from one village to another, we have to bring money to give to the NaSaKa, and we have to send the money for our shopping separately," said one Rohingya. "Economically, we are completely crushed."[57] Moreover, if a Rohingya is found to possess a Bangladeshi mobile phone, they have to pay a bribe of at least 100,000-200,000 kyats or face arrest. The NaSaKa often come to villages at night, to demand money or livestock. Typically the NaSaKa arrest people and then demand at least 1,000-2,000 kyats for their release. Another form of financial coercion is imposition of extensive taxes which may be termed as official extortion. Taxes are applied on a range of activities and agricultural productions. The exercise of land use rights obliges the tenants to pay a certain percentage to the government. The farmers must sell a definite percentage of their total

54 Karim, Abdul, op.cit.

55 Ibid.

56 Christian Solidarity Worldwide, "Burma: Visit to the Bangladesh-Burma Border," *Briefing*, 26-31 August 2008. Available, http://dynamic.csw.org.uk/article.asp?t=report&id=100&search

57 CSW Report 2008, Ibid.

harvest to the government at the price fixed by them. Since 1992 the GOM has imposed a new type of tax upon the Rohingyas. That is each of the families staying in the North Arakan has to pay a chili tax. It does not matter whether the family grows it or not. There are shrimp tax, vegetable tax, animal tax and bird tax. The Rohingyas have to register every single cattle and domestic animals and pay a certain amount of tax for each. The owner of a cow must pay 80 kyat per year, goat 30 Kyat and a fowl or duck 10 kyat.[58] Every birth, death, sale or purchase of animals has to be reported to the NaSaKa and to be paid a certain fee. The villagers have to pay tax to go to the market to sell their harvest products. A Rohingya has to pay 3000 kyat for each slaughtering of a cow.[59] There are taxes of fruit bearing trees, for cutting bamboos and firewood in the jungle, for fishing in the rivers. They need to pay kyat 200 for per betel nut trees and kyat 500 for each coconut trees. Fishing in the rivers of north Arakan and in the Bay of Bengal is heavily taxed. A fisherman has to pay 1,800 kyat per week to the NaSaKa and Military Intelligence. There are roof tax, house building tax, and repair tax, crossing bridge tax, crossing sea shore tax and even tax on football matches.[60] Even the students residing in Akyab have to pay a tax of kyat 2500 every week to renew their stay for continuing studies.[61]

A number of factors linked to legal, political, economic and social aspects have influenced the Rohingyas to cross the Bangladesh-Myanmar border and eventually become refugees. But then, how are they treated in Bangladesh?

2.3 THE LIFE AND DEATH OF THE ROHINGYA REFUGEES IN BANGLADESH

The Rohingya refugees have been experiencing the plight and solace, hopes and despair about their lives as refugees in camp and non-camp areas in Bangladesh. During the Operation King Dragon, more than 200,000 fled into Bangladesh as refugees in 1978. In 1992, 2,50,877 refugees from Burma braved the Arakan forests, hills and the Naf River to take shelter in Bangladesh. The Government of Bangladesh

58 Ibid, p.114.

59 Ibid, pp.108-110.

60 Ibid, p.13.

61 Ibid, p.112.

(GOB) with the support from United Nations stood by their side despite its own socio-economic problems. The GOB had originally built twenty camps for the Rohingya Refugee in 1992. Currently, there are two camps for the Rohingya refugees. Documented Rohingya refugees are living in those 'Kutupalong' and 'Nayapara' camps in Ukhia and Teknaf Upazila respectively. As Table 2.1 shows there are 23,107 documented Rohingyas in the camps while the number of undocumented/illegal Rohingyas is 1,09,962. However, the real number of undocumented Rohingyas is unknown and some estimate that it can be around 2,00,000 to 5,00,000. Everyday 5 to 10 families are trying to cross the border of Bangladesh. Undocumented refugees are living in the roadsides specially Teknaf and Cox's Bazaar highway. They were living in a makeshift camp named Tal. Recently they have shifted to new shelters of the 'Leda' camp through the help of GOB. The GOB maintains the camps with the help of UNHCR. The GOB is supposedly responsible for ensuring safety and security of the refugees both inside and outside the camps. While living in camp or non-camp areas, the Rohingya refugees face dismal living conditions marked by local hostility, violence, restrictive movements, lack of basic needs, insecurity, and various forms of discrimination.

2.3.1 Hostile Relations with the Local People

When the Rohingya refugees came to Bangladesh from Myanmar, the local people were sympathetic to them. They helped them through providing cloth, food and even shelter. Over the years, the situation has changed. Nowadays, the relations between the Rohingya refugees and the community people are not warm. The local people are becoming unhappy, if not hostile to the Rohingya refugees. The Rohingyas often involve in disputes and other forms of conflicts with the local people. The community people allege that the Rohingyas are responsible for all conflicts between them. It is reported that the local farmers and day labourers remain scared of the Rohingyas who live together and who organise very quickly and attack the locals.[62] Some local people argue that the problem of local unemployment has been created by the influx of the Rohingyas. The Rohingya labourers are low paid compared to the Bangladeshis. So, the opportunities of works for the local people have been decreasing day by day. The local people

62 Philip Gain, "Rohingyas: Who Really is their Friends," *Shetu Report 1*, Dhaka: Shetu, 1992. p. 5.

also think that the influx of the Rohingyas has caused the prices of essential commodities to shoot up. As a result, the local community is least concerned about the Rohingya refugee problem. It has been revealed during the field visits that a Rohingya generally receives Tk. 40 per day as opposed to Tk. 100 to 120 for a local person. The other problem is related to the accommodation issue. The Rohingya refugees have no place to make their shelters. Particularly, the undocumented refugees who do not get any chance to enter into the official camps often take shelters in open places. All these factors antagonise the local people against the Rohingyas as they confront more hardships in their lives due to their arrival in Bangladesh.

2.3.2 Violence against the Rohingya Refugees

The GOB has appointed the police and the Ansar Bahini for the security of the Rohingya refugees. It has been observed that the police have an aggressive presence in the camps and sporadic forced repatriations in the form of kidnappings and violent clashes are common.[63] Particularly, the Rohingya women and children are vulnerable to violence which is perpetrated in different forms. First, the Rohingya women and girls are tortured inside and outside the camps by the security officials and local people. "Anjuma, a 12 year old Rohingya girl who arrived in Bangladesh in 1996, told Reuters that she had been gang raped by three BDR soldiers who had previously ordered her family and six others staying in a village near Teknaf to return to Myanmar. An examination by a doctor confirmed that it was a sexual assault."[64] A small boy of the Kutupalong camp faced child abuse by a police man inside the camp. Nobody could protest against this crime.[65] The law enforcing members are deployed there for the security of the camps and the refugees, but they often violate the refugees' security. It is also reported that the refugee women are raped by the other camp residing refugee people. Four Rohingya women who arrived by boat in June 1997 told the BBC that they were robbed and then raped by some local Bangladeshi men on arrival near

---

63 Wipperman, Tom and Haque, Mahbubul (2007) "Between a Rock and A Hard Place: the Rohingya of Bangladesh and Burma" Neeti Gobeshona Kendra.

64 Jilani, AFK, *Human Rights Violation in Arakan*, p.104.

65 Hutut, Zaw Min (2003) "Human Rights Abuses and Discrimination on Rohingyas" Maruyama, Japan.

Teknaf.[66] During the field visits, a Rohingya refugee revealed, "Few days ago a Rohingya girl was raped by two men near the Nayapara camp. But when the victims go to the police, they usually do not get justice. Sometimes, the local people give false and fabricated complain about the Rohingya refugees to the local police. The police often arrest them. Even they are sent to the prison."[67] Some Rohingya women are forced to become sex workers by the local criminals or reasons of livelihood.

Second, the Rohingya refugees face physical torture often at the hands of security and management officials. The conditions in the two official refugee camps are very poor indeed. The camps are managed by the GOB but staffed with *mahjees,* who are recruited from the Rohingyas. They are known to force people to sign voluntary repatriation agreements, indulge in beatings, arbitrary arrests and confiscation of ration cards as punishments.[68] However, there is no *majhee* system in the camps now. Third, there have been false complaints of persecution against the Rohingya men. Most of these complaints come from the families of the accused persons. The law enforcing members exploit these cases to persecute the Rohingya refugees. Rohingya women often complain against the Rohingya men about physical torture and other forms of violence. Recently, the rate of divorce is becoming high in the camps. It has been revealed that women who aim for resettling in the third country often come out with false complaints against their husbands. The latter are often arrested and tortured by the police. Many of the Rohingya men have passed their life in jail on false cases of persecution. To make the matter worse, the Rohingyas do not get proper legal support to prove their innocence. Besides, it is also observed that crime and smuggling syndicates in this coastal region use the Rohingya youths to carry out criminal activities.

2.3.3 Restrictions on the Movement of the Rohingyas

The Rohingya refugees are restricted to move outside the camps. They cannot seek employment outside the camps. The refugees risk arrest

---

66 Hutut, Zaw Min (2003) "Human Rights Abuses and Discrimination on Rohingyas" Maruyama, Japan.

67 Interviews with the Rohingya Refugees, Cox's Bazar.

68 Wipperman, Tom and Haque, Mahbubul (2007), "Between A Rock and A Hard place: The Rohingya of Bangladesh and Burma" Neeti Gobeshona Kendra.

by the local police, or punishment by the camp police if they are caught outside the camp. For some, it may be worth the risk, since a little cash is useful to supplement and diversify their food ration and to purchase goods that are not available in the ration package.[69] There are many young children (39% of the population was born in the camp) who know no other world than its boundaries.[70] The refugees do not get permission for visiting doctor when the need is urgent. The Rohingyas are not allowed to form their own committees to manage services. They cannot arrange public meetings to discuss issues that concern them. Recently, a small number of refugees have engaged in works outside the camps. Some of them have started several road-side-type stalls inside the camps (mostly throughout Nayapara). These endeavours are only recently tolerated by the camp authorities, and there is no doubt that they are involved in these activities at risk.

2.3.4 Lack of Basic Human Needs

The Rohingya refugees are deprived from the basic human needs in their life. They have shortage of food, shelter, clothing, health care facilities, water and sanitation. Their lives are highly insecure. The economic condition of the undocumented Rohingya refugees is even worse than the documented ones. Their only hope for living is to earn money through work. They do not find work everyday. It is revealed from the field visits that sometimes undocumented Rohingyas do not eat for 2/3 days. Both documented and undocumented Rohingya refugees are surviving in conditions of utmost deprivation and insecurity. Several issues may be identified.

First, there is a problem of access to food for the Rohingyas. The majority of the Rohingya refugees are malnourished. Surveys taken in different times show the unacceptable high rates of malnutrition among the adult and child refugees. It is estimated that 58 percent of the total refugee children and 53 percent of the adults are chronically malnourished.[71] The food supplied by the camp authorities is insufficient for them. The Rohingya refugees do not have enough to

69 Medicines Sans Frontiers. "10 years for the Rohingya Refugees in Bangladesh: past, present and future," Medicines Sans Frontiers- Holland. March 2002.

70 Thomas Feeny, "Rohingya Refugee Children in Cox's Bazar, Bangladesh," 2001, p. 26.

71 Concern, ÒDRAFT Nutrition Survey in Kutupalong and Nayapara Camps among the Rohingya Refugees, November 2001, p. 2.

Figure 2.1: Prevalence of Acute Malnutrition, Refugee Camps, Bangladesh

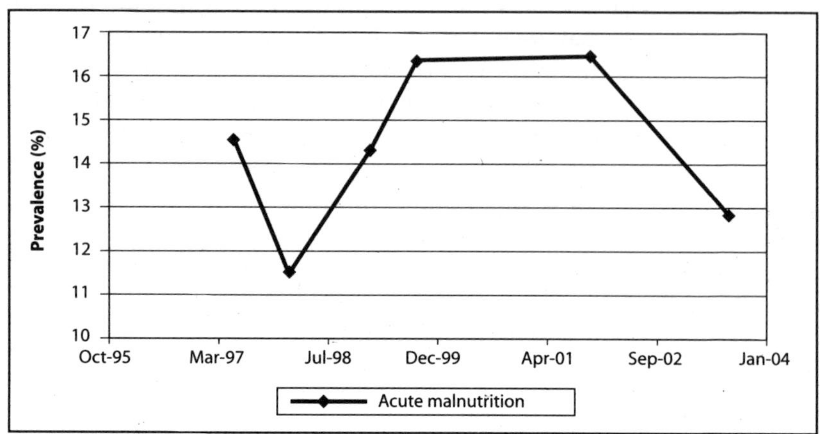

Source: http://www.unsystem.org/SCN/archives/nics01/index.htm accessed on 23 September 2008.

eat because of some specific reasons as observed during the field visits.[72] For example, almost none of the refugees are receiving their full ration.

The refugees are dependent on the weekly distribution of food. Newborn babies whom the government fails to register and households whose family books have been confiscated are denied their right to food assistance, and essentially left to their own devices to manage. WFP discovered in 2000 that the refugees were consuming an average of 1,600 kilocalories each day.[73] The Rohingya refugees complained that they were asked to get 6.30 kg rice per week but in reality they got only 5-5.5 kg rice. Every product they get is lesser than the chart. So, there is always a shortage of food in their family. Again food is used as a common bartering currency in the camps in lieu of money, because most of the inhabitants are unable to work.

Second, the Rohingya refugees have also acute shortage in getting clothes. As human beings, they need cloth for protecting themselves from sunshine, rainy season and cold. The refugees who are living in

---

72 Interviews conducted in Cox's Bazar during 14-20 June 2008.

73 According to the WFP, food security is defined as 'the ability of a household to produce or access at all times the minimum for needed for a healthy life.'

the camps get cloths from the camp authority every year, but it is not sufficient for them particularly for women and children. Every man gets a t-shirt, a pant, a lungi while each woman gets a thami and a blouse for one year. The quality of cloths is very pitiable. They also get a blanket for the cold season. They are given one blanket for six people in a family. For the undocumented refugees the situation is worse. They do not get any clothes from anyone. So they resort to begging. Sometimes they try to collect 'Zakat' from the local houses. The local people also donate blanket and warm cloths in the winter season. This does not fulfill the need for thousands of undocumented Rohingyas.

Third, the Rohingyas face severe problems in managing shelters for them. Initially, the Rohingya refugees took shelter in schools, colleges, madrassas and other institutions of Cox's Bazar and Bandarban areas. Subsequently, the government constructed temporary sheds in Cox's Bazaar district for their accommodation using khas lands, cornfields and forest lands. Those sheds are still in the camps and the refugees are using them living in an unhygienic situation. They are hardly adequate during rainy seasons. The houses are repaired after few years. The sheds are made for 6 to 7 people, but they are accommodating 12-16 persons. The camps, as stated by the WFP in its 1999 vulnerability report, "are small, crowded, and inadequate for healthy living."[74] The floor is covered with mud, so in rainy season it is barely livable in this house while they do not have any chance to leave this house.[75]

Fourth, healthcare facilities for the Rohingyas are very limited in refugee camps and outside. It is already mentioned that the population density of the camps is high. This has an impact on the general status of healthcare. MSF has documented a number of cases of communicative illness like common colds and the impacts of diarrhoea and skin diseases. The presence of MSF and the Irish NGO 'Concern' in the two camps is the main reason for healthcare conditions not being worse.[76] There are lot of complains about the healthcare system in the camps. The healthcare system does not have enough doctors and important lifesaving medicines. The Rohingya refugees allege that the doctors do not provide them with sufficient drugs.

74 WFP, "Vulnerability Survey of Refugees, September-October 1999," July 2000, p. 15.

75 Medicines Sans Frontiers. "10 years for the Rohingya refugees in Bangladesh: past, present and future," Medicines Sans Frontiers- Holland. March 2002, pp-19.

76 Wipperman, Tom and Haque, Mahbubul.(2007) "Between A Rock and A Hard Place: the Rohingya of Bangladesh and Burma." Neeti Gobeshona Kendra.

Fifth, the Rohingyas face problems regarding water and sanitation. In Nayapara camp, the supply of water has always been a major health concern. The water level of the Nayapara reservoir suffers from shortage during the dry season. From February to May, nearly 225,000 litres of water is trucked on daily basis from the nearby dam. Water rationing is often imposed throughout the year, with the dry season scarcity used as the explanation. Water is transported from the hilly forests through canals to a reservoir, and treated in water treatment plants.[77] The sanitation system in the camp is very poor. The refugees also do not know much about sanitation system. The Government prohibition of constructing semi-permanent structures in the camps has been hindering the construction of better sanitation system. MSF in Nayapara was responsible for the construction and maintenance of latrines and bathhouses, and for refuse collection and disposal, but after the MSF left the Rohingya refugee camps, the situation got worse in the camp areas. Besides, as there is no space to build new latrines, existing ones are patched up and emptied frequently.[78]

Sixth, there is an inadequate education and recreation facility in the refugee camps. During the field visits many parents expressed their deep concern about the education facilities in the camps. They complained that many students do not know how to write their names after completing their primary education from the camp based schools. Camp based schools do not have sufficient instruments for teaching the Rohingya students. The school does not have well educated teachers. Most of the teachers do not know the proper methods of teaching. The education level available to the refugees is from kindergarten to class five. After that most of the students continue their education by studying privately. Unfortunately, there is no scope for higher education for the Rohingya children. In addition, the facilities for recreation in the camps are extremely limited. In fact, there are no recreational facilities in the camps for the Rohingya refugees. There is no access to electricity in the refugee houses. The camp is dark after sun set. Sometimes they pass their times by gossiping, playing cards, playing football, etc, but they cannot watch television or listen to the radio programmes.

---

77 Medicines Sans Frontiers. "10 years for the Rohingya refugees in Bangladesh: past, present and future," Medicines Sans Frontiers- Holland. March 2002, pp-19.

78 Medicines sans Frontiers. "10 years for the Rohingya refugees in Bangladesh: past, present and future," Medicines Sans Frontiers- Holland. March 2002, pp-19.

Seventh, there is lack of safety and security of the Rohingya refugees in the camps as well as non-camp areas. The camps are not surrounded by any fence or wall. Anyone can enter into the camps and can harm people. The police and Ansars are deployed in the camps to protect the Rohingya refugees and camps, but they often become a source of insecurity for the Rohingyas. The law enforcing agencies argue that they are not sufficient in number for the security of the area. It was reported that when the *Majhee* system was in the camps, the security was in a precarious situation. *Majhees* used to force the refugees to sign the repatriation papers. It has been revealed from the field visits that they used to torture the camp people. Now-a-days, robbery, stealing, kidnapping, raping and physical torture have been rising in an alarming way in the camp areas. This has further deteriorated the security system in the camp areas.

2.3.4 Environmental Concerns

The Rohingya refugees are living in congested areas in the camps. The houses are bad in shape and the sanitation system is very poor. Hence, the environment around the camps and outside has been deteriorating over the years. The population density is extremely high in the camp areas. The environment is polluted by the camp people which is largely an outcome of their ignorance. Deforestation is the main environmental threat in the region which is linked to the livelihood of the Rohingya refugees. They depend on forests for collecting fuel, making huts and selling them as fuel for their livelihood. The forests department claims that the Rohingya refugees have destroyed forest resources. The forest department further alleges that the refugee camps are being erected on their plantation without their consent or knowledge. Besides, water pollution is another environmental concern. Water drainage systems of Bangladesh-Myanmar border area, Bandarban zone and Teknaf area have become polluted. There is no proper sanitation system in the camps. It also hampers the environment in the whole camp area and beyond.

2.4 CONCLUSION

This chapter has considered the historical background, the causes of the Rohingya refugee movements and their current conditions in refugee camp and non-camp areas in Bangladesh. The Rohingya refugee problem was created in the course of several historical trajectories as discussed in this chapter. It has been demonstrated that the Rohingyas are both stateless and refugees. First, they became stateless in their homeland and then eventually they had to embrace the status of refugeehood under conditions of persecution, discrimination and torture. The Rohingya refugees in Bangladesh have been continuing to remain stateless amid their refugeehood. The causes to their refugeehood can be categorised as primary factors (as enumerated in the 1951 Convention), secondary factors (as identified in the 1969 OAU Convention) and auxiliary factors (such as economic, ecological and demographic change). The denial of citizenship rights, denial of freedom of movement, eviction campaigns, forced labour, expulsion from their lands and property, violence and physical torture lead to the refugee movements by the Rohingyas. There are two critical points in understanding the Rohingya refugee problem. First, the causes and conditions of their refugeehood are becoming almost identical. The Rohingyas who fled to Bangladesh as a remedy to their sorrows and sufferings in Myanmar have been witnessing almost the same extent of miserable conditions of their life here. A camp dweller woman observes, "This country is like Burma. We are persecuted here just like we were persecuted there. We are like a football being kicked from one to another."[79] The field visits clearly show that there is an unbearable condition in the camps due to lack of access to basic needs, the abuse and intimidation at the hands of Bangladeshi local authorities and *majees* or camp volunteers. The Rohingyas are living in a state of impoverishment as refugees in camp and non-camp areas of Bangladesh. Second, the dynamics of current conditions of the Rohingyas are creating new questions about their identity. Who are the Rohingyas now? Are they just refugees or stateless people? It is true that the Rohingyas are dispersed in different countries of the world while a significant number of Rohingyas live in refugee camps in Bangladesh as well as their homeland. This gives a new dimension in their identity—a glocalised identity. "As stateless and refugees, within or beyond borders, the Rohingyas are as much local as they are global."[80]

---

79 Mike Thomson, "The Forgotten Rohingyas," *News Today*, 14 March 2006.

80 Imtiaz Ahmed, op. cit.

Appendix 2.1

The Geographical Location of Arakan

Arakan, the western periphery of Burma, is a narrow and long mountainous strip of land along the coast of Bay of Bengal. It is a natural physio-graphic unit completely separated from the rest of Burma by the long mountain range of Arakan Yoma peaks at almost 2000 meters. Arakan is situated between North Latitudes 17 degrees 15 minutes, 21 degrees 27 minutes and between East longitudes 92 degrees 15 minutes and 94 degrees and 55 minutes.[81]

Map 2.1: Myanmar (Burma)

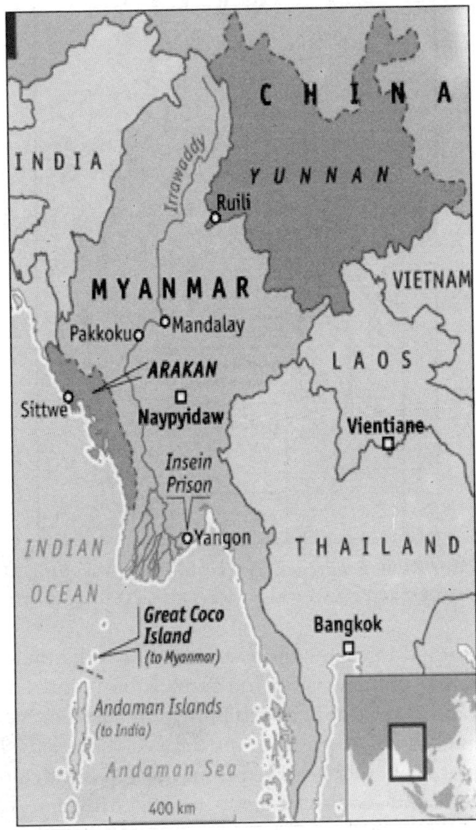

Source: Abdul Karim, *The Rohingyas: A Short Account of their History and Culture* (Chittagong: Arakan Historical Society, June 2000).

Map 2.2: Arakan

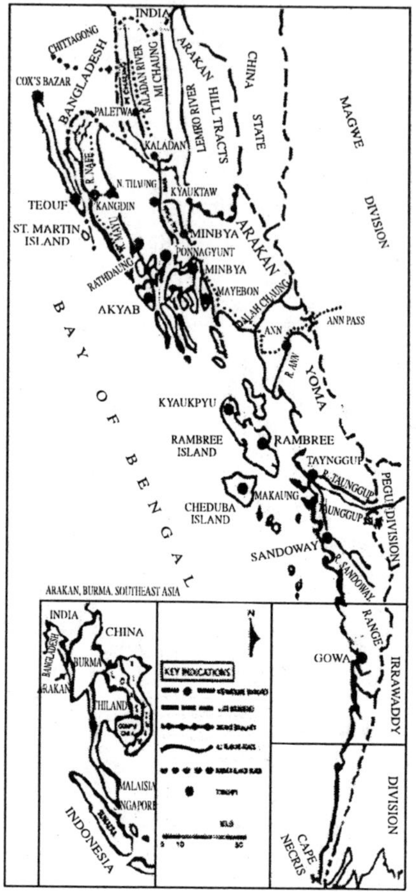

Source: Abdul Karim, the *Rohingyas: A Short Account of their History and Culture* (Chittagong: Arakan Historical Society, June 2000).

Arakan is bounded in the north by China and India, in the south west by the Bay of Bengal and in the west by the Yoma Mountains. The north and west Arakan have a common boundary with Bengal in the river Naf and the district of Chittagong which is still the borderline between Bangladesh and Myanmar. The old kingdom of Arakan is stretched from north to south along the coastline, divided by the high and inaccessible mountains of Burma. A few inaccessible mountain pass is the only way of land communication between Arakan and the rest of Burma; these two parts are however linked by water communication.

The total land area of Arakan is 20,000 square miles. Partitioning the 5,235 square miles of Arakan hill-tracts District and Southern part of Arakan, its land area has now been reduced to 14,200 square miles. No census was taken in Burma after the independence. So it is not possible to present the exact population figure, but the estimated population figure is 4 million. Of them 2 million are Buddhists, 1.8 million are Muslims and the rests are Animists.

Map 2.3: Ancient Cities of Arakan

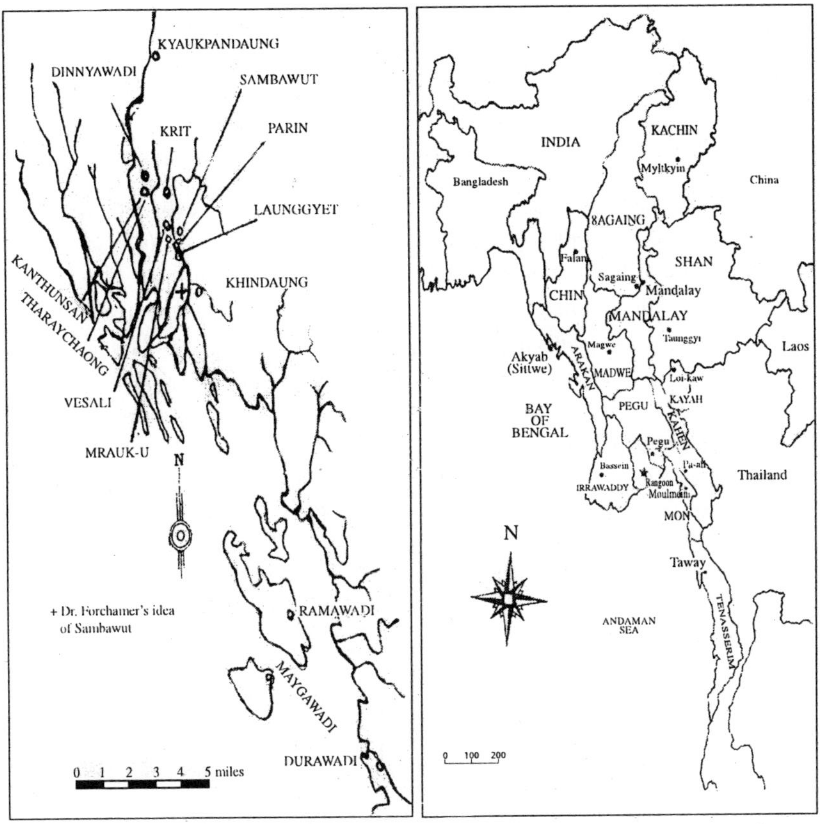

Source: Abdul Karim, the *Rohingyas: A Short Account of their History and Culture* (Chittagong: Arakan Historical Society, June 2000).

Appendix 2.2

Major Developments in the Rohingya Refugees Problem

1942	*1,00,000 Rohingya Muslims were massacred during World War ll. A large number of their settlements were uprooted.*
1948	*Arakan becomes a province of independent Burma. Since then Rohingyas have been driven out of Burma and now living in exile as refugees.*
1974	*Muslims in Northen Rakhine State (Arakan) are given foreign instead of National Registration card.*
1978	*'Dragon King' operation in Burma causes second Refugee influx (200000 persons).*
1982	*The Burma citizenship law of 1982, which violates several fundamental principles of customary international law standards, has reduced them to a position of defacto statelessness.*
1992	*Third refugee influx, 250000 persons hosted in 21 camps in Bangladesh.*
1993	*By November, 50000 refugee had been forcibly returned.*
1994	*UNHCR stops individual voluntary repatriation in August 1994, as thousands return to Burma each week. After this date reports of forced repatriation increase.*
2007	*Some refugees were resettled in Canada as part of a pilot resettlement programme.*

Source: Wipperman and Haque, op.cit., 2007.

Chapter 3
Trauma, Memory and Identity

Photograph by Md. Atiqur Rahman/IR/DU 2008

Refugees all over the world constantly face a reality where trauma, memory and identity capture a prominent place. They struggle with memory, dreams and hopes in everyday life. The lives of the Rohingya people are no exception to this reality. They have been experiencing traumas and different types of memories which are linked to their identities. This chapter gives an empirical understanding of the experiences of the Rohingya refugees in relations to trauma, memory and identity. The chapter is divided into five sections. Section one defines some basic concepts while section two discusses how the Rohingya people have been traumatised and how trauma affects their lives in the camp and non-camp areas. The third section deals with memories of the Rohingya people. The fourth section shows how identity of the Rohingya people has been constructed as a result of their traumatic experiences and their good and bad memories. The final section deals with their imagination of the future.

3.1 DEFINING THE BASIC CONCEPTS

3.1.1 Trauma

In conventional sense trauma means shock, upset, disturbance, pain, distress etc. A human being can be traumatised for many reasons. The causes of trauma may be the threat of death or serious injury, feeling of intense fear, helplessness or horror, threat to the physical integrity, terrorist bombings, shooting, arrests, forced labour, war, civil unrest, hunger, domestic abuse, rape, both natural or human made disaster and others alike. It is not necessary that a person who has experienced any of these occurrences should be traumatised. Though various reasons are responsible, some commonalities are found which cause trauma. If a person feels that his/her human rights and familiar ideas about the world is violated, and is put in a state of extreme confusion and insecurity then the person could be traumatised. In that case we can talk about the refugees who have survived in the world. The refugees of Bangladesh in 1971 got traumatised and most of them survived all the aspects of trauma. Usually the refugees get more traumatised than normal people. The main reason is that refugees face more traumatic situation, and their lives are always in great insecurity. Psychoanalysts tried to find the symptoms of trauma. The main symptoms of a traumatised person are repetition of disturbing memories, thoughts, dreams or images of the stressful events; feeling upset when something reminds the stressful events; avoiding activities or situations which remind the stressful events (psychologists call them triggers); feeling helpless, hopeless or powerless during or after the stressful events, flashbacks, which haunt the person and therefore nightmares, insomnia may occur.[1] These happen more in the refugee cases than in other cases. People, who have faced war, ethnic cleansing or civil war and became refugees, are affected by these symptoms. Feelings of despair, loss of self-esteem, and frequently depression may be found if some traumatised people become frustrated and helpless because of their belief regarding their static situation and trauma symptoms that it will remain unchanged.

3.1.2 Sources of Trauma in Home and Exile

For a refugee there may be many sources of trauma. The history of world refugees shows that four sources are prominent in creating traumas among the refugees. These are: rape; forced labour and displacement; armed violence and physical torture; and statelessness. Rape constitutes the leading source of trauma particularly for women. In terms of law, if a man forcibly subjects a woman to sexual intercourse against her will, he has committed the crime of rape.[2] Usually women are the main victims of this physical abuse, but men and children could be victims of this. In war or in ethnic cleansing rape has been used as a weapon, using attacks on women to humiliate and attempt to exterminate another ethnic group. Rape is often one of the ways in which women are targeted.[3] Although there are international

1 Available online http://en.wikipedia.org/wiki/Psychological_trauma

2 Available online http://www.hrw.org/women/docs/rapeinwar.htm

3 Available online http://en.wikipedia.org/wiki/Effects_of_rape_and_aftermath

agreements, such as the Geneva Convention which prohibits rape by soldiers during times of war or ethnic cleansing, it is found that in all kinds of war rape is encouraged, either as a reward for soldiers or as part of a campaign of terror. Rape, wherever it occurs, is considered an intense offense against honour of individual and society.

Empirical evidence of using rape as a tactic of terror in many wars is abundant. It was "a weapon of terror as the German Hun marched through Belgium in World War I; gang rape was part of the orchestrated riots of *Kristallnacht* which marked the beginning of Nazi campaigns against the Jews. It was used when the Japanese raped Chinese women in the city of Nanking and when the American G. I.'s made rape in Vietnam."[4] This is true for Somali women who have been raped and deal with not only the physical and psychological trauma of rape but also the likelihood of refutation by their families. The Liberation War of Bangladesh, 1971 is one of the examples of it. Pakistani soldiers raped more than 200,000 Bengali women in the Bangladesh war of independence.[5] In Bosnia, countless women have been attacked and brutally raped. In Second World War Nazis raped countless Jewish women. Soviet soldiers raped approximately two million women in eastern Germany in 1945.[6] One estimate claims that during the war against Kuwait, Iraqi troops raped as many as 3,200 women between August 1990 and February 1991.[7] In Kenya, 192 rapes of Somali refugees were documented from February to March 1993.[8] Thus, the histories of the war are the histories of the physical attack on women as well as children. Raped women are often stigmatised. Women, in most of the cases, are shunned by their own families and communities, viewed as tainted and a shame.

3.1.3 Memory and Trauma

> "We are only what we remember, nothing more. All we have is the memory of what we have done or not done; whom we might have touched, even for a moment."
>
> – *Romesh Gunesekera, Reef, 1994*

---

4 Cited in http://condor.depaul.edu/~rrotenbe/aeer/aeer13_1/Olujic.html accessed on 25 August 2008.

5 Hauchler,Ingomar,and Paul M. Kennedy (1994). *Global Trends.* New York: Continuum Publishers.

6 Available online http://www.hrw.org/women/docs/rapeinwar.htm

7 Enloe, Cynthia (1993). *Bananas, Beaches and Bases.* London: Pandora.

8 Available online http://www.hrw.org/women/docs/rapeinwar.htm.

Memory is embodied. It emanates from bodily experience that enacts the past. Memory is not simply a personal and subjective experience. It is socially constructed and present oriented, and thus reconfigures experience.[9] The experiences of life can be put to adaptive use only to the extent that they can be recalled at some subconscious in the absence of memory; learning is but the ephemeral and ad hoc adjustment of response to new conditions. The absences of it, perception is best the dazzling sense of a change in the environment. Memory provides meaning. It is the context in which all new experiences vie for the organism's attention. It is the basis of the concept of causation. Effects become orderly only through an awareness of their antecedents, the fuel of consciousness, substance of relegation. Scientifically, it has facile detention. Commonsense views are invariably homological. They define memory with new names rather than explain it in terms of principles, mechanisms, and lawful deeds. According to that, memory is recalling, remembering, knowing, recollecting, and having the knowledge of the past. They have a rather human surrounding quality which makes them seen out of place when applied to the behaviour of lower organism. The social and cultural networks that provide protective support, information and role models disintegrate when people are traumatised. Refugees and displaced persons are deeply affected not only by their exposure to violence, deprivation, and personal traumas such as the loss of family members, disruption of education employment and a clear path to future, but also by memories of the past life. There is a correlation between trauma and memory. Embodied memories of terror and violence create new meaning and reorder the world, but in doing so they encompass the inexplicable aspects of cultural processes that have allowed the world one lives in to become an unspeakable place and hostile.

3.1.4 Identity Construction

The concept of identity has generated significant academic debate. Identification from different forms of human collectivity or from different forms of established sets of values and principles fulfill

---

[9] Gay Becker and Others, "Memory, Trauma, and Embodied Distress: The Management of Disruption in the Stories of Cambodians in Exile", *Ethos*, September 2000, Vol. 28, No. 3, pp. 320-345.

necessary human needs. The ability to view oneself within a broader context is imperative in providing a sense of wider meaning and reason. Geertz defines identification as "a social assertion of the self as being somebody in the world."[10] So a vital purpose of identification is the need to overcome loneliness through a sense of belonging. Most academics concur that approaches to the concept of identity fall fundamentally into one of two camps, those that emphasise the primordial, essentialised elements of the concept (primordialist), and those that focus attention on situational, fluid and contingent characteristics (rationalists).[11]

For the understanding of the identity construction of the refugees and to some extent stateless persons, along with the two approaches stated above, it is important to see how 'place' has impact on the construction or molding of the identity of individual and a group. More importantly, the ignored part from the most of the literature of identity construction is the impact of the physical environment (Hague, 2007).[12] A place is often related with a certain lifestyle, social status and a definite group of people. People will prefer those places that have physical symbols which maintain and enhance self-esteem and avoid those that do not, for the purpose of maintaining a positive self-esteem (Hague, 2007).[13] The difference between the concepts of 'space' and 'place' was highlighted by Massey (1994)[14] in cultural geography. Space is defined as a timeless, absolute dimension, on the other hand place is defined as a space integrally tangled with time. This perspective on place makes room for the positioning of living beings in relationship to one another in such a way that new social effects may be produced. Precisely, Massey's perception of place gives

---

10 Geertz, Clifford. 1973. *The Interpretation of Cultures*, London: Fontana.

11 May, S. (2001) *Language and Minority Rights: Ethnicity, Nationalism and the Politics of Language*, Edinburgh: Pearson Education Ltd.

Kershen, A.J. (1998) *A Question of Identity*, UK: Ashgate Publishing Ltd.

Eade, J. (1997) *Living the Global City: Globalisation as a Local Process,'* London: Routledge

Gilroy, P. (1997) 'Diaspora and the detours of identity', in K. Woodward (ed) *Identity and Difference: Culture, Media and Identities*, London: Sage.

12 Hauge, A. L. (2007). 'Identity and place: A critical comparison of three identity theories.' *Architectural Science Review* 50 (1), 44-52.

13 Hauge, A. L. (2007). 'Identity and Place: A Critical Comparison of Three Identity Theories.' *Architectural Science Review* 50 (1), 44-52.

14 Massey, D. (1994). *Space, Place, and Gender.* Minneapolis: University of Minnesota Press.

an idea about how a place might influence the creation of identities that are particular to it.[15] As in other identity theories, social relations play an important role of creating the subject, but place is incorporated as a critical, supplementary element in shaping identities.

3.2 EXPERIENCES OF TRAUMA IN MYANMAR

The Rohingya people have vivid experiences of trauma in their lives in Myanmar. In Myanmar, the situation of Arakani Rohingya Muslims was just similar to the other war and civil conflict. While living in Myanmar they had been subject to rape, forced labour and displacement, physical torture and statelessness. Rape as a weapon of terror was systematically used against the Rohingyas. In 1992, government troops rounded up the men for forced labour and raped the women.[16] Rape was a part of a campaign to drive the Rohingyas out of the country. It has been revealed from the field study in camp and non-camp areas in Teknaf that women and children had been victims of rape at the hands of NaSaKa. A story from the field,

> "Amena Khatun was a 17-year old girl. She lived there with her mother and brother Aminullah. When the NaSaKa took her brother for forced labour, she begged them to save her brother. They released Aminullah but took her away. She was raped by 3 NaSaKa soldiers. She is now living in Kutupalong camp in Bangladesh as a refugee. Still she does not want to remember this painful confrontation. Sometimes she wakes up with her nightmare. She abhors red, because when they took her, she was wearing a red Thami."[17]

Interviews with the documented and undocumented Rohingya refugees demonstrate how terribly Rohingya women were treated in their homeland by the security forces. Psychologically, the effects of rape on children is different from women. "Sexual assault of children can lead them to the life-long depression, self injury, self-mutilation, borderline personality disorder, antisocial personality disorder, Post Traumatic Stress Disorder (which often leads to a reduced corpus callosum), flashbacks, psychotic breaks with reality, alcoholism, substance abuse, promiscuity, celibacy, prostitution, an inability to form intimate relationships, self-hate, guilt, anger (which is often directed inwards as well as outwards), emotional hypersensitivity, defensiveness, a lifelong inability to trust others, emotional numbness,

---

15 Massey, Ibid.

16 Available online www.cidcm.umd.edu/mar/chronology.asp?groupId=77501 - 48k

17 From field work by Fatema Hossain at Kutupalong Camp in Teknaf, 14-20 June 2008.

an attraction to partners who are dominant and/or abusive, and general mental deterioration including loss of IQ."[18]

3.2.1 Forced Labour and Displacement

Forced labour means work without any kind of wages or making somebody bound to do the job which he or she does not want to do. International Labour Organisation (ILO) is against the forced labour and always endeavours to stop such labour.[19] Forced labour in Arakan state is often accompanied by physical abuse by the military or NaSaKa guards who oversee the work. Arakan is an undeveloped region in Burma. The government of Myanmar thinks that as the Rohingyas are not citizens of the country, they must work as forced labour. In case of refusal to work they were subjected to torture and suppression by the NaSaKa. For instance,

> Manirullah was the victim of the physical torture of the NaSaKa. He was supposed to give labour without any wages. He carried goods from truck to truck. One day he was so sick that he could not carry goods. For this reason, they cut down his hand. He cried out but the security forces did nothing for him. In the twinkling of an eye, he lost his hand. After a while the screams stopped, the crying stopped and there was silence. That was his punishment. Although, subsequently he left Burma, he could not forget the torture.[20]

According to the UN Guiding Principles, the person or group of persons who have been forced or obliged to flee their homes or place of habitual residence in particular as a result of or in order to avoid the affects of armed conflicts, situation of general violence, violation of human rights or natural or men made disasters, and who have not crossed the internationally recognised state border, are displaced persons.[21] Since 1988, the government has established a program it calls "model villages" in Maungdaw and Buthidaung in order to "encourage" Rakhine families to settle in these townships. Under this program lands of the Rohingyas have been confiscated to accommodate Buddhist settlers. Until 2003, the government established 26 "model villages" of about 100 houses in Northern

---

18 Effects and aftermath of rape,accessed on 25th June, http://www.en.wikipedia.org/wiki/Effects_of_rape_and_aftermath

19 Available online www.burmalibrary.org/docs/HRDU2003-04/Forced%20Labours.htm

20 From field work by Fatema Hossain at Kutupalong camp in Teknaf.

21 Available online www.unhcr.org/publ/PUBL/44b5021d2.pdf

Arakan State. These villages were intended to reestablish Rakhine villages which had existed before the communal violence in the 1940s.

Though Rohingyas belong to Myanmar's largest ethno-religious minority groups, the military regime still does not recognise the Rohingyas as a distinct ethnic group. The political and constitutional identity of Rohingyas was abolished through the creation of the Citizenship Act of Burma in 1982 during the period of the military government of General Ne Win.[22] As the history shows that the government of Myanmar always dreams of an Arakan without Rohingya Muslims because they think that Muslims are not Burmese. They belong to the Bengali race and there has never been a Rohingya race in Myanmar though there is no historical evidence in favour of it. Thus they help Rakhine for rehabilitating in Arakan. As a consequence, the Rohingyas are becoming displaced from their home. The torture of the government and Rakhine made them refugee. Displacement from the habitual residence or home made them expatriate in their own countries. Memories of the home drive them to flashback and hopelessness which are the symptoms of trauma.

3.2.2 Armed Violence and Physical Torture

Armed violence can be defined as the use of armed force (usually with weapons) to achieve specific political, social and economic goals.[23] Torture is a particularly dreadful type of trauma because it is designed to destroy the will, personality and autonomy of the victim. Not only people may be tortured but they may be forced to witness their loved ones being tortured. In Burma, the Rohingya people faced both armed and physical violence by the government and NaSaKa. The government troops and the NaSaKa carried out several operations on Arakani Muslims and most of them were armed. There have been no less than 20 major operations of eviction campaigns directed against the Rohingyas that were carried out by successive governments of Burma. The major operations of such kind took place in 1942, 1949, 1978 and 1992 respectively. In pursuance of the 20-year Rohingya Extermination Plan, the Arakan State Council under direct supervision of State Council of Burma carried out a Rohingya drive operation code named Naga Min or King Dragon Operation. It was the largest, the

22 From Dr. Md. Yunus's interview, the President of the Arakan's historical Society.

23 Accessed on July 22,2008 http://www.undp.org/cpr/we_do/armed_violence.shtml - 21k

most notorious and probably the best-documented operation of 1978.[24] The operation started on 6 February 1978 from the largest Muslim village of Sakkipara in Akyab, which sent shock waves over the whole region within a short time. News of mass arrest of Muslims, male and female, young and old, torture, rape and killing in Akyab panicked Muslims in other towns of North Arakan. In March 1978 the operation reached Buthidaung and Maungdaw.[25] Hundreds of Muslim men and women were thrown into the jail and many of them were tortured and killed. Muslim women were raped freely in the detention centres. As revealed from the field visit, Md. Kashem was a school teacher in Maungdaw. In 1992 he was taken to jail. He was tortured by the Army. After many years of that incident he is still afraid of sound of any kind of vehicles. The reason is that when they took him his eyes were covered tightly and he could just hear the sound of the Jeep.

3.2.3 Statelessness

Under the military regime of General Ne Win, beginning in 1962, the Muslim residents of Arakan were labelled illegal immigrants who had settled in Burma during the British rule. The 1974 Emergency Immigration Act took away Burmese nationality from the Rohingyas, making them foreigners in their own country. Then came the Burma Citizenship Law of 1982 violating several fundamental principles of the international law and effectively reduced them to the status of Stateless. Although their ancestor lived in Burma, but after the Citizenship Law of 1982 the Rohingyas became stateless.[26] In Myanmar, the Rohingyas have been denied their citizenship, uprooted from their ancestral homes and forced to live as refugees and illegal immigrants in Bangladesh, Pakistan, Saudi Arabia, U.A.E., Malaysia and Thailand. A country that does not recognise the Rohingyas as a citizen despite the fact that their forefathers lived there for centuries, is enough for generating trauma in their minds. It was a big trauma to experience that half of their people have been forced to take asylum or refuge outside, and they may be the next in line to seek a way out of this living hell.

---

24 From Dr. Md. Yunus's interview, the President of the Arakan's historical Society.

25 'A Long History of Injustice Ignored: Rohingya: The Forgotten People of our time' by Dr Habib Siddiqui Accesed July 22,2008.http://www.islamawareness.net/Asia/Burma/ro_article003.html

26 Ibid.

3.3 TRAUMATISED MEMORIES AND THE ROHINGYAS

Like any other group of refugees, the Rohingyas are closely connected to their memories. The cultural and political constructs of the Rohingyas are deeply influenced by the memories of the past, mainly when they were in Myanmar. In their case, the aspect of their memories is still a wide open space for scholarly exploration. When the basic needs of the refugees are being undermined, their physical safety at stake, their future of returning home is being doomed and concerned international organisations, NGOs, governments and the United Nations are struggling to give them the minimum hope for their survival in the future, it is no wonder that, little effort has been given in listening to the refugees' tale. It is imperative that refugees should be treated from a more human centric approach and to do so an endeavour to understand their memories and analyse them with empathy to reach a compassionate solution is very important. This part of the chapter deals with the memories experienced by the Rohingya refugees both at home and in exile. It gives an understanding of how they react in different situations, their nightmares, sufferings, silence, joy and pain, dreams and how they see their future.

Traumatised memory of the Rohingyas is linked not only to their experiences of tortures at the hands of NaSaKa and other forces in Myanmar, but also being forced to witness their loved ones being tortured. Often these memories of extreme suffering are linked to their traumatic condition they are living with. When it comes to adolescent female, trauma has a totally different gender dimension and it impacts differently than on male. Rape has been a common feature of torture both in Myanmar and in the refugee camps in Bangladesh. Rape is not the only reason behind the traumatised memory for a female refugee but also the response she gets from the host country and her fellow refugees afterwards play a key role to bring back those memories and continue to reproduce the trauma. Sometimes other refugees even female ones are associated with rape. It was revealed from the field visit that a boy named Abdul was sexually abused in the camps. He is now an 11 years old boy who was born in the refugee camp of Nayapara in Bangladesh. He was assaulted by the BDR at the age of 5. After that he has been suffering from mental disorder.[27] Two stories as revealed from the field visits could give a vivid picture of traumatised

---

27 Interviews conducted in Refugee Camps during 14-20 June 2008.

memories of the Rohingyas. One is related to the memories of the Rohingyas in Myanmar and the other is in Bangladesh.

Zafar Alam, 40, Samitipara, Cox's Bazar[28]

"I am always in fear of safety of my daughter"

—*Zafar Alam*

"It was 1996. I was living with my wife in Arakan. Economic miseries, poverty, lack of jobs were the daily friends of most of the families. In addition, the harassment by NaSaKa was a bonus pain! Women were mostly vulnerable. Rape was an every day incident. Besides this, farmers had to handover 90% of their crops to NaSaKa. Forced labour for the construction works without any payment was another way of torture. And if anyone denied to work, he or she had to face unbelievable tortures. We had to pay gallons of patrol fuel to the NaSaKa on daily basis. Now you tell me, how could we stay there? But we did not make any plan to come to Bangladesh. One day, NaSaKa grabbed 11-12 families including me and my family and told us to leave Arakan at night. We had nothing to do, nothing to say. In October 1996 we came to Bangladesh crossing Naaf River at mid-night. In mid 2006, 5 NaSaKa people came to my house and demanded 2 gallons of fuels and 3000 Kyat. It was absolutely impossible for me to provide these things. I told them with tears to forgive me and leave us. But do you know what they did? They told me that—we'll leave, if you rape your own daughter (Fatima) right now in front of us. Otherwise we will set a rough cane inside your little daughter's secret place. At that moment, I was crying out loud and telling them I can't do this and I won't be able to tolerate that. But that bloody persons had no heart. May be they are the worst brutal creature in the world. They took away my little daughter and a rough cane was just about to push. Suddenly my wife took a bamboo stick and hit one of the NaSaKa. In action, they pushed their arms and fired. I then decided to do whatever they want from me but I planned to do acting. I tried to act as I planned. Oh Lord, her loud screaming ... unforgettable for me. After a while, one of the NaSaKa came to me and took my daughter to him. He then raped my daughter along with two other partners. My Fatima died. My Fatima died in front of me. I could not do anything. Just nothing. I lost my wife. I lost my Fatima. I might be happy if they kill

28 Interview by Md. Amirul Islam, 17 June 2008, Samitipara, Cox's Bazar.

me also. But they didn't. They left the place saying that -you have only two options left. Either bear this sorrow or kill your little daughter and commit suicide. I then came to Bangladesh. I think you can now imagine why I am always in fear of safety of my daughter."

Hasina, 17, Kutopalong, Cox's Bazar

Hasina Begum, age 17 currently living at the Kutupalong camp, was raped by three local Bangladeshi male in 2006. Another female refugee tricked her by saying that she will take Hasina to a marriage ceremony in the nearby Bengali village and her away to those three Bengali male for 10 taka each. In this case Hasina's trust was broken by a fellow refugee female. The broken belief on human makes her suspicious and angry about the other people who try to get near her. When the interview was taken she didn't want to cooperate with the interviewer, which was unusual as experience shows that almost all the Rohingya refugees were happy to tell their stories and be heard by someone. Although the interviewer was a female, Hasina looked disturbed and angry. On the other hand, Hasina got insensitive response from the police, as the police didn't believe her story rather she had to stay in prison for fifteen days. The doctor who examined her for the evidence gave a false report, bribed by the convicted, that Hasina was not raped. However later the truth was revealed and she got the justice. In this case first the instant impact of rape was critical. As an adolescent Hasina never expected to be victim of a rape, the idea of the outer world radically changed, when she was asked how does she feel when those memories come back, she replied, "I have nothing to say but this, that I was 15 then and I didn't know what relation a girl and boy could have, and they treated me like I am not a human being. Actually I don't know what I should answer." Her answer reflects that she was inexperienced about the sexual relation, let alone abuse of such kind. The shock she got from the incident and the response she got from the police was unbearable for her. She also thinks that her identity as Rohingya has to do with the response from the police, as she asked the interviewer, "Your (Bangladeshi) police didn't believe me because I am a Rohingya, could they disbelieve me if I were a Bengali?"

These narratives as mentioned above reveal how people strive to remember and see continuity of traumatic memories in their lives. The testimonies were provided by members of refugee families in the refugee camps and outside the camps. The oral testimonies reveal the common experiences, hopes and fears of the Rohingyas caught up in the violence, extortion and torture in Arakan by the government forces. The Rohingyas face trauma in both situations as non-refugee but stateless in Myanmar and as refugees and stateless in Bangladesh. There is commonality in their traumatic experiences of life as reflected in the narratives of the Rohingyas. In Myanmar the Rohingyas were vulnerable to violence, negligence, exploitation, and abuse in a variety of forms. They were denied of citizenship rights in their homeland. They were severely restricted in their movement in Arakan, not to mention in the whole Myanmar or abroad. The Rohingyas had been victims of rape and sexual violence. They had been subjected to systematic eviction campaigns in Myanmar for decades. They were forced into labour. They did not have religious freedom in Myanmar. They faced a financial coercion imposed by the GOM in the forms of extortion, arbitrary taxation and charges. The security forces particularly NaSaKa regularly traumatise both men and women. As a result, people have lost their self esteem and find themselves frustrated by inaction and powerlessness.

The Rohingya refugees arrive in Bangladesh exhausted, ill and traumatised. Before their arrival they have often witnessed extreme violence. In Bangladesh the refugee camps are also vulnerable to attack from outside and domination by violence within. The host people are showing rising discontentment about the presence of the Rohingyas which is fuelling resentment. The Rohingya refugees have been subject to rape and sexual violence mainly by the Police, Ansar, BDR and the local people. All this forms the bedrock of memories of the Rohingyas which are haunting them continuously.

3.4 IDENTITY AND THE ROHINGYAS

In the words of a Rohingya, "The regime is trying to take away our identity. We will not be there in the very near future. Our prime concern is that we must not be eliminated .... We are a people on the brink of extinction."[29] This indicates how important the question of identity is to the Rohingyas. There is a debate on the question of the identity of the Rohingyas. The most common identity of the Rohingyas is that they are an ethnic group from the northern Rakhine state

29 One Rohingya spokesman told Christian Solidarity Worldwide (CSW) during interviews. Available Online: http://www.rohingya.org/ accessed on 2 October 2008.

(formerly Arakan state) of Myanmar. They are Muslims. Broadly, on the one hand, the identity of the Rohingyas is linked with factors such as ethnicity, religion, place, and gender, on the other it is closely connected with statelessness and refugeehood. Ethnically the 'Rohingyas' tend to identify themselves as the Arakanese Muslims. They claim historical and ethnic ties with the state of Burma (Myanmar).

The word 'Rohingya' has a close link with the place where the Rohingya refugees have come from, it is Arakan, and is now officially known as 'Rakhaine state' situated in the northern part of Myanmar in Bangladesh-Myanmar border. The primeval name of Arakan was 'Rohang' and the people of Arakan later came to be known as Rohingya.[30] According to historian Phayre (1884), Arakan continued to be an independent kingdom until it was annexed by Burma in 1784 AD.[31] Some Arakanese scholar argue that Aryans from the west first came to Arakan for settlement, but for most of the scholars Kanyan tribe of Tibeto-Burman group first came to Arakan.[32] Unlike the other parts of Burma, Arakan has the longest history of ruling of dynasties back from 2666 BC.

The Arakanese were basically animists but over the centuries Brahmanism, Buddhism and Islam shaped and influenced their religious beliefs, as they did over the Burmans.[33] By the Arab merchants, Islam was first introduced in Arakan. So one school of historian suggests that Rohingyas are descendents of Moorish, Arab and Persian traders, including Mughul, Turk, Pathan and Bengali soldiers cum migrants, who arrived between the ninth and fifteenth centuries, married local women, and settled in the region.[34] It may be mentioned that there was regular arrival of Muslims from

30 Siddiqui Habib, 'A Long History of Injustice Ignored: Rohingya: The Forgotten People of Our Time,' sited in http://www.islamawareness.net/Asia/Burma/ro_article003.html accessed on 25th July, 2008.

31 Phayre, A P (1883) *History of Burma*, London quoted in Abrar C.R. 'Repatriation of Rohingya Refugees,' sited in http://burmalibrary.org/docs/Abrar-repatriation.htm accessed on 25th July, 2008.

32 Maung S L (1989), *Burma: Nationalism and Ideology*, University Press Limited, Dhaka.

33 Hall. D G E (1940) *A History of Southeast Asia*, Macmillan, London.

34 Ahmed Imtiaz 'Globalisation, Low-Intensity Conflict & Protracted Statelessness/Refugee hood: The Plight of the Rohingyas,' sited in http://programs.ssrc.org/gsc/publications/quarterly13/ahmed.pdf, accessed on 26th July, 2008.

Afghanistan, Persia and Turkey, as well as from north India and the Arabian Peninsula. They amalgamated with the Muslim society and became the Rohingyas. As a result, a distinct dialect was formed by the mixture of Persian, Urdu, Pushtu, Arakanese and Bengali.[35] To this school Rohingyas are a mixed group of people with many ethnic and racial relations. Thus a Muslim presence already existed in northern Arakan even before Islam reached Bengal in the 13th century.

Another school argues that ethnically, culturally and linguistically the Rohingyas are closely related to the Bengalis, and particularly the people of Chittagong area of Bangladesh. The Muslim population of the Rakhine State is the descendent of Bengali migrants from Bengal (now Bangladesh), with some Indians coming during the British period. It is also emphasised that most of them speak Bengali with a strong "Chittagongonian dialect," so they are regarded as illegal immigrants from Bangladesh. The Government of Myanmar, most of the Burman-Buddhist populations believe in this conception.[36] The military regime in Myanmar prohibits the use of the term 'Rohingya', arguing it is the "creation of Bengali insurgents", and refers to them instead as "Bengali intruders". The pro-regime scholars tend to argue that the cause of Rohingyas finds a little support outside their own community, and their claims of an earlier historical tie to Burma is insupportable.[37]

It is important to understand the origin of the word 'Arakan' to conceptualise the politics of identity between these two schools. 'Arakan' is a Bengali, Arabic and Portuguese version of the local word 'Rakhine', which is 'Yakhine' in Burmese.[38] In Chittagong dialect, Rakhine is pronounced as 'Rohong' or 'Rohang', thus the people from this land are named as 'Rohingyas'.[39] The use of different terms or identities for the people of this part was not merely linguistic reason,

---

35 Nicolaus, P 1995 'A Brief Account on the History of the Muslim Population in Arakan', (Mimeo).

36 Ahmed Imtiaz 'Globalisation, Low-Intensity Conflict & Protracted Statelessness/Refugee hood: The Plight of the Rohingyas,' sited in http://programs.ssrc.org/gsc/publications/quarterly13/ahmed.pdf, accessed on 26th July, 2008.

37 Aye Chan, The Development of a Muslim Enclave in Arakan (Rakhine) State of Burma (Myanmar) *SOAS Bulletin of Burma Research*, Vol. 3, No. 2, Autumn 2005, Available Online: http://web.soas.ac.uk/burma/3.2files/03Enclave.pdf

38 Joe Cummings and Tony Wheeler, *Myanmar: A Lonely Planet Travel Survival Kit* (Hawthorn, Victoria: Lonely Planet Publications, 1996), p.364.

39 Ibid.

rather their identity was politicised as Arakanese. Buddhists identify themselves as "Rakhines' and the Arakanese Muslims as 'Rohingyas'. Some also argue that the term 'Rohingya' derives from Rakkhasa, (rakking), Rakkhanpura, 'Rosang' (Alaol calls it), Ro-khing-yha (Arthur Phayre calls it). 'Gya' (meaning a resident in Bengali) similar to Chatgya (Chittagonian) 'gya' to the word Rokking "gya", which comes to Rohingya. It seems that 'Rakking', 'Rosang' etc are Arakani words and 'gya' is Bengali. Along with religion a colonial legacy also played an important role for the difference in identity among this population of Arakan. It actually inspired the Arakanese Muslim to seek a newer identity, 'Rohingya'. From 1824 to World War II; these years between them played an important role in the formation of the Rohingya identity. The year 1824 refers to the year of annexation of the Arakan by the British colonial power and World War II is marked by the expulsion of the British by the Japanese. In each of the two events Arakanese Muslims played a role which contributed to their separation with the Buddhist population of Arakan.

It is widely held that the British invaded Rakhine region in 1824 when the Burman army started pushing the Arakanese Muslims further west well inside the British colonised territories.[40] After this annexation many Arakanese Muslims started to return from Bengal or India to Arakan whose ancestors left Arakan because of the Burman conquest of Arakan at the end of the 18th century. Thus the British conquest actually encouraged migration of population in this British ruling period. In a way the position of the Arakanese Muslims entwined with the British colonial power. Thus when Japanese conquered Burma in 1942 a significant population of Arakanese Muslim escaped from Burma and Arakan and took refuge in Bengal. In this event the political attachment of the Arakanese became apparent, as Arakanese Buddhist supported Japanese and Arakanese Muslims supported the British. At the end of the day such affinity with the colonial ruler went against them, thus they started to identify themselves within a new identity, 'Rohingya', which distanced them from the Arakanese Buddhist and created a sense of unity within their own group of people to fight their weakened position and misery.[41]

The persecution against the Rohingya people has been linked to Buddhism followed by majority of its people in Myanmar. Buddhism

---

40 Imtiaz, op.cit.

41 Imtiaz, op.cit.

is known as a religion of peace. The Buddhist Samsara discourse in its subtle meaning is normally understood to work as an aid to pacify anger and promote peace. This is however not the case in the north western corner of Burma's Arakan province. Contrary to Buddhist precepts, in Arakan, Bhuddhism is used to promote antagonism and violence against the Rohingyas. In this type of use, the extremist Moghs have elevated their religion to the status of a political ideology. It has lately promoted the political conceptualisation of Buddhism to fight its perceived enemy, the Rohingyas. In this endeavour, they are using Buddhism to justify their political agenda of exclusivity and ethnic cleansing. It is similar to the Serb's use of religious discourse to commit genocide against Muslims in the former Yugoslavia.[42]

The question of identity of the Rohingyas is further developed by the link between Rohingya refugees' identity construction and the 'place' they were and now they are in. The Rohingyas having lived in refugee camps and outside camps in Bangladesh are not just supra-national but also multilingual, and multi-cultural. Imtiaz Ahmed invokes a new dimension of identity of the Rohingyas where the 'place' dimension is very much present. To him the question of identity of the Rohingyas is linked to global as well as local factors. In his words:

> In the light of this demographic diffusion, the Rohingyas have often been dubbed as Asia's "new Palestinians," imbibed with what could be referred to as local-global or *glocalised* identity. Indeed, as stateless and as refugees, within or beyond borders, the Rohingyas are as much local as they are global. There are not too many places for them to go, yet staying at one place puts them at risk if not in a serious state of uncertainty. The *glocalised* identity is of course in addition to their *social, cultural* and *political* identities, all of which were earned either one way or the other through systematic coercion, alienation and marginalisation, within and outside Myanmar.[43]

While Arakan has been at the centre of their awareness as a separate people in the world, the dispersion of the Rohingyas in different countries as refugees is an inescapable reality for them. There is no doubt that their presence in the refugee camps and non-camp areas in Bangladesh and Arakan shapes their identity. Gradually, their identity is becoming what Imtiaz Ahmed terms as multiformed and multilayered largely due to the impact of globalisation. The traumatic experiences of the Rohingyas in Myanmar as well as in the refugee

---

42 Bahar Abid, 'Burmese invasion of Arakan and the rise of Non-Bengali settlements in Chittagong of Bangladesh.'

43 Imtiaz op.cit.

camps in Bangladesh drive them not only to resettle in the third countries, but also to enter into the network of subaltern globalisation, including seeking military training from the Taliban and al Qaeda.[44] This adds a new dimension to the understanding of the Rohingyas as a community. It is true that only a small section of Rohingyas is getting involved in militant activities or subaltern movements, but the Rohingyas as a whole found themselves stigmatised, and governments of different countries became fearful of their presence irrespective of their position as stateless, refugees, migrants, or honest workers.[45] Amid statelessness, refugeehood and stigmatisation the identity of the Rohingyas will continue to remain as a major concern for addressing the Rohingya refugee problem.

3.5 IMAGING THE FUTURE

Dreams and hopes have a crucial meaning for the Rohingyas and without that there would not be much left for them. Loss of home and loss of land is synonymous with loss of identity. When the word 'refugee' comes up in the mind of anyone, it is normal to think of a life of despair. They are linked in such a way, which is surprising and also very refreshing to see some exceptions and also fascinating that after being in a damned condition how refugees refused to give up their dreams. It does not matter for them how unrealistic those dreams are or just some simple objectives to achieve under normal circumstances for any individual in the world. The pursuit of happiness or the hope for a better life is keeping the Rohingya refugees alive. The reality on the one hand is always telling them that they are forgotten people, on the other hand small achievements, gains, and happiness whatever they might find from their life in the camp is inspiring them to project their desired future. This dialectic link between their optimism and despondency can be explained by the fact that it is a typical response by human under extreme misery and a necessity for their survival. Each time they imagine a future and refuse to give up, they win a battle and these small gains take them to the next one. On the way they lose many but again they rebound and start again because the death of the dream means here, the death of life.

44 Imtiaz op.cit.

45 Imtiaz Ahmed, Globalisation, 2004. op.cit.

The biggest source of inspiration for the Rohingya refugees has been their young generation. Most of the young people at the camps are born in Bangladesh or can remember little about their ancestors' home Myanmar. For most of them Bangladesh is now the home as many of them are involved in different jobs (although unofficially), a big part is going to the camp schools and children are going to the primary school in the camps. But the reality is much harsher for a generation like them which want to rebound and lead a better life than their previous generation did. The camp schools only give the young Rohingya the opportunity to study till grade eight. After that officially it is all over for them, but life does not stop there. With time young Rohingyas like Mansurul Alam tried to find a way out to achieve their dreams. Like Mansur, who lives in Kutupalong camp many students are studying outside the camp in the government and non-governmental schools. After finishing his primary education in 2003, Mansur went to nearby Kutupalong High School and requested the Headmaster to get him admitted. The Head Master of the school gave him the chance to study in his school by hiding the refugee identity and in 2008 Mansur attended the SSC exam (Secondary School Certificate). Mansur had been studying with much difficulty for the last few years. He had to sell the ration to continue his study and his mother had to sell the gold chain, the last token of memory from her father-in-law's house. They had to sell the hatch's plastic they got from UNHCR. The members of the family had to starve. Yet, he did not give up. He is hoping that he would achieve an 'A' grade in his SSC examination. When he was asked what he will do after passing SSC he replied, "I will study H.S.C.", he was asked, 'From where?' and Mansur replied, 'I do not know yet.' When the interviewer asked him, 'What will you do after H.S.C?' he replied, "I will study Law." He explained, "I want to set my nation free. I want to discover in what law and for what right my nation has to suffer and die now. I want to know why we are stateless though all other nations on earth have their own states. We want citizenship, democracy in Burma, freedom of Aung Sun Syu Ki. We want our compensation." The interviewer asked him, 'Will you be able to do these?' Mansur replied, "Obviously I will, if you help." This case shows that whatever hopes the Rohingya refugees have it centres around the young generation they have. Everyday Rohingya refugees have to face the reality that in Bangladesh they can not even claim the minimal opportunities to dream any sort of future, still they try to grab anything that comes in their way just to have a dream.

Many of the interviewees were politically concerned in terms of their future. A great deal of their imagination was around the freedom of Aung Sun Syu Ki. All of them believe that the freedom of their great leader would bring peace in Myanmar and one day, they will be able to return to their country. For example, Md. Yunis, a 28 years old young man living in the Tal[46] was asked if he wants to go back to his country, he replied, "It depends on improvement of the situation in Myanmar. The great leader Aung Sun Syu Ki has to be released from captivity. Democracy has to be restored and the Rohingyas should be given citizenship of Myanmar. I intend to go back to Myanmar once the fundamental rights are established. Otherwise I will prefer to work as casual worker or pull rickshaw here in Bangladesh rather than go back to Myanmar. My only expectation at this moment is to get a chance to be transferred to Leda Camp so that I can be registered as refugee. This will give me the status of a refugee and will get ration and other facilities." This answer of Yunis projects the consistent dialectics of hope and reality, the whole Rohingya refugee community is facing inside them. On the one hand, he is hoping that someday he will get everything back, on the other hand, he is also prepared for the worse even if he has to pull rickshaw here in Bangladesh he will do that. With all these dreams for Yunis the reality is to get to Leda so that he can register himself as a refugee. Yunis is struggling to get the status of a refugee, still he can dream of his home and citizenship of his country.

Nurul Hakim is another Rohingya refugee who has dreams and hopes. When asked about his future plan, Nurul Hakim said, "I don't want to go to Burma. I want to stay here. I am saving money to repay the five thousands taka which I borrowed for being released from the jail. After repaying my loans, I will learn any technical work. Then I want to marry a Bangladeshi girl who has land in any village to build a house to live in."[47] Another Rohingya refugee, Nur Hossain also expresses his dream about future. Nur Hossain is optimistic about the future of young generation. When asked about the future, he said,

46 Tal is an unofficial camp for unregistered refugees on the bank of river Naaf bordering Myanmar, where most of the Rohingya refugees come as the first stopover.

47 Based on Interview of Nurul Hakim (undocumented Rohingya) by Ashraful Azad on 14-20 June 2008.

"One day they will be educated and they will talk about our right, about our torture." Nur Hossain added, "Some of our people would go abroad. We want to go as well. If we can go abroad, one day our children will grow up and lead a standard life. This is a poor country. Many of the indigenous people are suffering in this country. So, in this position, we do not have any hope in this country. If we stay in this country, we must live in this position and our fate will remain the same. If you want to know my wish, then I want to tell you, ultimately, we want a place beyond Bangladesh."[48]

The narratives of the Rohingya refugees clearly demonstrate that they dream a future where hope is the driving force. A democratic Myanmar or resettlement in a third country preferably a developed one or living in Bangladesh marrying a Bangladeshi girl capture some of their dreams, but certainly not all. This can be regarded as the greatest force in their lives. However, it does not mask their traumas they experienced in Myanmar and subsequently in the refugee camps in Bangladesh. Trauma and their traumatic memories will continue to influence their lives and shape their identity.

---

48 Interview of Nur Hossain by Mobasser, Nayapara camp, a registered refugee, 14-20 June 2008.

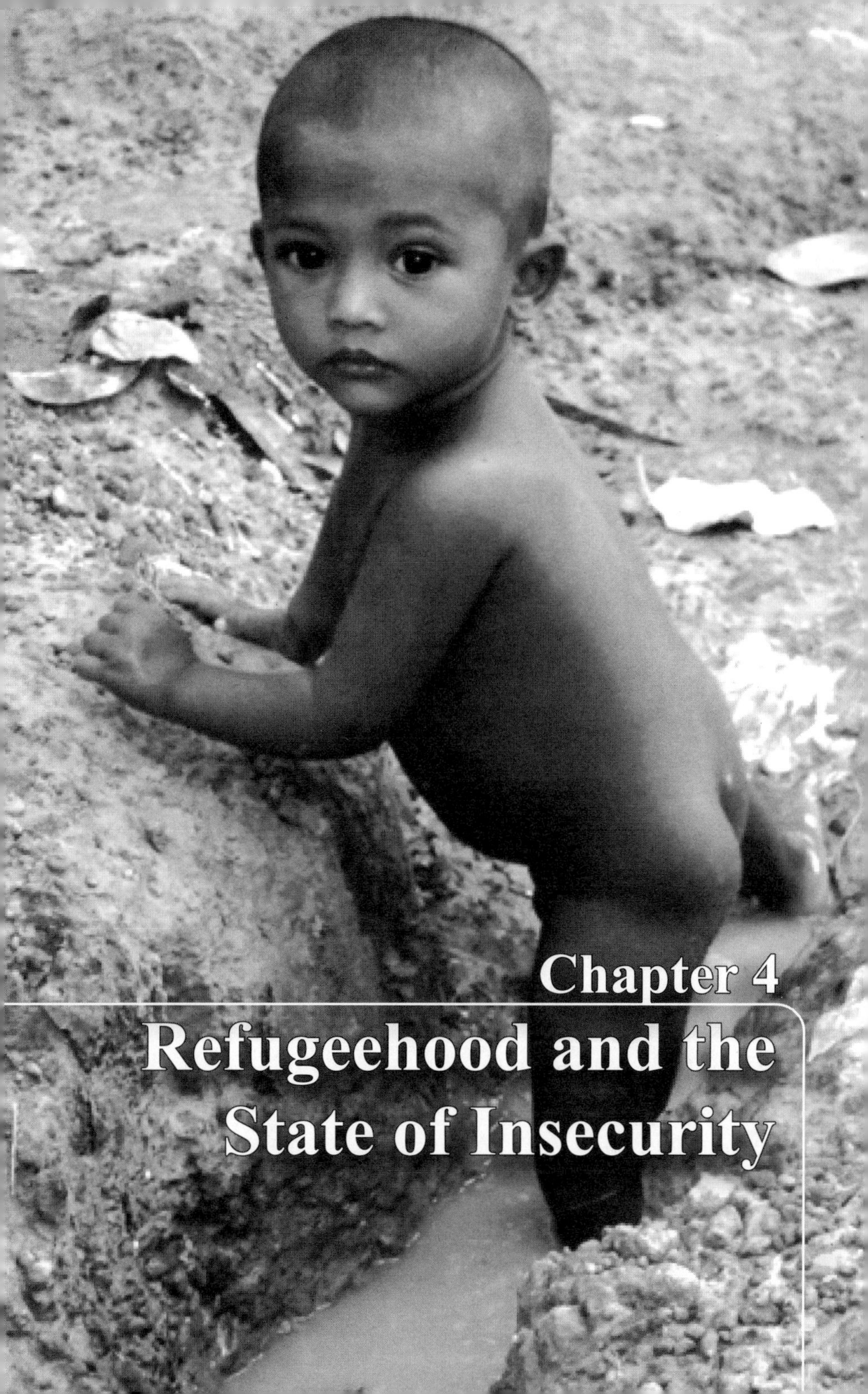

Chapter 4

Refugeehood and the State of Insecurity

Photograph by Jolly Nur Haque/IR/DU 2008

"I was born in Burma, but the Burmese Government says I don't belong there. I grew up in Bangladesh, but the Bangladesh Government says I cannot stay here. As a Rohingya, I feel I am caught between a crocodile and a snake."[1]

The Rohingya issue is not merely a refugee issue; it has critical security implications. The influx of Rohingya refugees into Bangladesh from Myanmar constitutes a major security concern for Bangladesh as well as the Rohingya refugees living in camp and non-camp areas. A report published by the Christian Solidarity Worldwide (CSW) states that hundreds of Burmese Muslim minorities, seeking refuge on the Bangladesh-Burma border, are in dire situation, despite escaping brutal repression by the Burmese military junta.[2] Many analysts in Bangladesh tend to argue that the exodus is a source of national insecurity in addition to an excessive economic and administrative burden for Bangladesh. Security is seen as the main factor influencing the whole process involving resolution of the Rohingya refugee problem. Moreover, with the ascendancy of new notions of human security and effective protection, the field of security has broadened, deepened and responsibilities have become operationally multilateral. The problem of security regarding the Rohingya refugee issue is complicated by the insurgency factors. Militant Rohingyas have reportedly taken up arms to fight for an

1 Burma Centre Netherlands, *Report of the Fact-finding Mission - April/May 2003*, Amsterdam: Burma Centre Netherlands.

2 Available on http://www.mizzima.com/news/regional/1021-rohingyas-in-dire-straits-csw.html accessed on 22 October 2008.

independent homeland in Arakan.[3] This chapter deals with the key question of what security vulnerabilities or threats the Rohingyas are facing while living in this country as documented and undocumented refugees. The chapter is organised into five sections. First section briefly sheds light on the conceptual understanding of security in a holistic sense. In the second section, political and strategic factors of security are identified while the third section focuses on economic factors. The fourth and fifth sections deal with social and environmental factors respectively.

4.1 WHAT IS SECURITY?

While security 'ranks prominently among the problems facing humanity', it remains a difficult concept to define.[4] What has been widely accepted is the link between 'threats' and 'security'. Insecurity is subjective, and is consequently rooted in the perception of a threat. As Jervis argues, the 'perception of a threat is certainly as important as any construction of an objective threat...'.[5] This is true even if the threat is misperceived and later proved to be without basis.[6] Thus, threat is central to an understanding of security. The word "security" in general usage is synonymous with "safety", but as a technical term "security" means that something not only *is secure* but that it *has been secured*. In this context, security is rightly defined as the condition of being protected against threats whether perceived or real. It also refers to a condition that results from the establishment and maintenance of protective measures that ensure a state of inviolability from hostile acts or influences. Protection is the basic element of security. From all perspectives security is an issue which gives the assurance of safety from all odds. From an individual's point of view, security means the assurance of all the basic human rights. On the other hand, securing the sovereign from opposing forces is the prime duty of the state. This,

---

3 Iftekharuzzaman, "Bangladesh: A Weak State and Power", in Muthiah Alagappa (ed.) *Asian Security Practice: Material and Ideational Influences*, London: Stanford University Press, 1998.

4 Buzan, Barry (1991) *People, States and Fear: An Agenda for International Security Studies in the Post-Cold War Era.* Second Edition. London: Harvester Wheatsheaf, p.1.

5 Jervis, Robert (1976) *Perception and Misperception in International Politics.* Princeton: Princeton University Press, p.6.

6 Berkowitz, Morton, and P.G. Bock (1968) 'National Security.' in David Sills (ed.) *International Encyclopedia of the Social Sciences.* New York: Macmillan and Maluwa, Tiyanjana (1995) 'The Refugee Problem and the Quest for Peace and Security in Southern Africa.' *International Journal of Refugee Law* 7 (4), p.654.

however, is a realist construct, the referent object of security here is the state.[7] The prevalence of this theorem reached a peak during the Cold War.

The traditional state centric notion of security has been challenged by more holistic approaches to security. Human security is one of such approaches which shows that sources of threats are primarily intrastate and they can be both direct and indirect. Human security shares with poverty, human development, human rights a concern with protecting the 'vital core' of human life.[8] It implies a remarkable shift in focus of security as a universal quest for human beings. It changes from an exclusive stress on national security to a much greater stress on people's security, from security through armaments to security through human development, and from territorial security to food, employment and environmental security. Another major category is non-traditional security. In a non traditional security paradigm an individual is provided with all the basic human needs, right to practice democracy, access to information, right to movement, right to speech, etc. The continuing debate between traditional and non-traditional security obscures the fact that from both perspectives security remains highly a state centric notion. In order to avoid the controversy, it is better to focus on four major dimensions of security whether it is traditional or non-traditional or human security. They are closely enmeshed with the Rohingya refugee issue. These are politico-military dimension, economic dimension, social dimension and environmental dimension (Table 4.1). It must be made clear that while understanding security we must avoid the mistake of *universalising* the conception of security by *privileging* widely held or dominant views on the matter.

4.2 POLITICO-MILITARY DIMENSION OF SECURITY

The politico-military dimension of security involving the Rohingya refugees has two basic levels: local and state. At the local level, militancy, insurgency, policing, and arms smuggling are the major threats to security while law and order, protection measures, counterterrorism mechanisms and others cover state level. The key

7 Ayoob, Mohammed (1995) *The Third World Security Predicament: State Making, Regional Conflict and the International System*. London: Lynne Rienner.

8 Sakiko Fukuda-Parr, "Gender, Globalisation and New Threats to Human Security." *Peace Review*, 16:1, 2004, 35-42.

Table 4.1 The Rohingya Refugees and Sources of Insecurity

Security for Whom?	Sources of Insecurity Politico-Military	Social	Economic	Environmental
States	National security/ Interstate security Counter-terrorism, counterinsurgency		Unemployment Rising prices of lands and essentials	Deforestation Water pollution Soil erosion
Societies, Groups, and Individuals	Local Policing Civil war, Ethnic conflict, Genocide, Terrorism Proliferation of small arms	Rape Violence Drug Abuse Survival of societies, groups, and individuals	Smuggling Money – laundering Unemployment Price hike	Deforestation Water pollution Medical conditions Waste

issues in politico-security dimension of security regarding the Rohingya refugees are briefly analysed in this section.

4.2.1 Insurgency and Islamic Militancy

Insurgency is increasingly becoming a critical security issue involving the Rohingya refugees, Bangladesh and Myanmar. Historically, two major operations by the military government in Myanmar have contributed to the exodus of the Rohingyas and related problems of insurgency and terrorism. The first major operation took place in 1978 when the Ne Win regime in Myanmar launched the "Nagomin Programme" which has been described as "a census operation,"[9] "a campaign against illegal immigrants,"[10] and "an attempt at national consolidation through forced eviction of the Muslims from Myanmar."[11] By May 1978, an estimated 200,000 Rohingya had to escape across the border to Bangladesh. The second major influx had resulted from military operation in 1991-92 when a new wave of over a quarter of a million Rohingyas escaped to Bangladesh because of widespread forced labour, summary executions, torture, and rape. Many other human rights violations took place in the context of forced

9 Ibid. p. 241.

10 David I Steinberg, "Constitutional and Political Bases of Minority Insurrections in Burma" in Lim Joo-Jock and S Vani (eds), *Armed Separatism in Southeast Asia*, Singapore, Institute of Southeast Asian Studies, 1984, p. 68.

11 HRWA, *Burma: The Robingya Muslims: Ending a Cycle of Exodus*, New York, Human Rights Watch/Asia, 8(9), 1996.

labour of Rohingya civilians by the security forces.[12] In addition, several other, albeit in small scale, exodus have taken place over the time.

Map 4.1: Presence of Insurgent Groups in Bangladesh and India

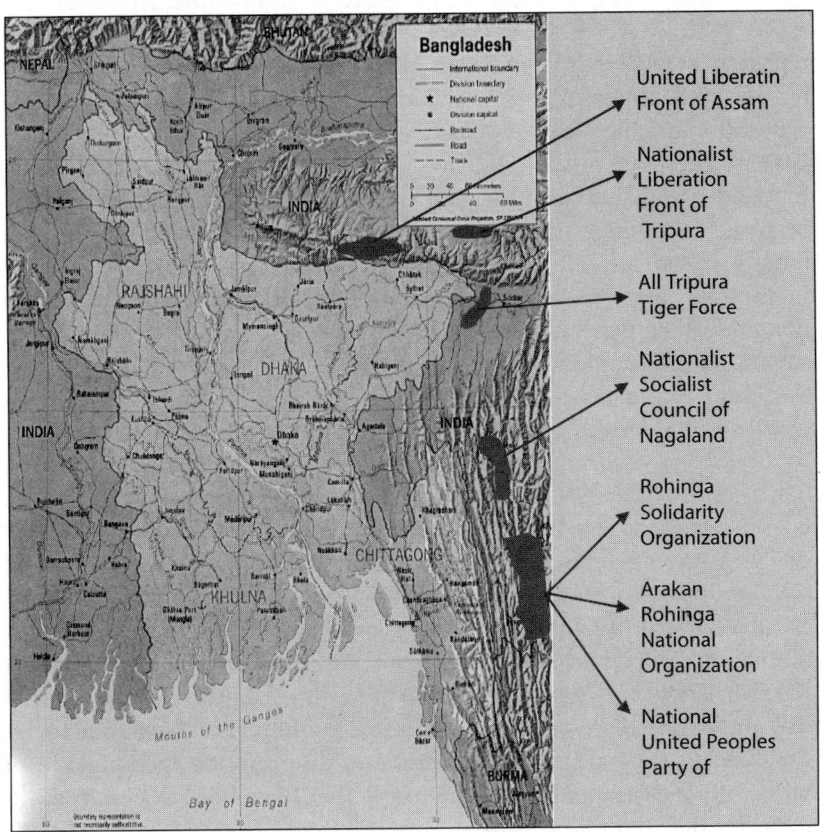

Source: ATM Amin, 2008, op.cit.

One of the major consequences of the military operations in Arakan and persistent torture on the Rohingyas is the establishment of several Rohingya armed groups over the last three decades. These include the Rohingya Solidarity Organisation (RSO) and the Arakan Rohingya Islamic Front (ARIF), both of which in 1996 jointly formed the

12 Ibid.

Rohingya National Alliance (RNA).[13] In 1998 two RSO factions and the ARIF merged into the Arakan Rohingya National Organisation (ARNO).[14] Particularly, following the 1991-92 influx of Rohingya Muslim refugees, some of the Rohingya armed groups became vibrant in the refugee camps, where they tried to recruit people. Subsequently, these groups were divided into several small factions. They are reportedly working from little bases in the Bangladesh-Myanmar border, and apparently do not have a great number of troops. It is estimated that the number of armed Rohingya insurgents is maximum 1,000.[15] There are also other armed groups which are operating in the Bangladesh-Myanmar border. Those include the National Unity Party of Arakan (NUPA) and the Arakan Army; both of these groups are mostly based among the Buddhist Rakhine population. It may be mentioned that there are allegations by some quarters that the Bangladesh government supports an armed movement against the Myanmar government which the former always denies. However, the Rohingya refugee issue has the potential to cause cross border clashes between Bangladesh and Myanmar.

Linked to insurgency Islamic militancy involving the Rohingyas has been on the rise. Over the past decade a number of extremist Islamist groups have become active in Bangladesh, with at least some of them having links to the international terrorist network. The Al Qaeda-allied group, the Harkat-ul-Jehad-al-Islami (HuJI), is believed to have a base in Chittagong. Some reports indicate that the Harkat maintains camps in the hilly areas of Chittagong as well as near Cox's Bazar.[16] They are also reported to be using camps vacated by the Rohingya refugees, and a number of Rohingyas are known to be involved in the smuggling of arms and ammunition in Bangladesh. Some other prominent Islamist groups that have been active recently include the Jama'atul Mujahidin, Shahadat-e-Al-Hikma, Hizbut Touheed and Islami Shashontantra Andolan.[17] There is little doubt that extremist groups have taken advantage of the disenfranchised Rohingyas, including recruiting them as cannon fodder for Al Qaeda

13 Press Statement by the Rohingya National Alliance (RNA), 28 September 1996.

14 Declaration of the Arakan Rohingya National Organisations (ARNO), 13 December, 1998.

15 Peter Van Wonterghem, 1999.

16 http://www.satp.org/satporgtp/sair/Archives/2_38.htm accessed on 15 October 2008.

17 Ibid.

in Afghanistan and elsewhere. In an interview with the Karachi-based newspaper, *Ummat*, on September 28, 2001, Osama bin Laden said: "There are areas in all parts of the world where strong Jihadi forces are present, from Bosnia to Sudan, and from Burma to Kashmir."[18] He was most probably referring to a small group of Rohingyas on the Bangladesh-Burma border.

Many of the Rohingya recruits were given the most dangerous tasks in the battlefield, clearing mines and portering. According to Asian intelligence sources, Rohingya recruits were paid 30,000 Bangladeshi taka ($525) on joining and then 10,000 taka ($175) per month. The families of recruits killed in action were offered 100,000 taka ($1,750).[19] Recruits were taken mostly via Nepal to Pakistan, where they were trained and sent on further to military camps in Afghanistan. It is not known how many people from this part of Bangladesh — Rohingyas and others — fought in Afghanistan. Others went to Kashmir and even Chechnya to join forces with Islamist militants there.[20] Thus, the emergence of insurgent movement associated with militancy in the subsequent period has built a global network of the Rohingyas and thereby creates a major security concern for Bangladesh with bilateral, regional and global implications. Imtiaz Ahmed captures this security question succinctly. He observes that while there is no doubt about the fact that the Rohingyas are stateless and refugees at the same time, the subaltern globalisation in the contemporary world has exposed the Rohingyas to the domain of terrorism and violence.[21] The Taliban and al Qaeda connections with a section of the Rohingyas, as mentioned above, make it evident that they are getting involved with militant activities with subaltern aspirations.

4.2.2 Drugs and Arms Smuggling

The drug trade poses another security threat for Bangladesh. Smuggling rings operate in Maungdaw and Sittwe in Arakan State and

18 For an account of the 1978 refugee crisis, see Bertil Lintner, *Burma in Revolt: Opium and Insurgency Since 1948*, Chiang Mai: Silkworm Books, 1999, pp. 317-8.

19 Bertil Lintner, Tension Mounts in Arakan State, *Defence Weekly*, October 19, 1991.

20 Ibid.

21 Imtiaz Ahmed, "Globalisation, Low Intensity Conflcit and Protracted Statelessness/ Refugeehood: The Plight of the Rohingyas", in John Triman, ed. *Maze of Fear, USA*: The Newpress, 2004, p. 183.

Teknaf, Cox's Bazaar and Chittagong in Bangladesh.[22] As Myanmar is a member of 'Golden Triangle', and is also located in the close proximity of another major narco-producing region, the 'Golden Crescent', drug trafficking becomes a common practice. In recent times, Yaba (madness medicine), a synthetic drug manufactured mostly in Myanmar-Thai border, constitutes a significant component of drug smuggling on the border. Bangladeshi authorities, the BDR, the police and other concerned authorities have already seized large quantity of Yaba. They have been trying to stop the inflow of Yaba to Bangladesh from Myanmar. It may be mentioned that Yaba from Arakan State are smuggled to Bangladesh through land and waterways.[23] In June 2009 it was reported that over 2,000 Yaba tablets worth one million Taka were seized by Bangladesh Rifles (BDR) on the Myanmar-Bangladesh border from a bus plying to Cox's Bazaar from Teknaf.[24] For smuggling heroin from Myanmar beyond the region and the continent, both India and Bangladesh are used as transit points.[25] This further aggravates problems related to narco-terrorism in the region. In fact, one critical problem arising out of the convergence of two major narco-producing and trading regions is the cementing of a diabolic relationship between insurgent groups, arms dealers and narco-terrorism. Such a relationship is quite common in and around Thai-Myanmar, Indo-Myanmar and Bangladesh-Myanmar borders. Not that all the insurgent groups engage in narco-production or narco-trafficking, but it has been found that almost all of them have regularly taxed and exhorted money from the traffickers while providing protection to the latter for conducting trafficking in drugs.[26] So, this nexus among the terrorist, drug dealers and insurgent groups operating within the region is creating a severe military threat for the security of Bangladesh. Besides, the local people allege that the Rohingyas in the camps give shelter to illegal outsiders and criminals and bring in arms through the hilly border areas. For them it has become a den for arms and drug business.

---

22 Altsean, Burma, *Report Card: Balancing Act*, March 2003.

23 http://www.kaladanpress.org/v3

24 *Kaladan News*, June 10, 2009.

25 Burma Country Brief (BCB), 2002, *Drug Intelligence Brief*, DEA Intelligence Division, Office of International Intelligence, Europe, Asia Africa Strategic Unit, Washington DC, May.

26 Ahmed Imtiaz, 'Small Arms & Subaltern Globalisation' in *CODESRIA Bulletin*, Nos 1 and 2, 2004, p.62.

The security problem with the insurgency activity in the border region centring the Rohingya refugees also crops up the issue of networks between international, regional and local Islamic terrorist organisations to help their own cause. As these groups need arms for their movements or operations, illegal arms trade and infiltration of arms into Bangladesh are common phenomena. The militant groups are trying to recruit men from the refugee camps and they are buying and selling arms from these insurgent groups operating in Bangladesh, Myanmar and Indian border area. It is reported that at least 37 illegal arms smuggling syndicates are active in Chittagong, controlling the illegal arms market and the supply to terrorist groups. A number of Rohingya and Arakanese groups are also involved in the arms smuggling. Around 60 kilometers of the border area at Teknaf in the Cox's Bazar district, where there is little Government security presence, is one of the main routes for arms smuggling. The gunrunners face little resistance here and maintain several offices in the port city of Chittagong, the hill districts of Khagrachhari and Bandarban, Cox's Bazar and Dhaka, where they maintain close contacts with various terrorist groups.[27] The kind of arms and ammunition recovered, however, suggest strong linkages with the growing force of radical Islamists in the country. Ordinary criminals in Bangladesh do not have a significant history of the use of such weapons, and partisan political violence in the past has not graduated to the level of sophistication reflected in the present arms cache.

4.2.3 Camp-related Security Issues

Inhabitants of refugee camps and surrounding areas suffer a wide range of security problems, including attacks by external forces, the militarisation of camps, and the breakdown of law and order. Militarisation in camps is increasingly becoming a security concern. The presence of combatants in camps undermines civilian authority and sources of law and order, and can lead to camps falling under the control of political agents or military elements. Refugees are then more likely to be deprived of their rights and otherwise be subjected to violence and intimidation. Inside camps, refugees are often subjected to intimidation, violence, and harassment from a variety of groups and individuals. Clashes also occur between refugees and local people,

27 *'South Asian Intelligence Review'* Volume 2, No.38 April 5, 2004.

usually outside the camp, and most often when there is resentment by locals towards refugees for perceived wrongdoings, such as theft or immoral acts, or for inequities resulting from refugees' access to relief resources.

As the Rohingya refugee camps are characterised by limited resources such as food, water and fuel, competition over these resources may therefore give rise to people resorting to violence as a survival means. In the absence of effective rule of law, petty and violent crime flourishes and can lead to camps becoming zones of drug smuggling, human trafficking, organised crime, illegal logging, and gun running, with the attendant problems of violence. When deprived of the assurance of protection, people do not have the confidence to approach the few police available and instead increasingly opt for self-help. Bad policing can also contribute to the breakdown of law and order in refugee camps. Excuses for not stopping impunity are many and varied in refugee camps. The presence of suspected criminals in the camps led to problems of both internal and external security. The enforcement of law and order in the camps became increasingly problematic as intimidators within the camps exercised greater control over the refugee population. Security in the areas surrounding the camps was also jeopardised. There were numerous reports of banditry and attacks on the Rohingyas as well as neighbouring people.

4.2.4 Policing in the Camps and Counter-terrorism Measures

As part of law and order protection in the camp areas and counter-terrorism initiative, the government of Bangladesh maintains wider presence of police, Bangladesh Rifles (BDR), National Security Intelligence (NSI) and the Directorate General of Forces Intelligence (DGFI) in Teknaf region of Chittagong where the Rohingyas are concentrated as documented and undocumented refugees. Both state and non-state actors are involved in the maintenance of the overall environment in the camps. Mainly, the Bangladesh government ensures safety and security of the refugees both inside and outside the camps. The GOB has appointed the Police and Ansar for the security of the Rohingya refugees. Every camp has a Camp-in-Charge (CIC) to maintain law and order in the camps. Apart from government security forces, camp management committee, block committee and security volunteers assist in managing the camps. These committees are playing a positive role for conflict management in the camps.

However, despite increasing role of local and informal institutions, the police as the state agency have an aggressive presence in the camps. It generates fear among the Rohingya refugees in the camps. It has been observed that there is a feeling of insecurity in the camps, about half of the refugees felt insecure, mainly because of fear of harassment by camp authorities or villagers.[28] As reported in a local newspaper, "an unidentified Rohingya was killed in a shootout with BDR. While trafficking illegal Burmese goods to Bangladesh, BDR had an exchange of gunfire with the traffickers. Two men died in the shootout, among them one was identified as a Rohingya by the BDR men."[29] According to UNHCR, camp authorities ceased using corporal punishment, fines, and the systematic withholding of food as punishment. In January 2008, however, camp police tortured a young Rohingya refugee to death after another refugee involved in a personal dispute with him claimed he was a terrorist.[30] It has also been revealed that authorities often falsely accuse many camp-based refugees of crimes and jail many refugees for a longer period than the actual term. For example, a person found guilty is punished over a year for charges with maximum sentences of three months. On the other hand, local authorities are also concerned over the firearms in the hands of refugees. Thus, the Rohingyas remain vulnerable amid law and order protection activity and counter-terrorism initiatives of government security forces such as BDR, the Police and Ansars.

4.3 ECONOMIC DIMENSION OF SECURITY

Economic security is extremely significant for both the Rohingyas and the local community. The major threats in the economic domain of security for the Rohingyas stem from smuggling, unemployment, rising prices, continuing poverty, money laundering, etc.

4.3.1 Smuggling/Illegal Trade

It is a fact that many of the Rohingyas are engaged in smuggling. The Chinese consumer products are commonly smuggled through the Bangladesh-Myanmar border in which the Rohingya refugees are allegedly involved (see, Box 4.1). Such involvement of the Rohingyas

---

28 http://www.unsystem.org/SCN/archives/nics01/index.htm

29 *The Daily Cox's Bazaar*, 18 May, 2008.

30 "Country Reports, Bangladesh," *World Refugee Survey*, http://www.refugees.org

Box 4.1: Report on Smuggling
On June 16, 2008 the Bangladesh Rifles (BDR), arrested a smuggler with 350-litre of soyabean oil while he was attempting to smuggle the same to Burma. At least 100,000 litres of diesel is smuggled to Burma from Teknaf and Ukhiya points per month. In Burma, a litre of diesel is sold at Taka 70, while in Bangladesh it is sold for Taka 45. People of Maungdaw and Buthidaung Townships depend on Bangladeshi diesel and in return contraband drugs and fishing nets are smuggled to Bangladesh, a trader in Teknaf Town said.
Source: http://www.kaladanpress.org 19 June 2008.

in this smuggling activity is well known in the region. Another practice is observed among the Rohingyas that they sell part of their rations received from the UNHCR in the local market although the government of Bangladesh has restricted the rights to trade for the refugees. Box 4.2 shows how much ration a Rohingya refugee normally receive from the UNHCR. It has been revealed that the Rohingya refugees believe that if they have a large family, then they would get a larger quantity of rations. Part of this ration can be sold in the informal market. However, the MOU between Bangladesh and UNHCR clearly notes that the refugees cannot take part in any sort of trade activities.

Box 4.2: General Food Distribution, Kutupalong Refugee Camps in Cox's Bazar Area, Bangladesh	
Food Items (bi-weekly)	Non-food Items
6.3 kg of rice	Laundry soap
560 grams of pulse	Bath soap
280 grams of soya bean oil	Kerosene
140 grams of sugar	Compressed Rice Husk
140 grams of salt	Cloths (Yearly)
700 grams blended food	Semai (Eid Festivals)
Source: Field survey, 7-10 June, 2008	

While asked about this illegal trade, one of the high officials from UNHCR (on the condition of anonymity) acknowledged the fact that it is a common practice among the Rohingya refugees. He further says that the UNHCR does not provide any protein items for the refugees, so they give the rations in such a quantity that could be sold after meeting some of the basic requirements of the refugees.[31] In this way, the refugees can meet their protein needs. There are examples of smuggling by the refugees. BDR has been active in stopping illegal cross border trade in the border regions. It is widely reported in the local newspapers. According to one newspaper, "Many Rohingya refugees are caught and accused of being involved in such activities. Twelve spots are being used as illegal trade routes in Ukhiya Upazila - Reju Mogpara, Deilpara, Chakboita, Tulatoli, Amtoli, Boroitoli, Fatragira, Koroibonia Ghumdhum, Tumuru, Farir Bil, Rahmater Bil and Dhamonkhali."[32] These spots are frequently used by the illegal traders around the camps. The refugees receive help from the local businessmen while engaged in such illegal trade. The local businessmen provide the refugee counterpart with the money or goods and the refugee has the duty to guide the transportation of the goods to the other side of the border. Local authorities are concerned with this illegal trade activity. The major items being smuggled include wood, diesel, soybean oil, cattle, sugar, shrimps, plastic bags, rice, medicines, fertiliser, salt, fruits, etc.

4.3.2 Employment Issues

Employment is another major area where the Rohingya refugees are considerably vulnerable. In fact, the abject poverty with poor living conditions is a direct consequence of massive joblessness among the Rohingyas particularly those who are undocumented refugees. The reasons behind their unemployment range from official restriction to illiteracy of the Rohingyas. The restrictions on wage earning employment extend to trade and self-employment. Refugees do not have the right to own moveable or immovable property. Besides, high birth rate among the Rohingyas is also another cause. It is observed during the field investigation that the Rohingyas are not conscious about the pitfalls of high population growth. High birth rate in the Rohingya families living in refugee camps and outside creates pressure on local economy. Most of them work as day labours, rickshaw pullers, etc and very few of them are businessmen. Generally, the Rohingyas are not allowed to get engaged in income generating works. However, the recent development is different. The refugees are now allowed to

31 Field interviews conducted during 7-15 June 2008.

32 *Banglar Jamin* (Cox's Bazar, Chittagong), 8 June, 2008.

move in and out of the camps more frequently than ever. They are engaged in many different income generating activities like day labour, restaurant jobs, carpentering etc. Some of the Rohingyas are working even in the cities of Cox's Bazar and Chittagong.

Understandably, this has an impact on employment opportunities of the local people for which they have already expressed their resentment. While the Rohingyas do not get enough job opportunities to survive in a decent way, sadly so, these limited opportunities are creating hindrance for the local people particularly the marginalised community. As one analyst states, "Only a few thousand Rohingyas are living in refugee camps while a sizeable number of them are living outside the camps affecting the local environment and destroying the balance in the labour market of Chittagong."[33] The local people allege that the Rohingyas are the cheapest of labours and hence the local labour market is being spoiled by their inclusion. Unsurprisingly, the employers are seeking for cheaper labour for which local people are losing their job opportunities as well as bargaining capacity.

4.3.3 Rising Price Levels

Price is another sensitive but vital area that affects the life of the Rohingya refugees as well as the local community people. Apart from the daily essential goods, the price of land is a critical issue. Due to the influx of the Rohingyas price of land has been increasing in the region. In recent times, the Rohingyas have been put into a dire situation as their food supply is close to being depleted particularly for the undocumented Rohingyas. With joblessness and marginalisation the Rohingya refugees have been badly hit by globally rising global food prices.

4.4 SOCIAL DIMENSION OF SECURITY

Several issues and concerns constitute the gamut of social dimension of security with regard to the Rohingya refugees. These include use of drugs, drug trafficking, violence against women and children, riots, decaying social values and gender discrimination. The drug trade is creating another security threat for Bangladesh. It may be mentioned

---

33 Based on Seminar held in Chittagong on Rohingya refugee problem on May 19, 2008. http://www.kaladanpress.org//index.php?option=com_content&task=view&id=1335&Itemid=2 accessed 5 October 2008.

that China, India and Bangladesh face the highest drug addiction in their areas bordering Myanmar. In China's Yunnan province, heroin use seems completely out of control and the UN estimates that up to 80% of the city's intravenous drug users are HIV positive.[34] Bangladesh has been facing an increased drug influx by land and sea since September 2002. Smuggling rings operate in Maungdaw and Sittwe in Arakan State and Teknaf, Cox's Bazaar and Chittagong in Bangladesh. The Bangladeshi press has been reporting that the political pressure upon the law enforcement agencies prevent them from taking any actions. Local drug traffickers are often extremely powerful, making government agencies helpless.[35]

Many women have been compelled to engage in prostitution to save their family from hunger. Besides, a few hundred Rohingyas, most of them inhabiting illegally are currently in custody. Some were arrested for petty criminal offences, but often on false charges made by Mahjees[36] or local police. Particularly, the undocumented Rohingyas in imprisonment do not receive any legal aid, and remain detained although they should have already been released. Moreover, there is a concern with regard to the state of the undocumented refugees living in the Teknaf 'makeshift camp'. More then 4,000 refugees live there under stressful situation with almost no access to food, drinking water, sanitation and medical aid.[37]

In many cases Rohingya women are victims of rape and domestic violence both within the camp and outside. As revealed in a local newspaper, "a woman from Taal camp was raped by a local, while she went to fetch water from the mountain stream (Cholera)."[38] It has been disclosed by the Rohingya refugees during the field study that rape has been commonly used as an instrument of violence against them. The members of security forces, the Rohingya men, and local villagers are the main perpetrators. Women who had to go for the collection of firewood and drinking water in areas surrounding the camps, female heads of household or young girls whose fathers/husbands are in jail are particularly at risk of rape and kidnapping. Rape and sexual abuse

34 See, "The Blood Ties That Bind," *Newsweek*, 28 October 2002.

35 *Narinjara News* (6 Oct 02) 'Tactics change, smuggling goes on'.

36 Group leaders in the Rohingya camps.

37 "Between the Crocodile and the Snake;,"Burma Centre Netherlands; May 2003.

38 *Ajker Desh Bidesh*, 4 June, 2008.

is also used as a measure to compel women into marriages against their will or as a means of taking revenge on male family members.

The sheds created for the refugees are too small to accommodate a family of two members, whereas the refugees have to live there no matter whatever the size of the family is. It may be mentioned that almost all of the Rohingya families have on the average five members. The reason for the big family is probably that each and every member receives equal amount of ration from the UNHCR. That means, the more member you have in your family, the more rations you get. Besides, there are some accusations that the refugees are involved in social crimes in the areas such as stealing, robbery, etc. These issues ignite instability in the society from time to time. The same accusations are also labelled against the local community people. The route to seek justice is also quite difficult for the refugees. They have to place a written complaint to the CIC of respective camps; the CIC would resolve the problems and if necessary file a case in the local police station. There are cases that men get rid of criminal cases by bribing the police personnel. Hence, the situation remains hostile for the Rohingya refugees when issues are related to their survival, not to mention about their dignity.

The scope for education in the refugee camps is very limited for the Rohingya children. The GOB shows negligence in providing adequate opportunities for education. In the camps the refugees are allowed schooling for only up to class five. The subjects taught are also limited as they get the opportunity to learn only English, Mathematics and Bengali. The right to education is somewhat violated in this regard. It was observed from the field study that the UNHCR took interviews of the selected refugees to resettle them in a third country. There is no doubt that the offer is highly beneficial for the Rohingyas as they will get chance to resettle in the developed countries like the USA, Canada, New Zealand and Australia. The point is that the UNHCR is selecting the educated ones and the most vulnerable women for this resettlement. It indicates how critically education is linked with the development of the Rohingya children not only as human being but also for getting good opportunities for resettlement in the third country.

4.5 ENVIRONMENTAL DIMENSION OF SECURITY

The documented and undocumented Rohingya refugees are often blamed for deteriorating environment in the region. The major issues regarding environmental dimension of security include deforestation particularly by cutting trees, water pollution and unhygienic living conditions.

4.5.1 Deforestation

It is generally claimed that the Rohingyas are clearing the forests, cutting the hills for their shelter, residing here and there, thus causing significant damage to the environment. They cut trees deliberately to earn their livelihoods. The lands of the two existing camps were 'Reserved Forests' of the Department of Forestry, Government of Bangladesh (as marked as Mochni Bit in the Survey Map of the Forest Department of Bangladesh). The unofficial camp for the unregistered refugees, Taal Camp, was also based in the reserved forest area. Before the establishment of the camps, the local people used to graze the land. Now due to the camps lands are totally lost. As the reserved forest is being destroyed, the local inhabitants are becoming 'internally displaced persons'. The situation is getting worse day by day, because the UNHCR used to provide firewood in the rations, but it has been stopped since 2004. This caused the refugees to cut down the forest trees and use them as firewood for the purpose of cooking. It is obvious that the uneducated refugees do not think or know about the importance of forest reserve; not surprisingly they cut down the trees without any hesitation. Largely due to deforestation, the ecosystem of that area is undergoing a massive change. The species that would inhabit in the area are slowly moving out or getting extinct.

4.5.2 Environmental Pollution

Different kinds of environmental pollution are commonly seen in the areas where both documented and undocumented Rohingya refugees live. The typical pollutants are probably absent in the refugee camps, for instance emission of chemicals that particulates into the atmosphere, but there are severe forms of genetic pollution in the camp areas. Specifically, water pollution is a major concern due to lack of access to sanitation and fresh drinking water. The sewerage management in the camps is obviously a major concern. Particularly, the location of the Tal camp is a great concern. All the sewerage flows into the Naf River, spoiling the purity of the river water. Moreover, the waterborne diseases are more likely to spread due to such flow. Water pollution otherwise makes the camp dwellers as well as the local people vulnerable to diseases. More generally, the environment is degrading. Partly related to deforestation soil erosion is becoming another major environmental disaster in this area. With growing number of cutting of trees in the forest, the ecosystem of the area is bound to change a lot and probably into a non-reversible position.

4.5.3 Living Conditions

The living conditions of camps raise the questions about medical and environmental aspects to which the Rohingyas are vulnerable. The refugee camps are very clumsy and dirty. They do not have adequate sanitation and water supply facilities. On September 5, 2008, the Kaladan Press Network ran a report saying that twenty nine unregistered Rohingya refugees died in the Leda camp in Teknaf Upazilla under Cox's Bazar district due to lack of proper treatment in two previous months (July and August 2008). There were 11 women and 18 men among the dead.[39] Box 3 shows water and sanitation condition in Kutupalong camp. It reveals the poor living conditions that the Rohingyas are facing.

Box 4.3: Information about Water and Sanitation in Kutupalong Camp

Total refugee population	14,777	
	Total Units	Population Ratio
Hand pumps tube wells	73	1:27
Units of latrines	545	1:20
Bath House (Units)	140	1:77
Garbage	57	1:189
Incinerators	05	1:2155
Medical incinerators	01	—

Source: Field visits, Kutupalong Camp, 7-14 June 2008.

4.6 CONCLUSION

The preceding discussion demonstrates that there is a close and critical link between the Rohingya refugees issue and security. It becomes more apparent if security is understood from a holistic sense. In this

39 *The Monthly Rohingya Review*, October 31, 2008.

context, four major dimensions of security have been identified in this chapter—politico-military, economic, social and environmental. While primary responsibility for refugee security clearly rests with the host government, it has been repeatedly stressed that the problem of security should be an issue for which a multiplicity of actors share responsibility—refugees themselves, local populations, country of origin, host country, donor states, regional organisations, the UNHCR and its operational partners. Currently, there are two main actors responsible for ensuring security in refugee camps—the host government and the UNHCR. The primary responsibility of the host states for the physical protection of refugees and the maintenance of security of refugee camps and settlements is a well-established principle in the international refugee protection regime. At the same time, however, it has been increasingly recognised by the international community that there is a need to support the host state which is unable to discharge such responsibilities. Host government can determine the fate of the camps, including whether or not they become militarised. On the other hand, the role of the Rohingya refugees is also critically important for protecting the security of all stakeholders, particularly the refugee community and host community. It is strongly stressed that the refugees themselves can "self-police" the camps through the creation of genuine refugee leadership. In this context, the recent changes in the management of the Rohingya refugee camps are remarkable as they are contributing to the development of law and order and conflict management. Particularly, the politico-military and social dimensions of security have been witnessing positive changes.

Chapter 5
Response of the State

Photograph by Shama Jahan/IR/DU 2008

"We came to Bangladesh because the Burmese army took our land, our cows, and everything we had. If I go back after all this time, they will put me in jail or shoot me. Here, at least they do not say anything."[1]

—*14-year-old refugee woman in Bangladesh*

The role of the Government of Bangladesh (GOB) is critical in tackling the Rohingya refugee problem. As a host country Bangladesh is in a position to facilitate or constrain measures to mitigate vulnerabilities of the Rohingya refugees in camp and non-camp areas. The existing government policy identifies voluntary repatriation as the only durable solution available to refugees, ruling out the possibility of local integration. However, so far, the major thrust of the response of the GOB is to ensure access to basic services for the Rohingyas through the active participation of the UNHCR and other implementing partners. It is often complained that while the GOB allows the donors to assist the Rohingya refugees who live in official camps, it prevents the international community from accessing undocumented refugees. Against this background, the main objective of this chapter is to understand the initiatives taken by the Bangladesh government in providing support to the Rohingya refugees living inside and outside the camps. The chapter will also focus on the various steps the government has initiated against the unlawful activities of the refugees, bilateral dialogues to resolve the problems including the problems of voluntary repatriation, the need for implementing the refugee law and governmental policing of the undocumented refugees.

1 *The Monthly Rohingya Review*, October 31, 2008.

5.1 FACILITATING THE DELIVERY OF BASIC SERVICES

Immediately following the arrival of the Rohingya refugees, the GOB took different steps to provide basic needs and to ensure minimum living standards to the refugees. In this context, five ministries are mainly involved: Ministry of Home Affairs; Ministry of Food and Disaster Management; Ministry of Health and Family welfare; and Ministry of Foreign Affairs. These ministries mainly provide workforce and keep an eye on the refugee situation. All kinds of financial support are provided by the UN agencies and various international donors. All staffs of Bangladesh government work under the Refugee Relief and Repatriation Commissioner (RRRC) of the Ministry of Relief and Disaster Management. At present there are 118 staffs collaborating with the funding agencies.[2] Main responsibility of GOB in the camps is overall coordination under the office of the RRRC, a Joint Secretary of the government. He works under the Myanmar Refugee Cell under the Ministry of Food and Disaster Management. Two Camp in Charges (CICs) at the level of Assistant Secretary and other staffs work under the RRRC. In the camps CIC coordinates the work of all international organisations, non governmental organisations, security forces, Ministry of Health staffs and camp committees. A breakdown of the responsibilities of these ministries is given in annex 5.1.

5.1.1 Shelter

GOB set up 20 camps in Cox's Bazar and Bandarban during 1991-92 influx to accommodate the Rohingya refugees. At present there are only 2 camps (Nayapara and Kutupalong) which accommodates around 23,000 documented Rohingyas refugees.[3] The sheds for the refugees are built under the supervision of GOB and funded by the UNHCR.

There are 826 sheds in two camps where 4956 families are accommodated, as per shed contains 6 families. The camps are not enclosed and are easily accessible, and as one report mentioned: "Housing provided in the camps is extremely basic (There are no permanent structures). Long bamboo sheds with plastic or aluminium roofing are subdivided into several small compartments containing

---

2 Information gathered from the Refugee Relief and Repatriation Commissioner's Office at Cox's Bazar, Bangladesh on 6 June 2008.

3 Ibid.

Table 5.1 Accommodation of Rohingya Refugees in two Camps

Type of Refugee Sheds in 2 Camps	Kutupalong	Nayapara	Total
Total No. of Refugee sheds	395	431	826
Newly constructed sheds	187	30	217
Under process new sheds	100	04	104
Total old sheds	208	401	609

Source: CICs of Kutupalong and Nayapara Refugee Camps during the field visit from 3-6 June, 2008.

one living area with an adjacent kitchen area to house a single refugee family, regardless of family size".[4] According to the WFP vulnerability survey in 1999 the huts, "are small, crowded and inadequate for healthy living."[5] From the beginning the GOB built houses on temporary basis, they maintain their temporary, emergency setup character. Though they can hardly survive a monsoon season, they are repaired once every few years. In between the repairs, the refugees manage the houses by taking the doors and partitions from the latrines or collecting strong plastic to fill in holes.[6] Thus, the conditions of housing for the Rohingyas are in bad shape and they can hardly live in this pathetic situation. When asked about improving their shelters, the authorities generally argue that better living conditions would counteract their drive to repatriate.[7]

5.1.2 Food Support

General food ration is distributed to all registered refugees. Since May 2002, fortnightly distribution has been implemented. Besides, there is Supplementary Feeding Programme (SFP) for malnourished children under 5, pregnant and lactating mothers, Therapeutic Feeding Programme (TFP) for severely malnourished children under the age of ten years, low birth weight and premature babies with their mothers

4 WFP (2005) 'Assistance to the refugees from Myanmar,' p. 5, www.wfp.org/operations/current_operations/project_docs/100453.pdf accessed on 12 November 2008.

5 *WFP Vulnerability Survey of Refuges,* September, October 1999, July 2000, p. 15.

6 MSF (2002) '10 Years for the Rohingya Refugees in Bangladesh,' p. 18 available at www.doctorswithoutborders.org/publications/reports/2002/rohingya_report.pdf accessed on 19 December 2008.

7 Ibid.

and other serious medical patients. The office of the civil surgeon selects participants, for SFP and TFP, school snacks programme where each student gets 50 gm. of locally produced fortified biscuits for each day of attendance up to 250 school days a year, Food for Training (FFT), where adolescent girls and women receive rice allocation for attending skill training activities, kitchen garden and for the production of non food items (mosquito nets, clothing soap, embroided items), Food for Work (FFW), where members of extremely vulnerable refugee families get chance to work for food within camps. All food programmes are jointly funded by the World Food Programme (WFP) and the UNHCR with close collaboration of the GOB.

According to the WFP, each registered Rohingya refugee irrespective of age receives 6kg 300gm rice, 560gm lentils, 280gm edible oil, 140gm salt, 140gm sugar and 700 powder food fortnightly. Food sanctioned by the WFP is distributed in the camps by Red Crescent Society. In 2008, the WFP allotted 3873 metric tonne rice, 327 tonne lentils, 180 tonne edible oil, 80 tonne salt, 92 tonne sugar and 405 tonne powder food items for the Rohingyas.[8] Some non-food items are also provided to the refugee families like soap (1-3 persons : 6 pieces per month, 4-6 persons: 8 pieces per month, 7 above: 10 pieces per month), Compressed Rice Husk—CRH (2 bags per family per month), Kerosene (1 litre per family per month).

5.1.3 Health Support

In the recent past, MSF-Holland and Concern Universal took the responsibility for providing health support in the camps. After their withdrawal in 2003 and 2004 respectively, the Ministry of Health (MOH) of the GOB, through the office of the Civil Surgeon have been providing curative health support for the entire refugee population. MOH services include Out-patient Department (OPD), In-patient Department (IPD), reproductive health care, immunisation, Family Planning, Annual deworming, Selective feeding programmes (SFP) etc. Besides this, there are health education activities in the camps on hygienic promotion, nutrition and reproductive health targeted to preventive health care. All refugee children under 10 are immunised,

8 *The Daily Samakal*, 15 May 2009.

and vitamin A is also distributed to prevent health problems resulting from nutrient deficiencies, including night blindness.[9]

5.1.4 Educational Facilities

Since mid-1996 the GOB allowed formal schooling in some camps except Nayapara, where it started in January 2000. There are different types of basic education for different age group like Play ground 4+, Pre primary 5+, Primary 6+, Non formal 12+ and adult literacy program. Education programs are funded by the UNICEF and implemented by Program for Helpless and Lagged Society (PHALS). There is also school snacks programme, which was launched in May 2002. Its positive impact is evident from the increased net enrolment rates (92 percent in 2005 compared to 88 percent in 2002) and attendance rates (currently 88 per cent compared to 76 per cent in 2002), which led to an expansion of the programme in 2004.[10] According to another estimate, there are 20 schools in the camps where about 9 thousand students are enrolled. Each camp has 10 schools.[11] The curriculum of primary and pre-primary education is largely based on textbooks approved by Bangladesh Textbook Board. In addition, they study a book in Burmese language.

Table 5.2 Basic Education Facilities at Two Refugee Camps

	Kutupalong	Nayapara	Total
No. of schools	9	8	17
No. of students	3343	3968	7311

Source: CICs of Kutupalong and Nayapara Refugee Camps during the field visit from 3-6 June, 2008.

Thus, the Rohingya refugees merely survive through the provision of basic health care, nutritional services, safe drinking water, and sanitation facilities. The GOB has employed its bureaucratic machinery for facilitating the delivery of these services where local

9 MSF (2002), '10 years for the Rohingya Refugees in Bangladesh,' p.16 available at www.doctorswithoutborders.org/publications/reports/2002/rohingya_report.pdf accessed on 19 December 2008.

10 WFP vulnerability survey of refuges September October 1999, July 2000, P.11.

11 *The Daily Samakal*, 15 May 2009.

NGOs and international governmental and non-governmental organisations are involved. One of the critical questions as pointed out by Imtiaz Ahmed is that does the GOB bear the economic cost of the presence of the Rohingyas? Referring to the report of the US Committee on Refugees, Ahmed states that Bangladesh has borne little of the cost of caring for the refugees. Apart from US $2.5 million that Bangladesh spent on relief prior to the UNHCR involvement, the entire relief operation has been funded by the UNHCR, donor governments, and NGOs. It is even argued that the UNHCR relief operation has led to a net financial gain for the Bangladesh government and its citizens, as it has increased employment.[12] The idea of 'burden' or 'gain' does not hide the fact that the Rohingyas are in dismal situations in the refugee camps. The basic services which are to ensure minimum living standards are far short of fulfilling the requirements. Even the delivery of basic services as sanctioned for them remains poor and ill-managed.

5.2 MAINTENANCE OF LAW AND ORDER

5.2.1 Security Inside the Camps

The 1993 Memorandum of Understanding (MoU) between the UNHCR and the GOB stipulated that the government was primarily responsible for "safety and security of the Myanmar refugees in the camps and outside and the UNHCR is here to assist the GOB for these purposes and for discharging its international protection mandate"[13] The Camp-in-Charge (CiC) is primarily responsible to ensure security in the camps and they are assisted by the police and Ansar. In the past, it was a difficult task to maintain security because of poor number of security personnel. In fact, several unwanted incidents occurred in and outside the camps. It is alleged that some of the registered Rohingya refugees are involved in illegal activities. Incidents such as arrest of militants have also taken place. Arms were also recovered from the houses of refugees. They have formed criminal groups in the nearby hills as the camps are constructed without walls.[14] Now the situation

12 Imtiaz Ahmed, "Bangladesh-Myanmar Relations and the Stateless Rohingyas," *The Daily Star*, 15 June, 2001.

13 MSF (2002), '10 years for the Rohingya Refugees in Bangladesh', pp. 24-25, www.doctorswithoutborders.org/publications/reports/2002/rohingya_report.pdf. accessed on19 December 2008.

14 *The Daily Samakal*, 15 May 2009.

has improved due to the increasing of the number of security personnel. Moreover, there are camp management committees, block committees and security volunteers involving the refugees living inside who work for maintaining law and order under the supervision of the CiCs.

Table 5.3 Status of Security Personnel in Two Camps

	Kutupalong	Nayapara	Total
Cox's Bazar district police	25	15	40
Ansar	44	98	142

Source: CICs of Kutupalong and Nayapara Refugee Camps during the field visit from 3-6 June, 2008.

5.2.2 Trouble-makers and Trouble-shooters

The experience of having refugee is not pleasant for any society. The case of Rohingya refugees is no exception. The place where they have taken shelters after arrival is one of the poverty prone areas of Bangladesh. Because of the mountainous location and lack of availability of cultivable land, most of the people depend on day labour. This creates pressure on the job market and simultaneously makes the eco system vulnerable. Immediately after the influx, the forest department of Cox's Bazar reported that the Rohingya refugees had destroyed forest resources worth Tk. 13.5 crore.[15] In a separate report they claimed that the refugees had destroyed forest resources worth Tk. 740 million, damaging natural forest of 2,021.11 acres and new plantation of 91.05 acres.[16] In contrast, the degradation of law and order situation is another anxiety for which the illegal Rohingya migrants are mostly blamed. The RRRC Office at Cox's Bazar reported in its letter to the Ministry of Home Affairs and the Ministry of Foreign Affairs that the illegal Rohingyas are creating various social problems in Cox's Bazar and Bandarban. Police Superintendent of Cox's Bazar, Mozammel Hossain, told the media that the Rohingyas have destroyed the peace of the peaceful city, Cox's Bazar. He also said that they are not only illegally capturing the trees and land but also degrading the law and order situation.[17]

15 *Dainik Bangla*, 28 April 1992.

16 Philip Gain, "Rohingyas: Who Really is Their Friend" in SHETU, October 1992, p.9.

17 *The Daily Prothom Alo*, 8 December 2001.

5.2.3 Dealing with Undocumented Rohingyas

There is no specific data regarding the number of unregistered refugees in Bangladesh. It varies from 200,000 to 330,000.[18] The government administration often makes a list of undocumented Rohingyas living in Cox's Bazar. For example, in July 2002 the Ministry of Home Affairs asked the District administration of Cox's Bazar to take necessary steps to prepare a list of unregistered Rohingyas. Consequently, preparation for making the list started from October 2002.[19] But the exact number is still unknown. According to local sources, more than 50,000 unregistered Rohingyas live in Ukhiya and Teknaf Upazilla and the number of unregistered Rohingyas living in different parts of Cox's Bazar will not be less than 1,50,000.[20]

GOB has no special policy to deal with the undocumented Rohingyas. According to the RRRC, these people are not refugees; they are illegal migrants of Myanmar as per the MoU signed between Bangladesh and Myanmar in 1992 which stipulated that Bangladesh would not recognise any other Rohingya as refugee. In spite of this, GOB gave shelter to more than 14,000 Rohingyas in an unofficial camp known as 'Taal' (Dumping spot) situated very close to Teknaf. In June 2008 these unregistered Rohingyas were shifted to another place named "Leda". Whether they are in Taal or Leda, their living conditions are extremely poor. They do not have access to basic services for their survival. Two international organisations, Islamic Relief and the Handicap provide them minimum health facilities. The place is very congested, unhealthy and unhygienic. According to Ayub Majee (one of the Shed leaders), 29 unregistered Rohingyas died[21] in the Leda camp in two months of its establishment. Most of them died due to pneumonia, fever, odema, malaria, asthma and starvation and lack of proper medical facilities. The unregistered Rohingyas are often blamed for many illegal activities like terrorism, cutting trees from the forest, engaging in day labour activities and many others. Since there is absence of monitoring from the government over these people, they can move around freely.

---

18 'The life and living of Rohingyas: problems and solutions', *Annual Magazine* (2001-2003), the Arakan Historical Society, p. 49, including refugees living in two present camps.

19 *The Daily Prothom Alo*, 22 November, 2002

20 *The Daily Prothom Alo*, 22 November, 2002

21 29 unregistered refugees die in Leda camp in two months, www.kaladanpress.org, 5 September 2008.

5.2.4 Prevention of Sexual and Gender-based Violence

Sexual and gender based violence is a major concern for the Rohingyas living in the refugee camps. Women are generally victims of different types of torture at the hands of members of law enforcing agencies. Besides, refugee men, including *Mahjees*, as well as local villagers are known as perpetrators. Rape is very common both within and outside the camps. Women who collect firewood in areas surrounding the camps, female heads of household or young girls whose fathers/ husbands are in detention are particularly at risk of rape and kidnapping.[22] The field visits clearly reflect that women and children always remain scared of violence. Hence, the GOB has responsibility to prevent the occurrences of sexual and gender based violence in the camps. Particularly, the role of CiC and law enforcing agencies is critical for reducing gender related violence.

5.3 DIS/SOLVING THE "REFUGEE PROBLEM"

Like any other host nation, Bangladesh has often shown reluctance to deal with the challenge of tackling the Rohingya refugee problem on her own. Even the GOB has been hesitant to bilateralise the problem. To Bangladesh, regional and global initiatives are preferable to resolve the problem on the long term basis. However, there is no doubt that a short term solution to the Rohingya refugee problem hinges on measures taken at national and bilateral levels. While the short term measures taken at domestic level are discussed in the preceding section, here the focus is given on bilateral and multilateral initiatives.

5.3.1 Bilateral Agreements and Dialogues

High official meetings between the two countries are held regularly to resolve the problems. The first major high level official meeting was held between the two countries in 1992 when they singed MoU. Another significant meeting took place on 28 February 1994 regarding the repatriation of Rohingya Refugees where the Myanmar authority gave permission to another 11,382 Rohingyas to return. Later, 135,000 Rohingyas were given permission to return to Myanmar. Bangladesh submitted a list of 250,877 Rohingyas to Myanmar. In this meeting both countries agreed to build a bailey bridge near Tumbre border so

22 UNHCR, *Bangladesh: Analysis of Gaps in the Protection of Rohingya Refugees*, May 2007, http://www.unhcr.org/publ/PROTECTION/46fa1af32.pdf accessed on 12 January 2009.

that Rohingyas could return home by walking to their own country. Following the meeting 2,36,599 Rohingyas got repatriated, but more than 20,000 Rohingyas stayed back in Bangladesh. Though the Foreign Minister of Bangladesh visited Yangon in 1999, there was no progress on the repatriation process. In 1999, Bangladesh Government requested the visiting Foreign Minister of Myanmar about the importance of repatriation of the rest of the Rohingyas. Subsequently, the Myanmar Foreign Minister said that all the Rohingyas would be repatriated during the next one and a half years. The repatriation process, however, could not be restarted. On 13 January 2000 Bangladesh sent a team of high officials to Yangon. During the meeting Myanmar showed interest in receiving back only 7,000 Rohingyas whereas the 21,000 of them were residing in Kutupalong and Nayapara camps. During the visit of the UNHCR Commissioner in Bangladesh on 27 May 2008, the latter emphasised the implementation of the MoU signed by the three parties i.e. Government of Bangladesh, Government of Myanmar and the UNHCR. The visiting UNHCR Commissioner also said that this problem could only be resolved through the implementation of the 1992 agreement.

The new Grand Alliance government led by Awami League[23] has already initiated a process to deal with the Rohingya refugee problem. As part of this process, the Foreign Minister of Bangladesh, Dipu Moni, visited Myanmar on May 16-17, 2009. At the end of her visit, the Foreign Minister informed the media that military leaders in Myanmar admitted that they (Rohingyas) are Myanmarese and agreed to take them back. She further mentioned that Myanmar government sought a list from Dhaka on the number of Rohingyas living in Bangladesh as part of the repatriation process.[24] The Foreign Minister emphasised that Bangladesh was in touch with Myanmar and the UNHCR to stop further inflows of the Rohingyas. However, the GOB is of the view that the refugee flow would not stop unless Myanmar authorities guaranteed "qualitative change" in the Arakan state—the place where most Rohingyas live in Myanmar.[25] This only reflects the positive approach of the new government in Bangladesh on the issue of Rohingya refugee problem.

23 The government came to power through their victory in the general elections held in Bangladesh on 29 December 2008.

24 Bdnews24, "Myanmar pledges to take back Rohingyas", bdnews24.com/krc/bd/1251h.

25 http://www.reuters.com/article/latestCrisis/idUSDHA137724

5.3.2 Voluntary Repatriation

Voluntary repatriation is a key element in resolving the refugee crisis. Though the 1951 Convention is silent on the question of voluntariness, the UNHCR Handbook on Voluntary Repatriation states that: "the principle of voluntariness is the cornerstone of international protection with respect to the return of refugees...A person with a well-founded fear of persecution is a refugee, and cannot be compelled to repatriate."[26] A Memorandum of Understanding signed between the GOB and UNHCR in 1993 stipulates that the UNHCR should provide protection to refugees from Myanmar and cooperate with GOB to ensure their safe and voluntary repatriation. The GOB has explained its reluctance to integrate Rohingya refugees in the country for the fear of a large refugee population.[27] The first major repatriation of the Rohingyas took place in 1978 as an outcome of a bilateral agreement signed between GOB and GOM on 6 June 1978.[28] During the second spell of influx of the Rohingyas in 1991-92, Bangladesh granted temporary asylum to the refugees and called on the UNHCR to assist in the provision of humanitarian aid. On 28 April 1992, GOB and GOM signed a Memorandum of Understanding (MOU) on a repatriation scheme. Both the parties declared that there would be no forceful and unsafe repatriation. In reality, it is alleged that the repatriation was not voluntary. Under the MOU nearly 35,000 refugees were repatriated by November 1993. In November 1993, UNHCR also signed a MOU with GOM which allowed the agency's access in Myanmar to promote the repatriation and monitor the reintegration of Rohingya refugees. After the unilateral withdrawal of Myanmar from the repatriation process, Bangladesh Government continued its effort to restart the process and complete repatriation through diplomatic effort. In June 2002, an inter-ministerial meeting decided to repatriate all the Rohingyas by 3 June 2003. The meeting also decided to establish army outposts on the border in addition to the BDR to prevent the influx of the Rohingyas.[29]

On the ground, the Rohingyas are opposed to the repatriation process on account of their fear of persecution by the GOM upon their

26 UNHCR, (1996), *Handbook on Voluntary Repatriation: International Protection*, (Geneva: UNHCR), p. 10.

27 UNHCR, *Report 2007*, op.cit.

28 Kaiser Morshed, 'Bangladesh – Burma Relations', http://www.idea.int/asia_pacific/burma/upload/chap2.pdf accessed on 25 December 2008.

29 *The Daily Prothom Alo*, 22 November, 2002.

return. They strongly resisted such moves by the governments and the UNHCR and partly succeeded on some occasions. As a result, the whole repatriation process turned into largely involuntary in nature. By 1996, refugees' reluctance to return home was reinforced as increasing numbers of Rohingyas including those previously repatriated were returning back with stories of persistent tortures and abuse. But the repatriation programme continued. It is alleged that some 350 refugees mostly women and children were rounded up overnight at gunpoint and deported in July 1997. This set off a 14-month long strike by the refugees who even boycotted humanitarian services which stopped the repatriation process.[30]

Despite several attempts by GOB and the UNHCR, around 21,400 registered Rohingya refugees are still living in the camps. The UNHCR formally proposed to GOB to resettle these refugees in third countries.[31] GOB refused the offer of increased assistance and resettlement packages. Then the UNHCR threatened to end its operations within the camps unless GOB started to resettle at least 5,000 Rohingyas under the UNHCR status determination prosecution. The GOB argued that the resettlement of 5,000 refugees would not bring a solution to this problem. Further talks took place between Bangladesh and Myanmar and an announcement came that GOM would reopen its border for the repatriation of 7,535 refugees who would be repatriated in a group of 400. As the repatriation resumed in November 1998, the Myanmar authorities had introduced a new set of restrictive, bureaucratic conditions and procedures, much to the consternation of Bangladeshi authorities. Myanmar also refused to accept 7,000 previously "cleared" refugees, and embarked on a new round of re-verification. Since then, repatriation has slowed down to a trickle, with only 454 families (2,740 individuals) sent home between January 1999 and December 2001.[32] In early 2002, the Myanmar authorities verbally agreed to accept approximately 5,000 cleared refugees. Among them, according to the UNHCR, the majority are prepared to return home. The remainders have attached conditions to their return. Last repatriation took place in 2005 when only 92

30 MSF (2002) '10 Years for the Rohingya Refugees in Bangladesh,' p. 23, www.doctorswithoutborders.org/publications/reports/2002/rohingya_report.pdf accessed 19 December 2008.

31 Ibid.

32 UNHCR *Repatriation Statistics*, (MSF, p.24).

Rohingyas were repatriated. Now most of the Rohingyas are more interested in resettlement in third countries than repatriation.

Table 5.4 Year Wise Repatriation from 1992 to 2008 (May)[33]

Year	No. of people repatriated	Year	No. of people repatriated
1992	5962	1999	1128
1993	46129	2000	1323
1994	82753	2001	283
1995	61504	2002	760
1996	23045	2003	3231
1997	10073	2004	210
1998	106	2005	92
Total			2,36,599

Source: Refugee Relief and Repatriation Commissioner's Office, Ministry of Food and Disaster Management, Dhaka.

Although the Rohingya refugees have expressed their strong reservations for going back to Myanmar, GOB maintains its policy of repatriation. Negotiations are currently underway for possible tripartite meetings between the GOB, the Government of Myanmar (GOM) and the UNHCR on the issue of voluntary repatriation. Iftekhar Ahmed Chowdhury, Advisor to the caretaker government (CTG) in Bangladesh, emphasised the need for holding a trilateral—Bangladesh, Myanmar and the UNHCR—dialogue to create a condition for voluntary return of the refugees. The current political regime in Bangladesh has been continuing the same policy on the tripartite agreement for repatriation of the Rohingyas.

5.3.3 Resettlement Programme

The use of resettlement as a strategic tool to provide durable solutions to vulnerable refugees was first employed by the UNHCR in 2006.[34] This has included the identification for resettlement of extremely vulnerable refugees with compelling protection concerns. Both the

33 Information received from the Refugee Relief and Repatriation Commissioner's Office under the Ministry of Food and Disaster Management, at Cox's Bazar on 3 June 2008 during the field visit of the team.

34 UNHCR Report 2007, op.cit.

GOB and the UNHCR agree on this point that the problem can be mitigated if the Rohingyas can be resettled in any other country. It may be mentioned that twenty-three refugees were resettled to Canada in 2006 and a further 79 in 2007.[35] Seventy eight refugees—28 adults and 50 children—were identified by the UNHCR as a priority group for resettlement. Both Bangladesh and the UNHCR are also closely working on this issue. For Bangladesh, any solution to the Rohingya refugee problem must not be based on the fact that the GOB would declare the Rohingyas "refugees" and be allowed to settle in Bangladesh permanently. This position has been renewed by the GOB time and again, and is still the current policy of the government. Needless to mention, such policy contributes to the statelessness of the Rohingyas. Another dimension of the resettlement programme is that it enjoys strong support from the Rohingya refugees. They have expressed their strong desire to settle in the third countries particularly the developed nations. While talking to a student of class five in a school at refugee camp, the student told that he wanted to learn English to settle in a third country.[36]

5.3.4 Border Fencing

The proposed barbed wire fencing along the Myanmar-Bangladesh border as part of the ruling military regime's plan to curb the movement of Rohingya minorities living in the region is a major challenge to resolve the Rohingya refugee problem. Myanmar's military government, in fact, plans to construct a barbed wire fence about 50 miles in length, along the border with Bangladesh.[37] It was reported that since 14 March 2009, the Myanmar authorities had reinforced military presence in the border town of Maungdaw, in western Burma, to provide security to the fencing project along the Bangladesh-Myanmar border. However, the GOB finds the border fencing a violation of the bilateral accord between the two countries. According to the bilateral agreement, neither Bangladesh nor Myanmar can fence along the border or mobilise troops along the line

---

35 http://www.fmreview.org/FMRpdfs/FMR30/34-35.pdf accessed on 26 May 2009.

36 *The Daily Samakal*, 15 May 2009.

37 Salai Pi Pi, "Border fencing may aim to curb Rohingya movement: Observers", http://www.mizzima.com/news/regional/1864-border-fencing-may-aim-to-curb-rohingya-movement-observers.html

without cause.[38] Interestingly, at the official level, both Bangladesh and Myanmar are silent on this issue. The GOB has not officially acknowledged the development of such an issue which has created newer tensions and uncertainties.

5.4 LEGAL DIMENSIONS

Absence of a more supportive and proactive role by GOB lies with legal constraints regarding the Rohingya refugees in Bangladesh. In fact, Bangladesh does not have any domestic or national law which can cover the issue of asylum seekers and refugees. In Bangladesh, foreigners irrespective of asylum seekers or simply visitors are treated under some old laws (e.g. Passport Act, 1920; Naturalisation Act,1926; Registration of Foreigners Act,1939; the Foreigners Act, 1946; Bangladesh Citizenship (Temporary Provisions) Order 1972; and Extradition Act, 1974)[39] which are inadequate to meet the needs of the Rohingya refugees. This is particularly caused by Bangladesh's refusal to be a party to the UN Convention Relating to the Status of the Refugees, 1951 or its 1967 Protocol.

However, Bangladesh recognised 258,000 Rohingyas as 'refugees' in 1991 through an executive order. The remaining 200,000 Myanmar nationals (including Rohingyas) who are not registered as 'refugees' are considered 'illegal foreigners' or 'economic migrants' by GOB. Nevertheless, Bangladesh is a signatory to various international legal documents like the Universal Declaration of Human Rights (UDHR), International Convention on Civil and Political Rights (ICCPR), International Covenant on Economic, Social and Cultural Rights (ICESCR) and signatory to the Charter of the United Nations, which ensure the state responsibilities of the refugees. Hence, the country is committed to the principle of non-refoulement by becoming a party in the light of the above mentioned international documents. The Constitution of Bangladesh also guarantees the rights of the refugees and the responsibilities of the state. Article 31 of Bangladesh constitution ensures the right to protection of law, right to life and personal liberty, safeguard to arrest and detention, prohibition of forced labour, protection in respect of trial and punishment. All of

38 http://priyo.com/news/2009/03/17/23016.html

39 Uttam Kumar Das, "Bangladesh's Obligation to Refugee Protection", *The Daily Star*, July 2, 2005.

these are equally applicable for people living inside the country.[40] Due to the absence of legal framework, there is a problem of coordination among the relevant departments regarding the treatment towards refugees. It is also difficult to understand and monitor the status of incoming and outgoing of the refugees.

5.5 EMERGING CHALLENGES

The Rohingya refugee problem has already turned into protracted refugee situations and it has been worsening in absence of effective short-term measures and long term solution. As far as the role of GOB is concerned, several challenges may be considered for further thought on the Rohingya refugee problem. One of the challenges comes from Bangladesh's relations with the UNHCR on the question of the Rohingya refugee. Although the GOB has been closely working with the UNHCR for ensuring minimum living standards of the Rohingya refugees particularly in the camps, it has refused to entertain some proposals suggested by the UNHCR. For example, in 2003 UNHCR took a decision to phase out its support for the 20,000 refugees remaining in the camps and forwarded to Bangladesh Government a "self-sufficiency plan", wherein the UNHCR proposed to integrate the Rohingya refugee population with the local Bangladeshi community. On September 2004, Bangladeshi authority rejected the self-sufficiency plan. In 2005, the UNHCR presented again a plan to the GOB that proposed temporary stay and freedom of movement of Rohingyas.[41] The GOB has not accepted this plan too.

Second, Bangladesh is criticised by international rights groups such as Human Rights Watch for its role in the Rohingya refugee problem. Brad Adams, Asia director at Human Rights Watch, says, "The Bangladeshi government is ignoring its obligations to protect Rohingya refugees and permit international relief agencies to assist with the humanitarian needs of Rohingya refugees."[42] Third, given the continuing entry of the Rohingyas to Bangladesh, it assumes a major challenge for this country to guard its 657 km long border with

---

40 Uttam Kumar Das, "Legal Dimension of Rohingya Refugee Issues: A Perspective from Bangladesh," National Programme Officer (IOM – MRF), Dhaka.

41 Mir Md. Amtazul Hoque, Rohingya Refugees: Some Legal Issues, *The Daily Star*, August 30, 2008.

42 http://english.dvb.no/news.php?id=25 accessed on 15 February 2009.

Myanmar.[43] Fourth, it is a challenge for a country like Bangladesh to ensure the delivery of basic services and to provide minimum living standards to thousands of registered and unregistered Rohingyas. GOB needs to address the problems of adequate food, sanitation, healthcare facilities, livelihoods and personal safety. It has been revealed in a survey that 58 percent of the refugee children and 53 percent of the adults are chronically malnourished.[44] Surveys conducted since 1992 have consistently found unacceptably high rates of malnutrition among the adult and children refugees. Almost none of the refugees are receiving his or her full ration.[45] Some allege that GOB tends to believe that free food can be an incentive to remain in Bangladesh and thus food has been used as a tool of coercion and intimidation in the past.[46]

Fifth, response of GOB may consider the social dynamics of the Rohingya people in Bangladesh in general and refugee camps in particular. Early marriage and pregnancy is a common feature in the camp life of the Rohingyas. The average age of marriage is 14 years; average age of first pregnancy is 16 years, and 10 percent of births result in low weight babies.[47] There are high rates of birth and pregnancy in the camps, even in recent years the birth rate has outnumbered the rates of death and repatriation combined. A major source of anxiety for the Bangladeshi authorities is the rising number of Rohingya population in the camps. MSF and Concern started wide-ranging family planning programmes in the camps in order to control the birth of Rohingyas.[48] Subsequently, MSF and Concern left. During the field visits, it was found that most of the refugees have complained about the services provided by the Ministry of Health (MOH) and they wanted the return of MSF-Holland and Concern.

---

43 Stated by Lt. Colonel Baizid Sarwar, Commandant Officer of Bangladesh Rifles, Teknaf while he was interviewed by a group of students of the Department of International Relations of the University of Chittagong on 5 June 2008.

44 Concern, DRAFT Nutrition survey in Kutupalong and Nayapara camps among the Rohingya refugees, November 2001, p.2.

45 MSF (2002) "10 Years for the Rohingya Refugees in Bangladesh," p. 13 available at www.doctorswithoutborders.org/publications/reports/2002/rohingya_report.pdf accessed on 23 December 2008.

46 Ibid, p. 5.

47 WFP vulnerability survey of refuges September October 1999, July 2000, P. 5.

48 MSF, (2002), "10 Years for the Rohingya Refugees in Bangladesh," p.16, www.doctors withoutborders.org/publications/reports/2002/rohingya_report.pdf 23 December 2008.

Sixth, the continuous presence of the Rohingya refugees creates an economic challenge for the GOB. Although documented Rohingya refugees have no legal rights to work outside the camps without permission, everyday they go outside the camps to work as day labourers, fishermen, salt field workers and rickshaw pullers. The administration could not stop such unlawful practices. What is of more concern is that camp officials are bribed to engage in income generating activities by the Rohingyas living in camps. Finally, the GOB faces a dilemma in maintaining law and order in the refugee camps and outside. The law enforcing agencies are employed to ensure security and safety by punishing the criminals or trouble makers. In reality, some of the members of law enforcing agencies get involved in criminal acts in the forms of rape, bribery and intimidation. Consequently, the experience of violence and coercion over the years has fostered an environment of fear and distress among the refugees.[49]

5.6 CONCLUSION

The preceding discussion demonstrates that generally the Rohingya refugees are portrayed as a burden to Bangladesh. The GOB often argues that there has been no tangible benefit from hosting them, only a drain of its limited resources. Despite this general perception, over the years the GOB has been involved in short-term and long term measures to address this problem. Apart from the management of the two refugee camps located in Cox's Bazar, Bangladesh has been active in bilateral and multilateral processes. Bangladesh has been closely working with Myanmar and the international community for its permanent and durable solution. Bangladesh shows strong support for multilateral initiatives in resolving the Rohingya refugee problem on the long term basis. For instance, Bangladesh has been supporting the Bali process to resolve this problem. The Bali process was originally set up at the Regional Ministerial Conference on People Smuggling, Trafficking in Persons and Related Transnational Crime, held in Bali in February 2002.[50] Bangladesh is involved in negotiation process for implementing the tri-party MoU signed in 1993, which enables the complete repatriation of the Rohingya refugees. On the

---

49 Ibid, p.25.

50 http://www.bangkokpost.com/news/investigation/136770/rohingya-a-regional-problem accessed on 19 April 2009.

other hand, continued bilateral dialogue between the GOB and GOM remains on the table. With a thrust on "Look East" foreign policy and active participation in the regional arrangements of BIMSTEC and ARF, Bangladesh can induce Myanmar in constructive engagement, and keep striving to resolve the problem with an active and concrete support of other regional countries.

What is of particular concern for the future is that laws governing refugees and asylum issues in Bangladesh remain the same which poses a major constraint for a more proactive and supportive role for Bangladesh. Besides, as the field survey reveals, there is a lack of awareness about the Rohingya problem among the government officials and more so about their responsibilities in dealing with the Rohingyas. Since there are several ministries involved in the management of camps, the officials often find it difficult, if not unwilling, to coordinate their activities and to ensure better delivery of basic services for the Rohingyas.[51] This can largely be attributed to the absence of well defined policies on the part of the government regarding the treatment of the Rohingya refugees.

---

51 Based on interviews with the Commandant Officer of the Bangladesh Rifles in Teknaf, police officials including Superintendent of Police, Cox's Bazar and Officer-in-Charge, Teknaf Thana during 18 May-20 June 2008. While speaking with Baizid Sarwar, Commandant Officer of the Bangladesh Rifles, regarding their responsibilities, he said that the responsibilities of the BDR was to protect the border of the country and in this special case, whenever they would find any boat from Arakan was crossing the border of Bangladesh, they would push them back but they are not responsible for those who are already living here illegally. Even when the Police Officials like the Superintendent of Police of Cox's Bazar and the Officer-in-Charge of Teknaf Thana were interviewed, they could not give any statistics regarding the criminal activities done by the Rohingyas.

Annex 5.1[52]

- Camp In Charge/ CIC (Ministry of Food and Disaster Management)
    - Maintaining law and order
    - Voluntary Repatriation
    - Shelter and infrastructure
    - Water management
    - Sanitation
    - Overall coordination
- MOH (Ministry of Health and Family Welfare)
    - Running out Patient Department (OPD)
    - Running Therapeutic Feeding Centre (TFC)
    - Running Supplementary Feeding Centre (SFC)
    - Immunisation, Family Planning
- Police camp (Bangladesh Police, Ministry of Home Affairs)
    - Assisting the CIC
    - Ensuring security
    - Investigating petty nature of complaints
    - Communicating to police station
- Ansar Camp (Bangladesh Ansar, Ministry of Home Affairs)
    - Assisting CIC
    - Ensuring security

52 Information is gathered from Mr. Shahanoor Alam, Camp-in-Charge, Kutupalong Refugee Camp, Ukhiya, Cox's Bazar, 26 May 2008.

Chapter 6
Responseof Civil Society

Photograph by Shama Jahan/IR/DU 2008

The Rohingya refugee issue has become intrinsically linked to the development and governance issues including trade between Bangladesh and Myanmar, sustainable development in the Chittagong region, environment, and poverty eradication. The magnitude of this problem has doubled, in terms of number of refugee mobility, in less than 20 years, and its increasing complexity has barely captured the attention of governments and society at large.

Considering the existing lack of attention from the society at large, this chapter seeks to identify the role of the non-state actors such as the civil society including NGOs and media in Bangladesh in shaping the Rohingya refugee discourse and the perception of various decision and policy making actors. It could be argued that for peaceful and meaningful settlement of the refugee issue civil society organisations (CSOs) could actively participate. Such actors are critical mediums to advocate the realities of the Rohingya refugees and dissipate confusions and encourage the government and political agencies to undertake a comprehensive strategy to resolve the refugee issue.

In Bangladesh, despite a vibrant and dynamic civil society, its role in the Rohingya refugee discourse has remained confined to offering urban-based pedantical supports while some national and international NGOs are offering operational assistance. Advocacy on formulating refugee or migration policies has been limited, particularly when compared to other fields such as the environment or human rights, for example, where the civil society has had a significant impact on policy development. Such dichotomy between thought and activities needs to be critically reviewed.

For the purpose of this chapter, the civil society and its organisations could be broadly defined as the area of voluntary collective action, driven by shared values and/or interests which operate beyond the state, the market and the family, and which provides the web of social relations linking these three spheres.[1] In view of its tight interconnection with the conflict structure, local civil society at times promotes the civic values and practices necessary for a peaceful transformation of tension, while at other times directly contributes to the causes and symptoms of international tension. As such civil society is not understood here as a normative concept but rather as an analytical category of actors to be investigated in order to ascertain what their precise impact on conflict is.[2]

Therefore, it could be assumed that CSOs are pivotal in providing the necessary support for peaceful settlement of (refugee) crisis, ensuring that any agreement negotiated by political leaders is ultimately accepted and implemented on the ground.[3] Besides, civil society can provide a vital push for change, especially when the governments in Bangladesh and Myanmar are failing to initiate change. This chapter focuses on the roles and responsibilities of CSOs and their related advocacy work. It looks at the current environment giving a bird's eye view of CSOs working on refugee issue and the scope and nature of existing policy structure in Bangladesh.

6.1 RESPONSE OF THE BANGLADESHI CIVIL SOCIETY ORGANISATIONS ON THE ROHINGYA REFUGEE ISSUE

In evaluating the role of Bangladeshi civil society in resolving the Rohingya refugee issue, one has to identify the wide variety of actors involved in this context. Eight different types of actors could be engaged directly or indirectly in the Rohingya issue: academics, economic actors, private citizens, training and education bodies,

---

1 Barnes, C. 2005. 'Weaving the Web: Civil Society Roles in Working with Conflict and Building Peace'. In Van Tongeren, P. ed. 2005. *People Building Peace II Successful Stories of Civil Society*. Boulder and London: Lynne Rienner. Also see, Fischer, M. 2006. *Civil Society in Conflict Transformation: Ambivalence, Potentials and Challenge*. Berlin: Berghof Research Centre for Constructive Conflict Management. *Berghof papers*. www.berghof-handbook.net

2 Tocci, Nathalie, 2008. *The European Union, Civil Society and Conflict Transformation*. MICROCON Policy Working Paper 1.

3 Miall, H., Ramsbotham, O. and Wodhouse, T. 1999. *Contemporary Conflict Resolution*. Cambridge: Polity.

activists, religion-based actors, funding bodies, and media.[4] Table 6.1 indicates the magnitude of intervention of various types of actors in mitigating the refugee situation in Bangladesh. We have used five levels of qualitative indicators to determine the levels of magnitude varying from No, Low, Relatively Low, Moderate and High. 'No' represents that almost zero level of participation, 'low' signifies very forlorn intensity of participation, 'relatively low' denotes some activities though not very sufficient, 'moderate' signifies some activities, and 'high' indicates satisfactory activities.[5]

Table 6.1 Types of CSO Actors in the Rohingya Refugee Discourse in Bangladesh

Actors	Examples	Visibility of Activities
Professionals engaged in human rights/ security	Technical experts and consultants,	Low
	Research centres and think tanks,	Relatively low
	Professional NGOs	Moderate
	Academics/writers	Low
Economic	Business associations	No
	Professional associations	No
	Cooperatives and self-help initiatives	Relatively low
Private Citizens	Individual citizens	Relatively low
	Diaspora groups	Relatively low
	Family and clan based associations	No
Training and Education	Training NGOs	Relatively low
	Schools and universities	No
Activism	Public policy advocacy groups	Relatively low
	Social movements	No
	Student groups	No
	Women groups	No
Religion	Spiritual communities	Low
	Charities	Relatively Low
	Religious movements	No
Funding	Foundations	Low
	Individual philanthropists	Low
Communication	Media	Low in National level and Moderate in local level

4 Marchetti, R. and Tocci, N. 2007. *Conflict Society and Human Rights.* No. 3/07. http://www.luiss.it/shur/wp-content/uploads/2007/10/shurwp03-07.pdf

5 Based on media coverage i.e. newspapers, academic articles, field visits in various refugee camps and interviews and focused group discussions with various stakeholders i.e. media personalities, academics, refugees, local opinion leaders and government agencies.

During this study it has been found that there are three broad reasons for lesser degree of participation of the CSOs in resolving refugee issues. These are:

- **Character and scope of CSOs in Bangladesh:** CSOs and particularly NGOs in Bangladesh do not receive much sponsorship and encouragement from the government in the field of refugee issue. Besides, the majority of CSOs in the country are dependent on external donor funding and the interests of donors often determine their objectives and causes—as such they may be described as ad hoc in their pursuits. The bulk of CSOs are involved in service delivery activities and relatively socio-politically sensitive areas. CSOs are largely constrained by lack of funds and sufficient expertise to engage the state on technical matters such as macro economic policies.
- **Relationship between CSOs and the Government of Bangladesh:** There is a growing trend where the government involves CSOs in processes of policy formulation and implementation. However, government has barely involved the CSOs as consultative partner in resolving the refugee problem in Bangladesh. The bulk of the CSOs are largely involved in service delivery rather than carrying out advocacy activities to mainstream the plights and consequences of the refugee problem in Bangladesh.
- **The political environment**: It has been observed that in Bangladesh, CSOs are not a homogenous category. Their constituencies, interests, methods of work and objectives are diverse. This problem is compounded by the fear or lack of "courage" by many civil society and media activists to confront or contradict the state on refugee issue. Lack of political will and consensus has become a key obstacle in resolving the protracted Rohingya refugee issue. For CSOs as a whole, such lack of political will or political consensus means that their activities and potency are necessarily limited to matters outside the explicit political arena and the arena of formal development agenda. However, the people and the government of Bangladesh, which has been extending shelter generously to the Rohingyas for a long time, should be vocal now against any proposal for having permanent shelter for them in Bangladesh.

The political parties should also take up the issue for the interest of the country.[6]

6.2 PARTNERSHIP OF THE NON GOVERNMENTAL ORGANISATIONS (NGOS) WITH THE GOVERNMENT AND UNHCR

As an effective organisational platform of the CSOs in Bangladesh, NGOs have played a significant role in preserving rights of the refugees in the field level. Despite the efforts assumed by the NGOs, Rohingya refugees are living in extremely precarious conditions, without access to adequate food, shelter, security or access to the range of social, economic, cultural, civil, political and legal rights they are entitled to. The scale and impact of this grim reality demands more efficient and active involvement of the NGOs and urgent global response. Currently six NGOs, both national and international, are functioning in the Refugee camps.[7] These NGOs are generally mandated to provide assistance to the 'documented' refugees.

Apart from the existing NGOs mentioned in the Table 6.2, 28 national and international NGOs provided services in the refugee camps. Table 6.3 identifies the NGOs and the types of services they had provided.

UNHCR provides support to the Rohingya refugees through two categories of partners. 1. Implementation partner, and 2. operational partner. Implementation partners are: Bangladesh Legal Aid Services Trust (BLAST), Bangladesh Red Crescent Society (BDRCS), Research Training and Management International (RTMI), and Technical Assistance Inc (TAI). Currently UNHCR has two operational partners: Handicap International, and Medecins Sans Frontieers (MSF) Holland (MSF Holland has suspended its operation since March 2008). Considering the number of NGOs involved in the camps, growing influx of 'undocumented' refugees and camp environments in Kutu Palong and Nayapara, it could be observed that there is a dire need to increase NGO involvements and diversify their services to the refugee population. Table 6.4 and 6.5 indicates that activities of the NGOs should be intensified to provide emergency health care and sanitation, drinking water, nutrition and supplementary feeding, shelter construction and clothing.

---

6 The Daily Star. *Rohingya Refugees*. Saturday, October 11, 2008. http://www.thedailystar.net/story.php?nid=25644.

7 According to the Camp-in- charge, Kutupalong Refugee Camp. Ukhia, Cox's Baazar. Date- 26-05-2008.

Table 6.2 Operational NGOs/INGOs in the Rohingya Refugee Camps*

No.	NGO†	Timeframe for Activities	Activities	Limitations
1.	Médecins Sans Frontières-Holland (MSF-H)	1993-94 & 2006-31st March 2008	Supporting and providing health assistance	Limited Working Period
2.	Technical Assistance Incorporated (TAI)	March 2005-Onward	• Self-help activities • Community services • Social awareness	
3.	Research Training and Management International (RTMI) [MSF- H is assisting RTMI	October 2007-2010	• Reproductive Health. • Operating the Patient Department (IPD) • Conducting Referral services to Refugee Patients • Essential Service Delivery (ESD)	Lack of adequate funding, lack of public confidence
4.	Handicap International	1997-Onwards	• Assisting to Disabled People • Community Awareness Regarding Disability	
5.	Programme for Helpless and Lagged Society (PHALS)	April 2008–2010 at Kutupalong. July 2008-Onward at Nayapara	Pre-primary and Primary Education	Lack of Funding
6.	Bangladesh Red Crescent Society (BDRCS)		Distribute the Food and Non-food Items provided by : • Government of Bangladesh • UNHCR • WFP	

* According to the Camp-in-Charge, Kutupalong Refugee Camp. Ukhia, Cox's Baazar. Date-26-05-2008.

† An NGO known as Al-Haramine is working in the camps. Islamic Relief International and ACRA has provided US$ 1.2 million to shift a refugee camp from Taal area to a new sight in Leda in Teknaf region.

Table 6.3 Non-Functional NGOs

Names of the NGOs	Operational Area	Types of Services
Care	Dhoa Palong, Dechua Palong-1 & 2. Maricha Palong, & Haludia Palong.	Sanitation
OXFAM	Dumdumia-1&2&Nayapara	Water and sanitation
Islamic Relief	Dechua Palong-2	Medical centre, supplementary feeding food distribution
Islamic Relief Agency (ISRA)	Dechua Palong-1&2	Health care
Medecins Sans Frontieers(MSF) Holland	Balukhali-1,2, Nayapara	Health & sanitation
Save the Children Fund (SCF) UK	Dumdumia-1&2	Health & sanitation
World Concern	Gundhum-3	Clothing
MSF-France	Dechua Palong-1 & 2 Maricha Palong, & Dhoa Palong	Nutrition & supplementary feeding
Caritas	Hankhola	Sanitation
Muslim Aid	Gundhum-1 & 2	Shed Construction
International Islamic Relief Organisation(IIRO)	Shailer Dheba	Shed Construction
TDHNL (Teredes Homes Nethelands)	Adarshagram	Sanitation
Gonoshasthya Kendro (GK)	Gundhum-1 & 2 Maricha Palong & Dechua Palong-2	Health & sanitation
EDM (Enfans Du Monde)	Gundhum-1&2 Nayapara and Jummapara.	Shelter construction
Church of Bangladesh	Harihola	Water and sanitation
ADMA(Association of Medical Doctors for Asia)	Dhoa Palong	Health care
Rabia-Al- Alam-Al-Islami	Dechua Palong-1&2 maricha Palong, KutuPalong & Dumdumia.	Health, Nutrition and Food distribution.
Concern	Kutupalong	Sanitation
Association for Social Advancement(ASA)	Nayapara-1,2	Shelter Construction
ADRA	Gundhum-3	Shed Construction
Al-Haramine	Nayapara	Shed Construction
World Vision	Balukhali-1,2 Kutupalong	Clothing, Health, Sanitation, Shelter Construction & Food.

Source: Refugee Relief and Repatriation Commissioner (RRRC), Cox's Bazaar.

Table 6.4 Level of Service Delivery in Kutupalong and Nayapara Camps

Assistance	Kutupalong Camp	Nayapara Camp
Nutrition	SEP: Children<2 years-57 Children 2 to<-5 years Pregnant women-92 Lactating mothers-192	SEP: Children<2 years-108 Children 2 to<-101 Pregnant women-169 Lactating mothers-220
TEP	TEP Total Beneficiaries-15	Total Beneficiaries-1
Water	Source: Underground water through shallow Tube-Wells Functional Plants :-40 Ratio(Person /day): 1:19 Functional Plants: 3 Ratio(Person /day):1:25	Source: Water treatment plant
Sanitation	Latrine: Functional: 292 Ratio: 1:29 Bathing Cubicles: Functional: 69 Ratio:-1:122 Garbage Pits: Functional: 97 Ratio:-1:87	Latrine: Functional: 614 Ratio:-1:22 Bathing Cubicles: Functional: 382 Ratio:-1:35 Garbage Pits: Functional: 171 Ratio:-1:78
Shelter	Total Shed:255 Total units:-1530	Total Shed:405 Total units:-2430
Education	Total School:-6 Total students:-1642 Boys:-937(57.06%) Girls:-705(42.94%)	Total School:-8 Total students: 2601 Boys:-1470(56.52%) Girls:-1131 (43.48%)

Table 6.4 suggests that despite being 'documented', refugees residing in the camps have inadequate access to sanitation and water facilities. Therefore, it is not difficult to comprehend that the living condition is far more miserable for the 'undocumented' refugees. It is evident that the improvement and reconstruction of the living areas, educational structures, community areas and recreational spaces depend on support from the international community and the

Table 6.5 Food and Non-Food Items Delivery in Kutupalong and Nayapara Camps[8]

Item	Quantity per Person	Time/Ratio
Food		
Rice	6.300 kg	
Pulse	0.560 kg	
Soya Oil	0.280 kg	Bi –weekly
Salt	0.140 kg	
Sugar	0.140 kg	
Blended Food	0.700 kg	
Non-food		
Soap	06 pieces per month	Family of 1-3 persons
	08 pieces per month	Family of 4-6 persons
	10 pieces per month	Family of 7+ persons
CRH (Compressed Rice Husk)	02 bags per month	Per family
Kerosene	01 liter per month	Per family

participation of the CSOs. Reconstruction of infrastructure, including community services such as schools and clinics, is important in creating conducive conditions for the refugees to return. When these conditions are not met, refugees would resort to violent and illegal means to sustain their lives and families. Despite their modest contribution to the lives of the refugees and influence over the government, civil society can still play an important role in improving the lives and provide a framework to resolve the refugee issue. However, major challenges for the CSOs, in this case, rest on government and its decision making structures.

6.3 RE-INVENTING THE ROLE OF CSOs

Despite common agenda between the politics and civil aspirations, civil society could not bring about any national political consensus on refugee issue nor has it been able to provide an alternative channel as intermediaries to make the political parties take concrete actions on the Rohingya refugee process. One can also argue that civil society could

8 Sources: Office of the camp in charge, Kutupalong Refugee Camp Ukhiya, Cox's Bazar. Updated on-26-05-2008.

not redefine the rules of the political game along the democratic lines. As we have observed in the earlier segments of this chapter, in most cases, civil society actors have little, if any role, in foreign policy making or charting a refugee policy. It is therefore necessary to examine the informal way and non-institutional pathways through which they can exercise influences.

In terms of organisational forms, a coalition, advocacy or national groups could be formed to effectively influence the government decision-making processes relating rights of the refugees and foreign policy towards Myanmar. In terms of non-institutional form, since CSOs in Bangladesh are closely tied to top-level policy-making through their interactions with parliaments, executives, big business, foundations and major media holdings, they can actively carry out advocacy, policy research, and negotiation support activities. This would help in easing tension and promote constructive engagement and press the government to modify the structural features of negotiation with Myanmar and international organisations.

The government and policy actors must actively encourage the CSOs to get engaged in the refugee issue. The government and the international communities should understand that the CSOs can mitigate the material or psychological *symptoms* of security threats posed by the refugees, by engaging in operational service delivery targeted to the needs of Rohingya refugees.[9] It is therefore important for the government to provide security to the NGOs working in the field levels.

UNHCR and CSOs should actively facilitate dialogue and consultation between government, NGOs, INGOs, and communities regarding resettlement and repatriation issues. In this regard, it would be important to formulate and implement a coordinated and cohesive national approach to the refugee issue. This would require political consensus and firm commitment from the political parties.

CSOs may initiate tracks two and three diplomacy activities which should be aimed at supporting official negotiations and working through differences between the governments in Bangladesh and Myanmar. It should include inter-state dialogue projects between people sharing similar professional roles and experiences (e.g., civil society representatives, media, private sector, academics, politicians,

---

9 Tocci, Nathalie, 2008. *The European Union, Civil Society and Conflict Transformation.* MICROCON Policy Working Paper 1.

NGO representatives) in order to foster cross-border trust and understanding, and subsequent changes in the perceptions of states.

UNHCR and its implementation and operational partners should design clear communications strategies, with the assistance from the CSOs, to inform the broader public about the strategies regarding the refugees, progress in the process of repatriation and publicise the problems and threats posed by and upon the refugees in Bangladesh. Such communications strategies must also address the education, housing and healthcare needs of both the 'documented' and 'undocumented' Rohingya refugees. Another purpose of such strategies could be to ensure that safety nets are in place so that the rights of the refugees are guaranteed and would protect them from social humiliation and exploitation by the criminal networks.

Such communication strategies eventually would open up paths for the CSOs to raise awareness of the protection and assistance concerns of refugees; support the education of local elected representatives and strengthen the role of local leaders to ensure that they are able to respond to the particular needs of refugees; ensure a ready flow of information to refugee populations about durable solutions and support refugee participation in decisions about their future; monitor the repatriation process and government responses for durable solutions.

Local CSOs, based in Chittagong region, can be directly involved in Rohingya refugee issue. Local CSOs can engage in activities pertaining to issues such as human rights, governance in the camps, security (human and national), justice, gender, education or political abuse and corruption. Engagement of the local CSOs would be more effective than the national CSOs in preventing organised crime networks to which the refugees are often vulnerable.

Coordination between the local and national CSOs needs to be strengthened. The local civil society in the region of Chittagong has always been concerned about the refugee issue. However, their concerns had barely been accommodated or have influenced the national CSOs. The civil society based in Dhaka or urban areas remained less active on the Rohingyas. Such gap between the locals and the nationals has perplexed the local CSOs from influencing the government.

Media has an important role in sensitising both the government and the CSOs. Media could portray the refugee problem to attract the attention of all the stakeholders both within and outside Bangladesh. Media could play an effectual role in removing or minimising the antipathy of the society and the CSOs by promoting and projecting the state of affairs. They can create a wave of enthusiasm among the academia. An in-depth co-ordination between the academia and media could be considered a supportive instrument to sensitise the refugee issue.

Since conditions of return of the refugees are solely dependant on political and economic conditions, it is important that the academia and media should monitor conditions of return and repatriation of the refugees. Civil society representatives could conduct inquiries and report violations of human rights; investigate complaints particularly concerning sexual harassment or restitution for property and violence, and discrimination against returnees; monitor and report on the implementation of bilateral agreements with particular regard to their provision for durable solutions; and advise the government on the rights of refugees.

6.4 CONCLUSION

This chapter has argued that CSOs could be an important actor in finding solutions for the Rohingya refugees and in contributing to peaceful and safe repatriation of the refugees. However, civil society does not act in a vacuum. In particular, the role of government in encouraging and providing security to the civil society actors is essential. Working with refugees during their migration can enable them to play important roles in the bilateral relations between Bangladesh and Myanmar. It is important to recognise that due to absence of a democratic government in Myanmar, civil society response from Myanmar may not be possible.

The CSOs, along with the international community and National Human Rights Commission in Bangladesh should undertake a formal role to monitor the protection of the human rights of the refugees. This would allow a structured platform, apart from governmental initiatives, to provide solutions to the difficulties faced by the refugees to either return to their country of origin or in settling to a third country. This would pave the ways for bilateral negotiations and will contribute to the peaceful repatriation process.

However, given the existing political settings in Myanmar and bi-partisan politics in Bangladesh politics, all civil society stakeholders seeking change in the refugee regime must assume that the task right now is fundamentally political. This means non-institutional civil society should put its energies into the construction of a new social and alternative movement prepared to challenge the status quo in order to bring a democratic consensus on the refugee issue. Only when civil society organisations, government and other social change makers would address this task, our effort to resolve the refugee issue, now slow and slower, will get momentum.

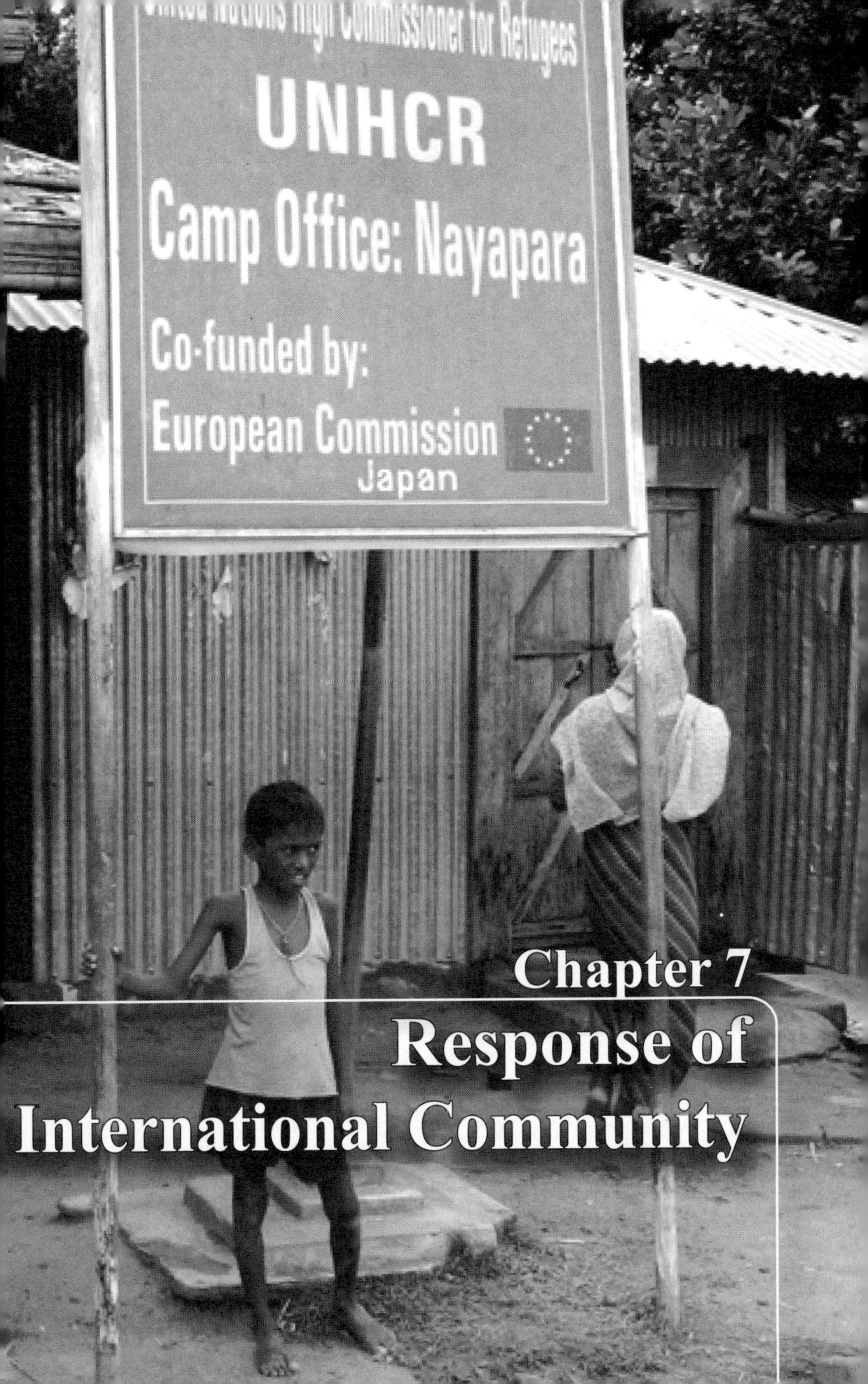

Chapter 7
Response of International Community

Photograph by Nazmus Saqib/IR/DU 2008

The response of international community (IC) is another crucial dimension in understanding the problem and solution of the Rohingya refugee issue. It is not only for the reason that the international community can put diplomatic pressure on the states responsible for the crisis, but also provide a critical support for survival of the Rohingya refugees in camp and non-camp areas. All the parties to this issue concur on the point that global support is must for the durable resolution of the Rohingya refugee crisis. One can also observe that the international community has already involved in this issue. The IC has been continuing support for the protection of Rohingya refugees in order to find permanent solution and to insure their human dignity. The reason behind the involvement of the IC is that the problems of the Rohingya refugees are multidimensional which includes political issues, domestic disturbances, social movements and many other elements. Besides, several countries such as Myanmar, Bangladesh, India, Thailand and Indonesia are directly affected by the Rohingya refugee issue making it an international problem. Since Bangladesh is hosting a significant number of Rohingya refugees for last 17 years it has created space for both the host country and the IC to be involved in the issue. Bangladesh faces numerous internal limitations that make it very difficult to assist the Rohingya refugees on its own. On the other hand, Myanmar is not willing or not taking proper actions to resolve this issue, which forces IC to extend its hands of cooperation to resolve this issue. The main objective of this chapter is to focus on the IC, their efforts to resolve the problems and how they are conducting their activities.

In this study, 'international community' is used as a loosely defined term which refers to a body of countries and organisations who get together to enact common policies that might otherwise be controversial or ineffective. The IC can be categorised into two groups—state and non-state actors. Geographically, state actors are represented by different regions of the world. Apart from Myanmar and Bangladesh, the major state actors involved in the Rohingya refugee issue include India, China, Indonesia, Japan, Malaysia and Thailand in Asia, USA and Canada in North America, UK and Germany in Europe, Saudi Arabia and UAE in the Middle East, Australia, New Zealand, ASEAN, and SAARC. The non-state actors can be divided into two categories—international governmental organisations (IGOs) and international non-governmental organisations (INGOs). The major IGOs involved in the Rohingya refugee issue include UNHCR, USAID and EU while INGOs comprise IRI, TAI, MSF, and Concern Worldwide. Though the national governments are the most important actors, there are groups and interest within the states that influence the state's policies.[1] Despite being non-state actors, they contribute to the development of the people. There are thousands of nongovernmental organisations (NGOs) that interact with states, some of which have political purpose, some have humanitarian and some have economic and technical purposes. Sometimes, states actions are also influenced by intergovernmental organisations (IGOs) whose members are national governments like, the UN and its agencies, European Union, and USAID. As regards the Rohingya refugee issue, the IC is primarily concerned with two major aspects of their interests—humanitarian and political. While apparently one contradicts with the other, in reality both the dimensions are clearly manifested in their policies and programmes.

7.1 STATES AND THE ROHINGYA REFUGEE PROBLEM

So far, different states in the world have responded positively to the Rohingya refugee problem in Bangladesh which ranges from direct

---

[1] Tocci, Nathalie, 2008. *The European Union, Civil Society and Conflict Transformation.* MICROCON Policy Working Paper 1, p.12.

financial and technical assistance to diplomatic pressure on the Myanmar government. The financial and technical support is channelled through the GoB. Another way of support is allowing the resettlement of a good number of Rohingyas to third countries and thereby lessening the burden on Bangladesh. Countries like Canada, Australia, the United States, New Zealand, South Korea and Thailand have provided significant contribution to the cause of the Rohingya refugees living in Bangladesh. Canada is one of the major countries which resettles refugees. In 2006, Canada resettled 10,651 refugees from over 60 different nationalities. The top five countries of origin were: Afghanistan, Colombia, Ethiopia, Myanmar and Sudan.[2] It is now well known that Canada is the highest recipient of the Rohingya refugees. Twenty-three refugees were resettled in Canada in 2006 and a further 79 in 2007.[3] As one of the largest donors of UNHCR, Canada donated US $ 33,409,634 for the year 2008. Australia is another major donor to Bangladesh. In 2007-08, Australia's aid budget for Bangladesh totals $32.4 million and includes programmes focusing on food security, nutrition and primary education, microfinance, health and others alike.[4] As a part of its development assistance to Bangladesh, Australia has confirmed its contribution for the Rohingya refugees in Bangladesh for year 2008-09. On May 22, 2008 the Australian government donated $1.4 million for the construction of 10000 new homes for the Rohingya refugees in Bangladesh. With this fund, the UNHCR will construct 10,000 new homes for Rohingya refugees living at Kutupalong Camp in Cox's Bazar. An Australia based NGO, Austcare is also working with Rohingya refugees in Bangladesh. It mainly works with Technical Assistance Incorporated (TAI) and Empowerment of Law through the Common People (ELCOP) with the aim of contributing to long term durable solutions for the Rohingya who are facing terrible problems in Bangladesh. Austcare includes education, vocational training, nutrition, sanitation and sports and

2 Reliefweb, Canada is first country to resettle Rohingya refugees from Bangladesh, available at: http://www.reliefweb.int/rw/rwb.nsf/db900SID/EGUA-72FPN6?OpenDocument, accessed on June 4, 2008.

3 Pia Pritz Phiri, Representative of UNHCR Bangladesh, mentioned this in the methodological Workshop on "Mainstreaming the Rohingya Refugee Problems in Bangladesh: The Needs for Networking and Capacity Building" organised by Centre for Alternative on 10 May 2008 at Dhaka.

4 Official Website of Australian High Commission in Bangladesh.

recreation programs. All these are good indicators to measure the Australian contribution for Rohingya refugees in Bangladesh.

A number of Rohingyas are now living in Australia. Australia is a country that has a strong tradition of resettling vulnerable refugees. Amnesty International along with UNHCR requested the Australian Government to increase its annual humanitarian quota for 2008-2009 from 13,000 to 20,000. In 2008-09, Australia government plans to resettle 100 Rohingya refugees from Bangladesh to Australia.[5] New Zealand has expressed its willingness to resettle Rohingya refugees from Bangladesh. The first batch of 23 Rohingya refugees from five families, including men, women and children reached New Zealand on June 30, 2008. Of the 23 refugees, five were from Nayapara camp and 18 members from Kutupalong refugee camp.[6] The selected families were trained in New Zealand culture by the International Organisation of Migration (IOM) earlier.

The resettlement of the Rohingya refugees in the United States has been hampered in the post-9/11 era due to new legislations such as the U.S. Patriot Act of 2001[7] and the Real ID Act of 2005. These laws have placed restrictions on the persons who could be considered eligible to resettle in the US. Under these Acts, "anyone who has provided material support to an armed resistance movement regardless of whether it was voluntary or coerced is to be considered a supporter of terrorism, and as such not permitted into the US."[8] However, things have started to change since early 2006. A delegation from the US travelled to Thailand, Bangladesh and Burma to monitor and evaluate conditions in four refugee camps.[9] During the Bangladesh trip, the team closely observed the living conditions of the refugee camps, sanitation and water supply system inside the camps. The team also visited the makeshift, unofficial refugee camp called 'Taal' at Teknaf.[10]

5 Available at: http://www.minister.immi.gov.au/media/speeches/2008/ce080620.htm

6 Arakan Rohingya National Organisation, *First batch of Rohingya refugees resettled in New Zealand*, available at: http://www.rohingya.org/index.php?option=com_content&task=view&id=191&Itemid=28, accessed on July 15, 2008.

7 Available at: http://epic.org/privacy/terrorism/hr3162.html, accessed on September 14, 2008.

8 Human Rights Documentation Unit, *Burma Human Rights Yearbook 2006*, available at: http://www.ncgub.net/BHR Y/2006/Refugees.html, accessed on July 12, 2008.

9 Monitoring and Evaluating Refugee Camps in Asia, available at: www.state.gov/g/prm/rls/65215.htm.accessed.

10 Ibid.

This unofficial camp is highly vulnerable to flooding as it is situated on the west bank of the Naf River. Besides, the US Ambassadors in Bangladesh have visited both the camps in Nayapara and Kutupalong on a number of occasions. The present US Ambassador James F. Moriarty after arriving here visited several Rohingya refugee camps.[11] It clearly demonstrates concern expressed by the US government. The cornerstone of the US position is to facilitate voluntary repatriation of the Rohingya refugees from Bangladesh to Myanmar.

Thailand is also one of the host countries of Rohingya refugees. There are 150,608 Rohingya refugees living in official camps in Thailand while approximately 200,000 living outside the camps. It is also true that Thailand has a poor record in supporting the Rohingya refugees in its territory. Recently, the Thai military has come under harsh criticism for its brutal mistreatment of over 500 Rohingya refugees fleeing persecution in Myanmar and seeking refuge in Thailand. Having arrived in small boats from Myanmar, the refugees have been pulled ashore by the Thai military, beaten and then towed back to sea with little or no food or water.[12] The Thai government is determined to stop this influx and they even want to place the Rohingya refugees living in Thailand in a deserted island. It is reported that Thailand also prevented UNHCR from meeting with the refugees, as well as stopping them from providing food and other humanitarian assistance to these refugees. In response to international criticism, the Thai Government has come forward with some positive initiatives. The Thai Foreign Minister Kasit Piromya took a diplomatic initiative for consultation with all concerned countries, including Burma, Bangladesh, Malaysia, Indonesia and India to find solutions. After meeting with the Ambassadors from these five countries the Thai government stressed that this is a regional issue that would need joint common efforts.[13]

South Korea is also getting involved to support the Rohingya refugees in Bangladesh. Until now South Korean assistance is confined to financial and technical support. This country does not show any interest about the resettlement of the Rohingyas in its territory. The Government of Malaysia is also sympathetic to the Rohingya refugees.

---

11 Embassy of the United States of America, Dhaka Office Press Release, July 10.

12 http://www.reliefweb.int/rw/rwb.nsf/db900SID/VDUX-7PUVFP?OpenDocument accessed on 9 June 2009.

13 http://www.nationmultimedia.com/2009/01/26/opinion/opinion_30094144.php

An estimate shows that about 12,000 Rohingyas live in Malaysia, some of whom are said to have resided there for more than 10 years. The Government of Malaysia earlier declared to provide the temporary settlement status to the refugees and asylum seekers registered with the UNHCR which will facilitate their legal employment and access to education for their children but the process is still unimplemented.[14] Recently, Indonesia has involved in the Rohingya issue particularly when it was revealed that an Indonesian fishing boat rescued 198 Rohingyas off the coast of Aceh, on the northern tip of the island of Sumatra. It was reported that these refugees spent three weeks in the ocean after Thai authorities denied them entry into Thailand, leaving them in the open sea in a 12-metre boat that had no engine.[15]

7.2 REGIONAL INSTITUTIONS

As time passes, the Rohingya refugee issue is becoming regionalised. Regional institutions such as ASEAN and SAARC have already been engaged with this issue. Understandably, ASEAN has particular responsibility in resolving this issue as one of its member nations, Myanmar, is the source of the Rohingya refugees while Thailand, Malaysia and Indonesia are major destination countries. It is often argued that ASEAN can be a key mechanism to create pressure on Myanmar. It is voiced in the diplomatic circle that Myanmar has become a problem for 10 nations group because of its poor human rights record.[16] Although non-interference in the internal affairs is a fundamental principle, ASEAN members have already shown interests to create pressure on the military regime in Myanmar to improve its human rights record. As one Indonesian political leader asserted, "It is time for the Indonesian government to take firm action against the Burmese military junta government to uphold democracy and respect human rights".[17] One can also refer to Article 1 of the

---

14 http://www.aliran.com/index.php?option=com_content&view=article&catid=34:2007&id=254:rohingya-refugees-dilemma-remains-unsolved, accessed on September 14, 2008.

15 Weena Kowitwanij, Rescue for 198 Rohingya refugees abandoned by Thailand in open sea, http://www.asianews.it/index.php?l=en&art=14387.

16 VOA, ASEAN Head Says New Charter Will Put Pressure on Burma, available at: http://www.voanews.com/english/archive/2007-07/2007-07-24-voa25.cfm?CFID=245737009&CFTOKEN=10397856, accessed on May 29, 2008.

17 Burma Review, ASEAN Charter and Burma's Democratic Agenda, available at: http://burmareview.com/2007/07/29/lost-promises-of-asean-asean-charter-and-burma%E2%80%99s-democratic-agenda/, accessed on May 29, 2008.

Chapter 1 of ASEAN Charter where it is emphasised that member states and the peoples of ASEAN are to live in peace with the world at large in a just, democratic and harmonious environment[18] and to promote and protect human rights and fundamental freedoms.[19] The Bali process is an example of ASEAN involvement in the Rohingya refugee issue. Leaders of ASEAN countries during their 14th summit in 2009 decided that the issue of Rohingya boatpeople is of regional concern and agreed to bring it under the Bali Process on People Smuggling, Trafficking and Related Transnational Crime, that was launched in 2002 in the hope of addressing the issues though regional cooperation. ASEAN Secretary-General Surin Pitsuwan termed the Rohingya issue a very complicated challenge to the entire region of Southeast Asia.[20] Thailand and Indonesia are playing a major role in advancing the cause of the Rohingyas under the Bali process. Terming it a regional problem, Thailand's Prime Minister Abhisit Vejjajiva stated that regional governments would take up the issue of Rohingya refugees at the Bali process.[21] Issues such as the type of humanitarian assistance and involvement of UNHCR and the International Organisation for Migration (IOM) are being discussed to mitigate the sufferings of the Rohingyas. However, doubts are also cast over the Bali process as the critics argue that it has not been giving adequate attention to this problem. So far, no initiative has taken place to grant refugee status to the Rohingyas. Adequate consideration has also not been given to the human rights and protection needs of the Rohingya population in the Asia Pacific region. Apart from ASEAN, other regional institutions such as South Asian Association for Regional Co-operation (SAARC), BIMSTEC, and Organisation of Islamic Conference (OIC) can provide support for the Rohingyas. One of the major destinations of the Rohingyas is Bangladesh which is a member of SAARC and BIMSTEC. India as a major regional power and a neighbour of Myanmar is also linked with the Rohingya refugee issue making SAARC as another regional institution to deal with the Rohingya refugee problem.

18 See Chapter 1, Article 1, Section 4 of ASEAN Charter.

19 See Chapter 1, Article 1, Section 7 of ASEAN Charter.

20 http://www.bangkokpost.com/print/136770/rohingya-a-regional-problem

21 Mizzima News, Bali Process' to take up Rohingya issue, 22 February 2009, http://www.mizzima.com/news/regional/1752-bali-process-to-take-up-rohingya-issue.html

7.3 NON-STATE ACTORS AND THE ROHINGYA REFUGEE PROBLEM

Since the beginning of the problem of the Rohingya refugee, the GOB has been working very closely with several non-state actors to ameliorate sufferings of the Rohingyas. It should be mentioned here that several ministries of GOB provide necessary workforce to implement programmes in the refugee camps. All kinds of financial support come from the UN agencies along with various donors.[22] Among the non-state actors, the most important one is the UNHCR. There are other IGOs and INGOs who are involved in this issue, but most of them depend on the UNHCR for their operations. The following section gives a brief discussion on the role of some IGOs and INGOs.

7.3.1 The United Nations High Commissioner for Refugee (UNHCR)

The UNHCR has the primary responsibility to provide international protection to refugees and to seek acceptable solutions for refugees all over the world. It has been working for the Rohingya refugees in Bangladesh for a long period of time. UNHCR is the principal partner of the GOB for providing protection and other assistance, to the refugees inside the camps. This relationship has been formalised through a Memorandum of Understanding (MoU) between the two parties in 1992. Within this framework a number of other specialised agencies also work. Basically the UNHCR provides the humanitarian and economic assistance to the Rohingya refugees in Bangladesh. As the donors do not provide fund for the refugees directly, the UNHCR works as a coordinator of the donor countries and agencies without having any political motive. Generally, donors disburse their grants to the UNHCR and then the UNHCR utilise these funds for the refugees. Currently, the implementing partners of the UNHCR include the Ministry of Food and Disaster Management, GOB and NGOs namely Bangladesh Legal Aid and Services Trust, Bangladesh Red Crescent Society, Research Training and Management International, Technical Assistance Inc. The operational partners include Austcare, Handicap International, Médecins Sans Frontières-Holland, and World Food Programme (WFP).

---

22 Information gathered from the Refugee Relief and Repatriation Commissioner's Office at Cox's Bazar, Bangladesh on 6 June 2008.

However, the UNHCR has been working to improve the conditions of the Rohingya refugees in Bangladesh. The UNHCR provides shelter, food, security, education, health service and so on for approximately 27,000 Rohingya refugees in the official camps, namely, Nayapara and Kutupalong with the coordination of the Ministry of Food and Disaster Management of the GOB. Most of the refugees living inside the camps are satisfied with the performance of the UNHCR. It should be mentioned that these two camps are only for the documented Rohingya refugees in Bangladesh. The UNHCR also provides assistance to the undocumented Rohingya refugees living inside the camps. The annual budget of the UNHCR to the Rohingya refugees in Bangladesh is about $3.7 million to $4.4 million in 2008, and it may change, according to Marin, the UNHCR representative of the local office of the UNHCR in Cox's Bazar in Bangladesh.[23] It provides primary education for the refugees inside the camps and they are taught English, Bengali, Burmese and Mathematics. The Secondary education is not allowed for the refugees. There is also a health care facility provided for the refugees by the UNHCR inside the camps. It also arranges voluntary repatriation of the Rohingya refugees to their own country, Myanmar. The UNHCR has also been pursuing a resettlement programme as a strategy of durable solution to the Rohingya refugees since 2006. This includes identification for resettlement of extremely vulnerable refugees with compelling protection concerns.

As mentioned above, the UNHCR deals with the registered or documented Rohingya refugees in Bangladesh. It does not deal with the unregistered Rohingya refugees in Bangladesh. But the unregistered Rohingya refugees suffer more than the registered ones. The conditions of their lives are extremely miserable and pathetic. Though the UNHCR claims that it provides assistance towards the unregistered Rohingya refugees inside the camps, but most of the unregistered Rohingya refugees inside the camp say the opposite. It may be mentioned that the UNHCR office in Bangladesh is aware of the fact that there is a limitation for this organisation to resolve the problem. As Pia Prytz, the former Head of the UNHCR in Bangladesh, said: "The UNHCR does not have any political power to solve the Rohingya problem in Bangladesh."[24]

23 The information was collected during the field visit and discussion with the UNHCR official in June 2008 by the project students.

24 Mentioned in the Methodological Workshop on "Mainstreaming the Rohingya Refugee Problems in Bangladesh: The Need for Networking and Capacity Building" at Dhaka on 10 May 2008, organised by the Centre for Alternatives.

However, the UNHCR actions have undoubtedly improved the efficiency of repatriation and they have also enabled UN officials to monitor the situation in the camps and on the ground in Arakan.

7.3.2 The European Union (EU)

The EU is one of the major donor agencies which provides humanitarian assistance of various forms to the people who are largely up-rooted by the military junta in Myanmar. The EU has taken several attempts to normalise the situation in Myanmar not only for the Rohingyas but also for the mass people living there. The EU has undertaken four official-level EU troika missions to Yangon. Restoration of democracy is a primary goal of EU towards Myanmar. EU wants to see an elected political government which will respect human rights in the country that is linked to the creation of the Rohingya refugees.[25] A Common Position was adopted by the EU in April 2003 where the EU stated that the Burmese government has no reason to disagree to restore the democratic environment within a definite timetable. Thus, the Common Position was aimed at strengthening EU's pressure on military junta to restore democracy. Above all, the EU pressurises the military junta to stop their discriminatory activities against different ethnic communities in Myanmar. The EU has also contributed for the betterment of economic and social life of the refugees who have been driven to the neighbouring countries by the repressive attitude of the military regime.

The EU also provides strong financial support for the operations of the refugee camps in Bangladesh. During the year of 1999-2000, EU contributed 66% of total budget (over €13 million) for both Rakhine state in Myanmar, and Cox's Bazar area in Bangladesh.[26] On December 6, 2006, the UNHCR singed a contribution agreement with EU in Dhaka under which the EC would provide a donation of 3.9 million Euros (over USD$5.7 million) to end the plight of the Rohingya refugees.[27] According to UNHCR, the EC has long been the largest donor for UNHCR's operations in Bangladesh, which costs $54 million

---

25 Europa, the EU's Relation with Myanmar, available at: http://ec.europa.eu/external_relations/myanmar/intro/index.htm, accessed on May 26, 2008.

26 Anais Tamen, *the European Union's sanctions related to Human rights: the case of Burma/Myanmar*, available at: http://www.burmalibrary.org/docs/Memoire-AT.htm#_Toc54419312, accessed on May 26, 2008.

27 EU Provides 3.9 million Euros for the Rohingya Refugees, available at: http://www.mizzima.comcomponent/content/archive.html?year=2007&month=12, accessed on Sept. 11, 2008.

since the arrival of the Rohingya refugees from Burma in 1991 and 1992.[28]

7.3.3 World Food Program (WFP)

The World Food Programme (WFP) is another UN agency which provides food aid. The WFP provides food, on average to 90 million people per year, 58 million of whom are children. WFP was formally established in 1963 by the FAO and the United Nations General Assembly on a three-year experimental basis. The WFP has undertaken different activities to lessen the sufferings of Rohingya refugees. Particularly, the WFP is responsible for distribution and supply of food in the refugee camps. It has been assisting the GOB since April 1992. A survey reveals that 58 percent of the refugee children and 53 percent of the adults are chronically malnourished.[29] To address this problem, all registered refugees are given general food ration in the camps. Since May 2002, fortnightly distribution of food is being implemented. The different food supports as provided under the WFP are as follows:

- Supplementary Feeding Programme (SFP) for malnourished children under 5, pregnant and lactating mothers.
- Therapeutic Feeding Programme (TFP) for severely malnourished children under the age of ten years, low birth weight and premature babies with their mothers and other serious medical patients. The office of the civil surgeon selects participants for SFP and TFP.
- School snacks programmes where each school going student gets 50 gm. of locally produced fortified biscuits for each day of attendance up to 250 school days a year.
- Food for Training (FFT) programme where adolescent girls and women receive rice allocation for attending skill training activities, kitchen garden and for the production of non food items (Mosquito nets, clothing soap, embroided items) etc.
- Food for Work (FFW) programme where members of extremely vulnerable refugee families get chance to work for food within camps.

---

28 Ibid.

29 Concern, DRAFT Nutrition survey in Kutupalong and Nayapara camps among the Rohingya refugees, November 2001 p.2.

All these programmes for food are funded by the WFP where the GOB, Bangladesh Red Crescent Society (BDRCS), and Technical Assistance Incorporated (TAI) work as the implementing Partners of the WFP. Besides, the WFP managed the supply of pure water to the refugees in Nayapara camp in 2005 with the assistance of UNHCR that helped them to get water from hilly areas. The WFP has two Assistant Field Officers employed in both the camps. There is also a food committee that meets in every two months in Cox's Bazar, led by WFP with participants from UNHCR, BDRCS and TAI.

7.3.4 Intervention of INGOs in the Camps

In addition to the UN agencies, there are several INGOs which provide various types of support to the registered Rohingya refugees in the camps. Majority of these organisations mainly provide various categories of health support, basic training for self help activities, adult education, sanitation etc. Technical Assistance Incorporated (TAI) provides training for self help activities like home gardening, poultry, tree plantation, skill development, tailoring, carpentry, school bag making and social awareness; adult education; sanitation management; and Food Basket Monitoring. Bangladesh Red Crescent Society (BDRCS) distributes food and non- food items supplied by the GoB, UNHCR and WFP. Research, Training and Management International (RTMI) funded by the MSF Holland mainly provides health support like In-patients Department (IPD); referral patients; promote and protect the reproductive rights and choices of the people and Essential Service Delivery (ESD). After the withdrawal of the MSF, Holland, the Islamic Relief International has started providing primary health care facilities to the refugees. Handicap International and its implementing partner Programme for Helpless and Lagged Society (PHALS) provide support to the both registered refugees and the unregistered refugees living at 'Taal', which include assistance to disabled people; community awareness regarding disability; mainstreaming the disabled people; and pre primary and primary education.[30] Moreover, there are health education activities in the camps involving hygienic promotion, nutrition and reproductive health. These activities are targeted to ensure preventive health care.[31] Besides, INGOs like

30 CICs of Kutupalong and Nayapara Refugee Camps, June 2008.

31 MSF (2002) '10 years for the Rohingya Refugees in Bangladesh' p.16 available at www.doctorswithoutborders.org/publications/reports/2002/rohingya_report.pdf

London-based Amnesty International has always shown strong support to the cause of the Rohingya refugees. It has voiced concerns about the Rohingyas on various occasions. Sam Zarifi, Amnesty's Asia-Pacific Director, states that Burma must immediately stop the persecution of the Rohingya minority, which is the root cause of the crisis[32] and urged the leaders of Southeast Asian Nations to formally include the Rohingya refugee issue as part of the agenda. It also calls for all governments with Rohingya people in their territories to allow them immediate access to the UN refugee agency (UNHCR).[33] INGOs have shown considerable degree of concern about the Rohingya refugee problem.

7.4 CONCLUSION

This chapter has demonstrated that the response of international community to the Rohingya refugee issue is positive and proactive. The support from the IC is reflected in three areas—humanitarian assistance, diplomatic support and resettlement programme. While the humanitarian assistance in the form of financial and technical support is contributing to the survival of the Rohingyas in the refugee camps, the diplomatic support remains vital for its long term solution. The resettlement programme which is most liked by the Rohingyas is also contributing to mitigate their sufferings. Among the actors in international community, the UNHCR is playing the key role in addressing this problem. The major challenge for the international community is the large number of unregistered Rohingya refugees in Bangladesh who cannot live in the camps. Besides, there has been rising number of Rohingyas who cross the Bangladesh-Myanmar border every day. The engagement of global and regional actors in this issue is also linked with other cases of refugee problems in the world. Particularly, for the UNHCR it is becoming difficult to cope with worldwide refugee situations emanating from intrastate and inter-state conflicts. Critics also argue that humanitarian support will not bring an end to the Rohingya refugee problem. It is evident from the field visits that most of the Rohingya refugees are unwilling to go back to their own country. On the other hand, the allure of resettlement in

32 http://www.bangkokpost.com/breakingnews/136080/amnesty-burma-must-respect-rohingya-minority

33 http://www.amnesty.org.au/refugees/comments/20296/

the third countries mainly in the developed world has created tensions and instability in the camps. The Rohingyas are often cheated by the false information regarding resettlement. The bottom line is that the international community has a lot to do regarding the Rohingya refugee problem.

Chapter 8
Conclusion: What is to be done?

Photograph by S. M. Mobassherul Alam Chowdhury/IR/CU 2008

The repatriation of the Rohingya refugees is a complex undertaking that places an enormous burden on Bangladesh, the UN and other entities involved. Successful repatriation of the refugee population and protection of their rights in Bangladesh largely depends on the GoB, active involvements of the international community and support from the civil society. Based on the findings of this research, following recommendations and proposals could be forwarded for immediate consideration:

8.1 NATIONAL, REGIONAL AND INTERNATIONAL RESPONSES TO THE ROHINGYA REFUGEE ISSUE

In order to develop a concerted and comprehensive framework to resolve the Rohingya refugee issue, it is important to identify the areas of intervention from national, regional and international actors. These are:

Adopt a comprehensive national policy and guideline on the Refugee issue: Currently Bangladesh government does not have any national policy or guideline on the refugee issue. Besides, government has no effective mechanism to identify a refugee, monitor and provide services to the refugees coming from Myanmar. Moreover, government lacks concrete policy to provide strategic guidance to various stakeholders dealing with the refugee issue. Therefore, GoB, in consultation and technical support form the UN agencies, international organisations and local CSOs may design and adopt a comprehensive national policy and framework on the refugees. Adoption of such policy will enhance the government's ability to mitigate the problem and strengthen inter-agency coordination, collaboration and cooperation in this regard.

Strengthening Bangladesh-Myanmar Diplomatic Efforts: Multilateral diplomacy with the donor community to share the burden of caring for refugees needs to be strengthened and should be seen from a broader development approach. So far, Bangladesh government has undertaken moderate and persistent outlook to resolve the Rohingya refugee issue. Protracted refugee problem is increasingly becoming connected with the development and governance agenda in Bangladesh. Therefore, GoB may consider the following options:

- The government should engage in bilateral diplomacy with international donor community to expand services and remove barriers to self-reliance for both the 'documented' and 'undocumented' refugees coming into Bangladesh.
- It is imperative that the government should continue to generously support the refugees for their livelihood development, and pursue fast track diplomacy for repatriation involving various stakeholders, i.e. China, India, developed countries, UN and other international organisations.
- The government may encourage third country resettlement as a practicable solution for those for whom repatriation is not an option, and for those who face legal and security protection tribulations in Bangladesh.[1]
- Actively explore with UNHCR more aggressive and creative opportunities to support voluntary repatriation.
- Possibilities to engage third party mediation could be explored by Bangladesh. Major powers in international politics or regional organisations like SAARC or ASEAN could come forward as a third party mediator.
- Continue and increase assistance to skill development projects for both the 'documented' and 'undocumented' refugees to make them skilled labours for their home countries and for the third countries.

---

1 Canada, Australia, EU countries may provide assistance to UNHCR and GoB to facilitate third country settlement.

- Bangladesh-Myanmar bilateral trade needs to be improved to strengthen confidence between these two countries. Bilateral trade may facilitate track II diplomacy that would eventually help in accelerating Rohingya repatriation. Bangladesh-Myanmar Joint Trade Commission and Chambers of Commerce can play active role in this regard.
- GoB should facilitate more active involvement of civil society and NGO at the local and national level into refugee repatriation process via both Track I and II diplomacy

Involvement of the International Community and Development Partners of Bangladesh: International community and development partners of Bangladesh may consider the following recommendations:

- Along with UNHCR, SAARC, the EU, the World Bank, the United Kingdom, Canada, Australia, Germany, Japan, Scandinavian countries, the Netherlands, and the People's Republic of China can play a significant role in facilitating repatriation and improving the livelihoods of the Rohingya refugees.
- The international community needs to approach the refugee issue within the context of broader development agenda. International and regional level donor conferences could be organised to discuss and find possible means and ways to resolve the Rohingya refugee crisis.
- International community, in particular, may consider providing more funds for reconstruction of accommodation and educational infrastructure, strengthen health services, and efforts to develop skilled labours. While some international donors are helping in these areas, the funding is still too low and the donor community in general has not stepped up to the plate.
- All the stakeholders involved in the refugee regime should broaden their support to include the refugees who are without documentation and living outside the refugee camps.
- GoB and UNHCR should ensure active collaboration among the national and regional level CSOs in developing/ implementing refugee protection and repatriation programs. GoB and UNHCR should undertake consultative linkages with the representatives of civil society particularly experts and representatives of

independent research centres, in the decision making processes relating refugee protection, rehabilitation and repatriation.

Contribution of the Philanthropic community: In addition to the international funding sources, the philanthropy community such as corporate, private and community foundations should be encouraged to play benevolent roles by providing grants and other type of resources to non-profit organisations, social service providers and community organisations that deliver services to the refugees.

Facilitation of Community based Resources: A list needs to be compiled of nonprofits, faith based organisations, government agencies (all levels form national to local) etc., that have culturally specific or language specific programs (sorted by activity area) available for both the documented or undocumented Rohingya refugees. This compiled list should be distributed to Voluntary Agencies, NGOs, faith based organisations, government agencies, philanthropic community, the community at large, and especially to the local civil society. The contents of the list should effectively provide bilingual/bicultural services for the refugees.

Dynamics of National Security of Bangladesh: The relationship between internal security and the refugees is a complex subject to comprehend. On the one hand, the refugees are the victims of insecurity, and on the other, they are often involved in criminal activities. Inhabitants of the refugee camps in Kutu Palong and Nayapara and surrounding areas suffer a wide range of security problems, including incidents caused by law enforcement agencies and due to breakdown of general law and order situation. It has been observed during this research that the refugees are often politically used for electoral motives, engaged in criminal activities, and manipulated by ideological extremist groups and insurgent groups from the Northeastern region of India and Myanmar. It could also be noted that due to physical similarities between Rohingyas and Bengalis, and influx of unmanageable size of Rohingya refugee population into Bangladesh, it has become virtually impossible to distinguish between the legitimate and illicit political dissents. Given such complexity, following measures could be considered:

- There is lack of coordination between different law enforcement agencies to monitor and evaluate the refugee situation.

Therefore, UNHCR in cooperation with the government may develop a multi-prong strategy to meet the security needs, impart security assessment and develop a security plan.

- The UNHCR, in collaboration with international donor agencies, could offer 'security package' to meet the cost of posting of more police officers in and around refugee sites and provide these officers with special allowances, equipment, vehicles, fuel and accommodation.
- Failure to provide physical protection occurs due to lack of capacity of the law enforcement agencies. Bangladesh does not have sufficient or adequately trained and equipped forces, either police or military, to provide adequate and appropriate physical protection in the Rohingya refugee camps. Therefore, training and capacity building programs to strengthen the law enforcement agencies to deal with refugee camp security and humanitarian laws would improve the efficiency of these agencies in dealing with the refugees.
- Hiring and deployment of private security firms could be an alternate and effective solution to provide security in the refugee camps.
- Bangladesh and Myanmar shares a porous border which is a major contributing factor for cross-border arms, drugs and human trafficking, informal trade and concealed access for the Rohingya refugees into Bangladesh. Border management system should be strengthened to monitor the access of the refugees which would have spill over effect on controlling arms, drugs, and human trafficking. Myanmar, however, is recently building a border fence, albeit within its own territory. This could impact upon two things. Firstly, as found in the case of Indian fencing of Bangladesh border, Myanmar could bring the flow of smuggling, including narco-trading, to its advantage, that is, allow the smuggled goods from Myanmar to enter Bangladesh by opening the gates while fencing off the smuggled goods from Bangladesh entering Myanmar. It may be mentioned that save illicit arms and drugs the informal trade between Myanmar and Bangladesh is in favour of Bangladesh at this stage. Secondly, since there are over 300,000 unregisterd Rohingya refugees living in

Bangladesh, Myanmar would be able to disown them once the fencing is done, claiming that these people were residing on the other side of the border. To offset the impact of border fencing by Myanmar immediate negotiation between the two countries ought to start on these two issues, including silently 'registering' the unregistered refugees.

Tangible Support from the Private Sector: In collaboration with Bangladesh Rifles and local government, private sector can put forward plans to set up markets in Bangladesh-Myanmar border. Such markets will increase legal trade and decrease illegal trade between these two countries. Besides, private sector organisations could provide tangible supporting aid, for both documented and undocumented refugees, such as improved diet to the pregnant, winter clothing, improved food during the festival seasons etc. in collaboration with the government and agencies working in the camps.

8.2 REPATRIATION, PROTECTION, LEGAL AND SECURITY CONCERNS

This research has found that durable solutions for the refugee situation depend on freedom from the fear of persecution from the Burmese government. The governments in Bangladesh and Myanmar should understand that voluntary repatriation or return in safety and dignity is in general the preferred durable solution for refugees. The rights of return and protection are enshrined in international law. GoB has performed commendable responsibility by hosting the refugees and by not exercising any forceful measures to repatriate the refugees. However, it is important to provide sufficient attention in the following areas:

Organised Voluntary Repatriation: Given the economic, social and environmental conditions, Bangladesh is reluctant to host refugees. This is often accompanied by the desire to see rapid repatriation, which can in turn translate into deliberate non-protection ("humane deterrence") as a way to encourage repatriation. Such approach would not bring in any sustainable solution to this problem. Myanmar gives mixed signal about their seriousness regarding repatriation of the Rohingya refugees. Therefore, negligible repatriation has taken place between Bangladesh and Myanmar. There has been a status quo in refugee repatriation process since 1998. Any aggressive voluntary repatriation strategy will also fail. Therefore, for the policy makers it could be suggested that organised voluntary repatriation should be preferred to ensure a durable repatriation process.

Protection of the Refugees: UNHCR has done commendable work in providing protection, assistance and support to the Rohingya refugees residing in Bangladesh. UNHCR and international organisations have developed guidelines, best practices, and other measures to improve protection of the refugees in Bangladesh. However, weaknesses in its staffing process and training limit the effectiveness of these measures. Therefore, it is advisable that UNHCR should make better use of partnering arrangements with nongovernmental and international organisations to boost its protection capacity.

Gender based Violence: Gender based violence is a major issue for the Rohingya refugee women. This could occur in their country of origin, where it may form the basis of their refugee claim, or since they arrived in Bangladesh. Therefore, there is a need to address this issue with proper attention by the law enforcement agencies, and a variety of responses are needed which should include counselling services, specialist legal support, appropriate refugee accommodation and the provision of general information and advice.

Combating Child and Women Trafficking: During this research, it was found that insufficient monitoring and protection mechanisms are in place to deter or identify refugee child and female trafficking. The government agencies, particularly the law enforcement agencies, in collaboration with UN bodies and other stakeholders involved in service delivery need to develop comprehensive monitoring and protection mechanisms to combat child and women trafficking.

Legal Aid and Counselling to both the 'Documented' and 'Undocumented' Refugees: During this research, it has been identified that legal aid and counselling services are very inadequate. However, there are some facilities for the 'documented' refugees while 'undocumented' refugees do not have any access to such services. Therefore, the government may consider engaging NGOs specialised in legal services to provide legal aid and counselling in a wider scale to the refugees.

8.3 LIVELIHOOD SERVICES AND SKILLS DEVELOPMENT

UNHCR has provided a significant level of assistance to strengthen the capacity of the Rohingya refugees to absorb the conditions of their livelihoods in the camps. However, several assistances are yet to be strengthened to lay the foundations for sustainable livelihoods and self-reliance for the Rohingya refugees. To support repatriation and third country settlement, GoB, UNHCR, INGOs, NGOs and other institutions need to provide support in the following areas:

Camp Management: To ensure effective management of the refugee camps and services, staffs working in the camp needs to be properly trained in the field of refugee laws and should be provided with adequate incentives, vehicles, office supplies, salaries, rent and utilities. There is a need for training programmes and workshops to improve the camp management skills of the staffs.

Camp Infrastructure: In the camps Nayapara and Kutu Palong overcrowding and poor hygiene are major factors in the transmission of diseases with epidemic potential (HIV/AIDS, STDs, skin diseases etc.). There is an urgent need to improve the accommodation and sanitary infrastructures that constantly expose the refugee population to serious health hazards. Poorly planned and insufficient accommodations in the camps spare the most pathogenic environments possible. Such problem is much more in the undocumented Rohingya refugee settlements. The undocumented Rohingya refugees suffer from inadequate shelter which means that the population is deprived of all privacy and constantly exposed to the elements (rain, cold, diseases, natural disasters etc.). Prompt actions must be undertaken by GoB and UNHCR to improve the camps and its-facilities for both the documented and undocumented refugees. Sufficient spaces for shelters must be provided as rapidly as possible to protect refugees from the health and environmental risks, and infrastructure installed for the necessary health and nutrition facilities, water supply installations, latrines, etc. needs to be improved without further delay. GoB, UNHCR, UNDP, WFP, IRC and other donor communities may provide financial and technical assistance in reconstruction of the camps and its facilities.

Lack of Information regarding Services: The Rohingya refugees are not conscious about their rights and responsibilities. Lack of information about services and rights constantly expose them to legal harassment and physical threats. Therefore, it is recommended that UNHCR, GoB, NGOs and the media should undertake programs to sensitise the refugees regarding their rights, entitlements to services, and responsibilities in general.

Lack of Credible Census and Profiling of the Undocumented Refugees: There is lack of credible and verifiable census relating documented and undocumented refugee population in Bangladesh. A systematic census program needs to be undertaken to identify total number of refugees in Bangladesh.

Health Services: It has been identified that there is a lack of delivery channels for health care services to the Rohingya refugees. Therefore, there is a need for health service enhancement (including publicly funded services and supports from International Organisations) in order to address the complex needs of refugee population. It could be recommended that all refugees should have access routinely to comprehensive health services that could be provided by experienced organisations like MSF or IRC.

Health Education/Outreach Programs: It has been found that the camps provide inadequate facilities for basic health education to children and adults. UNHCR, the government and local partners should develop health education and outreach activities that are culturally appropriate and sensitive to the Rohingya population. In this regard, NGOs may provide training and education modules for health care providers, refugees and partner agencies.

Mental Health: There is a need to engage psychologists, social workers and counsellors by the government agencies and non profit agencies to assist the refugees to provide mental health services. Trauma centres could be established in the camps and its surrounding areas to provide services to both the documented and undocumented refugees.

Family Planning: NGOs, INGOs and donor agencies can provide technical assistance to build awareness on family planning. This should be aimed at every adult member. Although there are such awareness programs in the camps, they remain largely ineffective. The extremely high population growth rate among the camp people proves this beyond doubt. As such, new strategies need to be implemented.

Childcare: The lack of childcare provision was identified as one of the major problems in terms of accessing services and being able to ensure health of the minors in a family.

Education, Language and Training: Lack of access to education impacts on the refugees' ability to become skilled and thus has an exclusionary effect. Therefore, it is imperative for all the agencies involved in the Rohingya refugee repatriation to focus on providing basic education, developing language skills and facilitating vocational trainings for children and adults. Vocational trainings to the adult population would assist them to become skilled workers. Education could be provided in Bangla, English and Arakanese languages. The government should also ensure the entitlement of all minors to access primary level education.

Workforce Development: The Rohingya refugees are hard workers but those with limited English proficiency or formal education continue to face many challenges in becoming skilled workers. An organisational structure could be developed to provide training programs to develop their skills. INGOs and NGOs in collaboration with the government can fund to establish an organisational structure, i.e. vocational training centres, adult education basic education schools, English language training centres. This will have great success in helping refugees find employment at livable wages with employers in their own country and in the third countries. In this regard, there will be a need to develop and fund collaborative partnerships between the government, donors, NGOs and academia.

Micro-finance and Income Generation for the Rohingya Refugees and the Camps: GoB and UNHCR should explore the possibilities of introducing new initiatives for income generation and improving livelihoods in the camps, particularly for women and children. Income-generation and loan schemes do instill new professional skills in refugees, permit them to enjoy a limited degree of financial autonomy and introduce money into a poorly monetised environment. In order to foster refugee self-reliance and the promotion of sustainable livelihoods, micro-finance programs would help in the long run.

8.4 ENGAGING CIVIL SOCIETY ORGANISATIONS, ACADEMIA, MEDIA AND ROHINGYA DIASPORA

During this study it has been identified that civil society has played little role in bringing the Rohingya refugee issue in the development discourse in Bangladesh. In the democratic setting of Bangladesh, civil society, academia and media could impart consultative support by providing strategic guidance to various stakeholders, policy inputs to the government and NGOs, and sensitising the national and international regarding the plights of the refugees. Therefore, CSOs, academia, media and Rohingya Diaspora should carry out activities in the following areas:

Establishing an Institutional Mechanism: Civil society representatives should form an institutional mechanism to discuss, examine and provide strategy or recommendations on the Rohingya refugee issues and to monitor and support the activities of NGO networks. Such institutional mechanism would strengthen cross-sector cooperation and set up events between civil society and relevant authorities to promote accountability and coherent responses to the refugee issues and needs of the refugees in close cooperation with various stakeholders.

Assist in Formulating a Coherent and Comprehensive Strategy: Civil Society should actively take initiatives to formulate a coherent, concrete and comprehensive strategy and policy framework relating refugee regime in Bangladesh adhering to international law and global best practices.

Advocacy and Research Support: CSOs should undertake campaign and advocacy initiatives to sensitise the stakeholders and international community regarding the plights of the refugees. Civil society and academia should conduct research and facilitate debate on the Rohingya refugee issues. Therefore, civil society organisations can undertake independent research and facilitate debate between international, national and non-governmental actors on refugee issues.

Political Consensus on the Refugee Issue: Civil Society and media should undertake aggressive initiatives to build political consensus regarding the Rohingya refugee issue. They should actively resist any attempts to abuse the refugees for political gains.

Bridging the Involvement of NGOs: Civil society in Bangladesh may work as a bridge to increase collaboration at the region/international level of NGOs with relevant experience on refugee issue.

Supporting the Grassroots Activities: Civil society should work together with grassroots organisations supporting and participating in the human rights activities focusing on the rights of the refugees. Civil society, academia and media should support initiatives which facilitate spaces to advocate and monitor the protection and promotion of human rights for the refugees.

Support Community Involvement: Civil society should actively support initiatives to establish special centres or community unions/organisations in bordering areas with the aim of fostering ties between communities (including economic ties) and to promote negotiation processes both at the official and unofficial levels.

Capacity Building in the Field of Education: Academia and media should actively support the government and NGOs to build their capacity to support/implement educational programs for the refugees. Therefore, civil society and academia could play an important role in strengthening the linkages between theoretical experts and practitioners in the area of Refugee concerns.

Collaboration between Civil Society and Media: Media should undertake programs to support contacts between civil society and all the stakeholders to ensure regular and informed coverage of issues and the work of civil society in the context of Rohingya refugee issues.

Refugee Journalism: Media should build its capacity on Refugee journalism in Bangladesh.

Rohingya Diaspora: Rohingyas who are living in the developed or middle income countries should take campaign projects for third country resettlement of the Rohingya refugees. Rohingya Diaspora could build worldwide advocacy networks to sensitise the matter and gain international supports to pressurise the Myanmar government to resolve the refugee crisis.

Practical and Tangible Supports by the Diaspora: Rohingya Diaspora may provide funds to GoB and expert NGOs to improve livelihoods of the refugees. They can also provide material and tangible supports such as clothing, food, educational materials, medicines, entertainment equipments to the refugees.

8.4.1 Capacity Building of the Tertiary Level Students

As Bangladesh is one of the frontline countries facing the problems of refugees, there is a need to bring refugee issue in the mainstream social science education. The academic curricula may adopt a refugee-centred course to promote critical thinking within policy- and practice-related debates. While conducting this research, students from three major public universities, i.e Dhaka University, Jahangirnagar University and Chittagong University, were brought together. What emerged from this networking, within research contexts, is unique and dynamic activism and engagement in activities independent of existing statist structures. The students involved in this study are now equipped with knowledge of the causes and consequences of prolonged refugee situation, problems of conflicting identity crisis and functioning of existing humanitarian aid structures. Similar thematic studies should be encouraged to prepare the future leaders to respond to refugee crises which transcend borders, local cultures and the humanitarian aid regime.

8.5 CONCLUDING REMARKS

The recommendations discussed above are issue specific those require immediate attention from all the stakeholders identified in this report. The government, along with UNHCR should support and encourage the bilateral donor countries to continue and expand their roles in bringing conducive environment for repatriation to Myanmar. To deal with the refugee issue for a poor country like Bangladesh, international community may actively participate in burden-sharing to build refugee-protection and reception capacities. To meet the recommendations, a series of policy revision targeting development assistance by the government, UN agencies and international donors is required. The main obstacle to provide assistance to the refugees has been the reluctance of donor agencies to provide more resources. A crucial task for UNHCR, therefore, would be to mobilise donor commitments to support the durable solutions and facilitate greater coordination across the branches of GoB. Therefore, the importance of mainstreaming the Rohingya refugee issue in Bangladesh should be discussed from a broader development context.

Case Studies

Photograph by Nazmus Saqib/IR/DU 2008

Case No: 01

Case Title: Dream
Name of the Refugee: Khodeja Begum
Status: Documented
Location: Nayapara Refugee Camp- 2
Age: 17
Project Student: Md. Atiqur Rahman
Institution: Department of IR, University of Dhaka

Innama Al a'malu binniyat.

[Results of all work depend on the niyat (wish)]
from Hadith, Bukhari Sharif.

It was raining for the last few days. The rain made the days icy and lifeless. But we were excited. The incident took place on the 16th. We were all prepared to start for Kutupalong and Nayapara after breakfast. All of us were abnormally excited because we were going to visit a population, about which we have only read and heard about a lot but never seen before. We all wondered what would they be like? How would they behave? Would they hijack our money, mobile or camera? Would we understand their language? In a word, there was excitement, uncertainty and fear in all of us.

In the microbus, everyone was planning what they would do or what case they would work with etc. I got the impression from everyone that they all wanted to take very complex and attractive subjects to work with.

But, from the very beginning I wanted to work with a very simple and humble character who could still dream.

Would I get anyone like that? I could not guess. But, that was my aim.

Just after entering the camp, I saw the others getting busy after having a talk with the CIC or Camp-In-charge. I thought, it was fruitless to just keep standing there. I started to walk around inside the camp with an umbrella. At that moment, a boy came towards me with a smiling face. He looked almost like me. Later, my Apu (elder sister) remarked that he was like my twin after seeing his photo.

His first question was, 'Do you study?' I said, `yes, I do. Do you live in this camp?' He said. 'Yes,' I asked. 'What do you do?' He answered proudly looking at me, 'I appeared for the S.S.C. exam this year.'

Without wasting another word, I held his hand and said, 'I will go to your house. Will you take me?'

He hesitated. I told, 'I have come to talk to someone who studies in the camp. Let's go to your house. I shall talk to you and your parents there.'

'But you cannot sit at our house.'

'Why?'

'The whole house is flooded in the rain.'

'Let's go. I will sit there.'

What could he do then! He started to walk along with me.

'Are your parents alive?'

'Yes, they are.'

'Are they in this country?'

'Yes.'

'Have you come here with your parents or were you born here?'

'I was not born here. I was born at Arakan's Yong Shong area. That area is called 'Boli Bazar' in Bangla. I was only two months old when we came to this country.'

'What year was it?'

'December of 1991.'

'Have you ever been to Burma later?'

'No.'

'Do you feel like going?'

'Yes, very much. Burma is my country. I will go. Obviously I will go.'

'Bravo!'

I silently uttered that, 'Innama Al-a: - malu binniyat' - I got my character!

On the way to his house the boy showed me the police and Ansar[1] camps, the UNICEF office, youth club, Refugee Primary Schools, soap industry, women's training centre, and many other things. I saw a neighbourhood near the Refugee Primary School—1, which looked deserted. Later I heard from him that all the houses of that neighbourhood would be built anew.

I was introduced to one of his friends at the Primary School. He also appeared for the S.S.C. examination this year. His name was Mustafa. He was at one of the schools that were directly under UNICEF before. But then this duty was executed by PHALS or Programme for Helpless and Lagged Society with financial assistance from UNICEF. Talking to some teachers, I understood that they were not pleased with the activities of PHALS.

When I first entered into the classroom, I saw that several male students were sitting at three pairs of tables on the left, and on the right some female students were curled up on the floor and writing 'Ka' 'Kha'. Discrimination, yes, it was clearly discrimination. I did not get any explanation about it from Mustafa.

Farther ahead from the school was the 293 no. house of G block. The house was almost like a bug's house- slightly above earth level with just a little open

---

1 Para military law enforcing agency.

space. I couldn't understand whether it was a door or a window. I entered there, almost crawling.

The room was damp, wet and dripping with water. I was in a Ruku[2] position because the room was not high enough for me to stand up. Some were peeping out from here and there. I had to bear with a stink while I sat on the mat given by UNHCR.

'What is your name?' I asked the boy for the second time.

'Mansurul Alam.'

'Father's name?'

'Mokbul Ahmed.'

'Mother's name?'

'Mahmuda Khatun.'

'Will you call your parents here for a while?'

'Yes. I will.' His sentences were in clear Bengali.

Mokbul Ahmed came. He was more than 50 years old. Mansur's mother Mahmuda Khatun also came along. She was approximately 40 years old. She said something while entering the room, but I could not understand her. It sounded like some complain. Later Mansur translated it. A movement took place at Kutupalong camp in September, 2008. The main issues of the movement were– (1) abolition of 'majhi' system; (2) form a camp committee with the consent of all and (3) stop forceful entrance. In this movement, three people died from police firing. The police tortured her at the time. The bones on her hand and leg broke because of that torture. She was in great pain - that was what she was trying to tell me. But I could not guess what she was thinking about me. It was more difficult for me to figure out whether I seemed sympathetic or ridiculous while listening to these personal woes of an unknown person. So, I glanced at her with a sympathetic look so that she could not understand my miserable state. It should be mentioned here that on the second week of January 2008, the 'Majhi system' was abolished. At present there is a camp committee of 18 members in this camp, 10 of whom are male and 8 are female.

I looked at Mokbul Ahmed, a gentleman with a beard. White beard, black and white hair. Red betel juice was rolling down from the sides of his mouth. His teeth were reddish. He was wearing a blue lungi and white Guernsey. For a long while, he was stroking his hair and beard with his fingers. A little girl gave him a white 'tupi'[3] while coming in. He looked at her with a face that was both smiling and dismal.

'How are you?' I asked him. I thought he understood me, but it was difficult for me to understand him. I asked him again. 'When did you come in this country?' 'In 1991.' Was that the first time you came or did you come before?' I looked at his son. The boy was very intelligent. He translated his response.

---

2 A position in Namaz...bending down and touching the earth with forehead.

3 Traditional hat for Muslim.

His father came to this country in 1975 at the age of 20 or 22. His father Nazir Ahmed, who was at that time 50 years old, was with him. The year before this, which was in 1974, the army of Burma forcefully took away Mokbul's mother to their camp. They begged the army earnestly and offered a good bribe. But all were in vain; after 9 days his mother's naked dead body was discovered in the jungle, a part of which was distorted by the attack of wild animals. Mokbul's elder brother Mostak Ahmed died cruelly while protesting against it. All other members of the family also fell under threat. So, it became essential for them to flee to this country.

Meanwhile, a boy brought some 'chanachur'[4] on a glass plate while I was listening to this. Mansur's mother told me something very affectionately. I understood she was showing hospitality. I smiled a bit.

Mansur's father was talking. I was looking at Mansur. The entire time that followed was like this. I looked at Mansur just when his parents' speech ended. He translated. I told Mansur's father, 'tell your story from 1975 to 1992.' He was talking and I was looking at Mansur.

After coming here in 1975, Mokbul and his father stayed at Saint Martin for a few days. Their earning was not great. Besides, they had 4.5 dun or about 50 acre fertile agricultural land in Yong Shong. They again returned to Arakan for the sake of that land. But the situation there was worse than before. The torture inflicted by the Moghs[5] had increased. So, they again came back to Bangladesh in 1978. In 1979, they returned to Burma for 16 months on the basis of mutual understanding between the two countries. But the situation in Burma had not changed. There was neither security, nor freedom there. Death and torture was a constant companion. They had to be prepared for death at any time. The marriage law was very strict. One had to pay high taxes for marriage. So, marriage almost stopped for the Rohingya Muslims. One could not use the word 'my' about any property. One had to report to the army or police about his paddy, his cow, his goat etc. One had to inform the police station if a new calf was born or any domestic animal died. In both cases, one had to give taxes. In one such situation, one day 55 year old Nazir Ahmed saw a cow grazing on his paddy field. He drove away the cow. But the cow belonged to the Moghs. According to them, it was a sin. The Moghs killed him on that land with the help of the police. This incident occurred in 1983.

On 10th September 1991, Mansurul Alam was born as the fourth child of Mokbul Ahmed. After about 2/3 months of his birth, they took shelter in Bangladesh as refugee with other Rohingyas. The boy did not know that he was born as a stateless child. The boy did not know that just after two months of his birth, he had to flee as a refugee to another country, leaving his own land.

---

[4] Kind of snacks.

[5] Rakhaine.

Mokbul Ahmed left. I was then talking to Mansurul Alam. I asked him, 'you have a card, so where is it?' He brought an old, torn book. The date of issue of the card was 4/4/1992. They are four brothers and three sisters. His youngest brother is Shafiqul Alam. He is 14 years old. He had great merit and will power, but because he was unable to continue studying after Primary School, he left the camp in 2007. He is still missing. The other younger brother and sister are studying in class 5 at Refugee Primary School—1.

Mansur completed his studies from Refugee Primary School—2. Here, at the camp there is no opportunity for study after primary education. But Mansur had dreams. He wanted to study more.

One day, Mansur visited the headmaster of Kutupalong high school, M.A. Mannan, who had left the camp. He was very kind. He got Mansur admitted at his school while hiding his identity. It was 2003.

Now it is 2008. Mansur has been studying overcoming great difficulty for the last few years. He had to sell his rations to continue his studies and his mother had to sell her gold chain, the last token of memory from her father-in-law's house. They had to sell the hatch's plastic they received from UNHCR. The members of the family had to starve. Yet, he did not stop. He appeared at the S.S.C exam this year. He hoped he would achieve an 'A' grade.

I asked him. 'What was your role in class?'

He replied, 'Three.'

'What will you do after S.S.C.?'

'I will study at the H.S.C level.'

'From where?'

'I do not know yet.'

'What will you do after H.S.C?'

'I will study Law.'

I was writing. I stopped writing and directly stared at his eyes. There was flair in those eyes. I asked, 'Why?' He replied, 'I want to set my nation free. I want to discover, due to what law and for what reason my nation has to suffer and die now. I want to know why we are stateless though all other nations on earth have their own states. We want citizenship, democracy in Burma. We want freedom of Aung Sun Syu Ki. We want our compensation.'

I asked. 'Will you be able to do these?'

He replied firmly, 'Obviously I will, if you help.'

I said, 'Do not wait for anyone's help. You proceed on your own way. Certainly you will be able to accomplish your dreams. *Innama-al-a: malu binniyat.*'

Case No: 02

Case Title: Shame
Name of the Refugee: Hasina Begum
Status: Documented
Location: Kutupalong
Age: 20
Project Student: Md. Atiqur Rahman
Institution: Department of IR, University of Dhaka

'I will not go anywhere leaving this country. I am one of the people of this country. This Bangladesh is my country. My husband, my son and me all of us are Bangladeshi. We would rather die in this country. We would rather starve here than go back to Burma.'

There was a heavy rainfall. With the help of an umbrella I was saved from rain, but in the cottage I could not save myself because it was almost broken. Raindrops were falling on my head from the broken thatched roof. There was no dry place to sit in. It was a tiny cottage; one side of it was blocked by firewood and stove. There were two pots for cooking-one is new and another is almost broken. Plate, glass or other things could not be sighted anywhere in the room. But two lungees[1] were hanged from the roof. In another side of the room Yeasmin, her one year old son and I were talking to each other. For getting close with them I sat on the wet floor. And then all of a sudden a mouse passed me through one side to another.

I was afraid. But nothing happened to be afraid of. Yeasmin was a very simple woman. So there was nothing to be afraid of. But she was colourless, hopeless and hapless. I could not find any similarity between her and me. *Innama Al a' malu binniyat* For this reason, I got startled, because she was speaking very fiercely, disavowing her past, culture as well as her motherland. What a shame that was! In fact, it was like disavowing one's entity.

'But you said you have come from Burma.'

'Yes.'

'So?'

'But that was ten or twelve years back.'

'You were born in Burma, weren't you?"

'Yes, at Monduk in Arakan.'

'You are a Rohingya then, aren't you?'

'Yes.'

---

[1] Traditional dress for the male in South Asia and South east Asia.

'But you are emphasising that you are a Bangladeshi.'

'Really I am a Bangladeshi.'

'But you are blowing hot and cold in the same breath. So far I know there is no tribe in Bangladesh named Rohingya.'

For a while, I forgot the advice of Professor Amena Mohsin[2] about the technique of collecting information. Being excited, I asked her a lot of questions directly. I was a new comer in this subject, so it was very normal to be excited. Yet she did not show her envious and furious mode fortunately. Only she looked at me with full of fear in her eyes. I could realise, one fact seized her—'Are they going to drive us away from this country?' So I tried to be easy.

'When did you come to this country?'

'Ten or twelve years ago. Probably a flood happened at that time in this country..'

I guessed she was mentioning 1998.

'Have you been staying since then?'

'Yes.'

How did you come to this country?'

'By a boat.'

'Why did you come?'

'We were oppressed by the Mogh[3].'

'Couldn't you file any case against them in police station?'

'There is no law to file any case against them.'

'Who came with you then?'

'My parents.'

'Where are they now?'

'They have died six years ago.'

'How?'

'They became old and it were natural deaths.'

'How old were you then?'

'May be fourteen. They died one year after my marriage.'

'How old are you now?'

'May be seventeen.'

Laughing I asked her, 'If you were fourteen six years ago, you should be twenty now.'

She was also smiling. I could realise she was very weak in arithmetic. There was also a fact which I realised; documented Rohingyas in the camp were very much smarter and more aware of their needs and interest compared to undocumented Rohingyas. Generally documented Rohingyas were also

---

2 Professor of Department of International Relations, University of Dhaka who took a class on the techniques of interviewing a refugee.

3 Rakhaine.

more expert in speaking Bengali and some also in English. Rohingyas in 'Taal' were very much hesitant in talking to strangers and also unconscious. Their dialect was also very hard to understand. To understand their dialect, I had to listen to their answer twice or thrice.

'Where is your husband?'

'He is in his work.'

'What is his name?'

'Younus.' At the time of answering she veiled herself. I observed a sublime affection in her.

'How old is he? What does he do?'

'He is thirty. He carries the goods in the harbour (may be in the port of Teknaf), goods that come from Burma. I also do the same job there.'

'How much do you earn per day?'

'In total, we get almost Tk.100.'

'Can you survive with this amount of money?'

'Yes.'

'What if your son gets ill?'

'There is a hospital. We can get free treatment there.'

I was very much surprised, a hospital in such a populous slum! Later I had visited that hospital. Besides, there was also a therapeutic feeding centre which works for nutrition, run by the 'MSF'- a non-government organisation. We got information that they were going to be shifted from this area to another place after the day I took the interview. They were going to be shifted to 'Ledaa'. 'MSF' will then hand them over to 'Islamic Relief,' which gets its funding from UK. But we have seen prescriptions in the hands of the people of 'Taal' attached with the logo of Islamic Relief. That means Islamic Relief has already started its mission.

The son of Yeasmin was very cute. He seems to be a very much affectionate son from a well off family. He was looking at me with a mysterious look. Putting my hand over his head I asked-

'What is his name?'

'Yeasir Arafat.'

I was surprised and astonished. This could well be a plot for cinema! His father named him Yeasir Arafat after the name of the famous leader of Palestine. His father wanteed his son also to fight for the freedom of his community when he would grow up.

'Who named him?

'His father.'

'Why?'

She was impressed by the question and answered,- ' Everybody needs a name.' She was also smiling.

'No, I like to know, why his father named him Yeasir Arafat?'

'It was his wish.'

'Does your husband know anything about his name?'

'Once two foreigners came here. One of them was named Yeasir Arafat. He liked the name very much.'

'Do you know that there is a famous leader with such a name?'

'What?'

'A team leader!'

She looked puzzled. I was bit disappointed. Although the charge of my camera's battery was weak, I restarted and clicked the face of Yeasir Arafat.

'Do you like this country?'

'Yes, very much.'

'The people of this country?'

'They are very good and I like them.'

'Do you like to stay in this country forever?'

'Yes, we will live in this country. This is our country.'

'Don't you like to go back to Burma?'

'No.'

'Why?'

'They are very bad and oppressed us very much.'

'If Burma fights against Bangladesh, whom will you support?'

'Of course Bangladesh.' She answered.

'Will you fight against your country Burma?'

'Yes.'

'If Bangladesh government try to drive away all of you from here?'

'We will not leave this country. We will stay here. They can hurt us, kill us but we are prepared to die here, but we won't leave this country.

Suddenly Yeasir Arafat started crying very loudly extending two hands in the air. What was he crying about? Death or freedom?

Case No: 03

Case Title: Void on a Merciless World
Name of the Refugee: Khaleda Begum
Status: Documented
Location: Nayapara Refugee Camp
Age: 15
Project Student: Shagufta Mahjabin
Institution: Department of IR, University of Dhaka

Around the huts there is an outlandish void. Not a single empty space left but still it seems like an inert emptiness is swallowing the place. A number of small houses with thick mud walls—covered by thin plastic blue sheets can be seen as one passes by. In a corner, a few children are reciting Arabic continuously. Some raise their eyes in astonishment and again concentrate on the recitation. The *Moulavi* wearing a faded white *tupi*[1] tries to control his class in husky voice.

This place is slightly higher than the rest. While walking on the winding road, I finally found the H block and the shed that I was looking for. Men, women and children of various ages gathered around me and started talking in a language unknown to me. I tried to calm them down and some one approached and asked them to move aside. The curious people stepped aside in disappointment.

I poked my head through the door. An invitation inside took me in. The dwellers inside were busy in finding me a suitable seat. I smiled and sat on the mat placed on the floor. From guest, I turned into a host and offered them a seat beside me. An old man sat in front of me. I was never good at guessing ages, but it seemed to me that he had walked a long way and reached the final stage of his life. He kept staring at me.

I said, "I have come to hear from you, will you talk to me?" The man kept staring at my probing face. I glanced at the other members in the room. A woman amongst them said, "Father cannot talk." I was shocked. The old man's wife sat next to him and asked me hoarsely, "What do you want to know?" A bit demoralised I said, "I want to know how you ended up here, and since when are you living here." After a pause I said, "I have heard about your daughter and I have come to meet her." She understood and took a long breath. After a while the woman started her story...

This family used to live in Burma about 17 years back in a small village in Arakan. Ali Akbar, the old man who was unable to speak, was the head of the

[1] Traditional hat for Muslim.

family. They had their abode, farm, land and everything there. They inherited a fruit orchard as well. They used to produce various fruits and crops and sell them in the market. Ali Akbar had a shop there too. Evidently they were well off. They had five children, all of whom studied in *moktob*[2] apart from the youngest. There is a saying that good times never last for long. Like other villages of Arakan, NASAKA battalion invaded their village too. They seized and captured everyone.

The soldiers burned down the village market and Akbar's little shop was burned to ashes. Because he was better off, he became one of the capsized and was taken to camp where they tortured him and demanded money. They captured Akbar's wife and raped her in the camp. It went on like this for 15 days and then the camp was shifted to another village. Before leaving, they burned the village down including his house. Their kids hid in the forests. After the soldiers had left, the villagers rescued unconscious Akbar and his tormented wife. He would not had survived...only he had to live. He lost his speech and his hands were paralysed. Maybe Almighty kept him alive to see even worse days. The family was ruined and desperate. Handicapped Ali Akbar lost his earning. The children were too young to earn. They stood in the line with those who had decided to move to Bangladesh so that they can survive.

Sneaking past the eyes of the military, they walked for miles, sometimes using boats to cross waterways and finally reaching the Bangladesh territory. They took shelter in a forest on the border, living in tents with some families there. They hid for days in jungles in dread of being captured by the BDR.[3] The BDR finally captured them. They did not send them back to Burma but brought them to a refugee camp in Damdamia. After few years they were shifted to Nayapara Refugee shelter.

I looked at old Ali Akbar. His hands were shaking. The eyes were still. I took a pause and asked, "Where are your children?" The wife replied that they were living with them now—three sons and three daughters. After coming to Bangladesh she had given birth to another daughter. The eldest son's family lives in the shed beside them, and the two youngest children are not married yet. The second son Nasir asks me "Apa would you like to talk to Khaleda?" I nodded. Nasir asked Khaleda to come in. Khaleda is the youngest who was born here in Bangladesh.

A little girl with a covered head entered. Watching the 13 or 14 year old girl standing in front of me was like receiving a blow—a small face with large innocent eyes. In November 2007 she was raped by Bengali inhabitants. I took her hand and asked her to sit. Her eyes were still lowered to the ground.

2 A kind of school where Muslims get religious education.

3 Border security force of Bangladesh.

Sitting next to me she raised her eyes, swarming with countless questions. Khaleda's brother left the room with others.

The conversation started. I asked, "Have you recognised them?" After a pause she replied, "Yes, I knew them before, they live beside the camp." It was an outcome of a dispute with the husband of Khaleda's eldest sister Kashim. That evening they forcibly grabbed her from the shed. Hearing her scream, Rozina, who lives next-door, as well as others came out. There was a fight; her brother still had the mark of a cut on his head. They filed a case against the four perpetrators at the camp police station. They were arrested, but were bailed out in a few days. As a result they started to threaten Khaleda's family. They had bribed the police with 30 thousand taka, and were free to do anything they wish. "I am always afraid; I can not go out of the shed. I always stay around my sisters," said Khaleda with fear in her eyes.

I was speechless; I did not know what to say. I held her hands and said, "Do not be afraid". She continued, "These men are now all free of charge and loiter around the camp. It scares me even inside the camp. Now I am a bad girl in every one's eyes... No body looks at me, even no one likes me like before." Her eyes were brimming with tears. But she quickly controlled herself. Looking at me she smiled and said, "Have you come to see me for this?" I answered after a short silence; "I came here to be with you for a while." She sat beside me holding my hands and smiled with strength. Suddenly I felt that the girl had a strong will to survive and live. She told quietly, "I want justice *Apa*[4]. I want those four perpetrators to be punished for what they have done." Few moments passed and all other members of her family entered. Her brother told instantly, "*Apa*[5] we were much better off in Burma. We studied, had good clothing and had no shortage. Here we are in great despair. We live by days. Living is hard and managing food is tougher. On top of that there are troublesome people. We filed a case against them, and now they are threatening us. They paid 30 thousand *taka*[6] at the police station and now want us to repay them!"

"How will I marry off my daughter? She is spoiled in everyone's eyes. She was not to be blamed for anything, I am a mother but I could not save my child from those evil eyes." The mother started crying. There was no enclosure around there, no wall. Anyone could enter. Last month one of her brother's sheds was set on fire, with all the dwellers sleeping inside. All of them could have been burnt alive. The Bengalis set the fire to take revenge for the case they have instigated.

I asked if the police have helped them or not. "People from UNCHR came, wanted to know what had happened, and then nothing happened. Can people

---

4 Sister in Bengali.

5 Ibid.

6 Bangladeshi Currency.

live like this in constant fear?" Nasir replied. He asked me again, "*Apa,* can you not help us in any way?" I was stunned by this question. What will I answer? Who was guilty for the injustice? I looked at Khaleda's innocent face. How old was she? She had already seen the harshest sides of life. Would she ever be able to forget this? Would it not haunt her year after year? The look in people's eyes and the panic of the terrorised family are already casting dark shadows on her. One could tell this by her pale, helpless face.

These people went through such cruelty only because they were refugees. They have become worthless to the world only because they were uprooted. It seems that the world has denied them and refused then a happy life. My cell phone brought me back to my world, and I stood up. Holding her hands I told, "Do not be afraid, Khaleda, it will be all right soon. You will not have to be afraid." I could not assure her any more than that. What more could I say? I stepped out into the lifeless sun. The void seems even larger now. Has Almighty tied up their lives in a whirling cycle? The horrifying memories of the mother seems to have caught the daughter after 17 years. Has anything changed after 17 years except the faces? Will she ever get justice? The culprits have only changed faces and names. But the fear in their lives is the same. Even crossing the border does not save human lives.

Case No: 04

Case Title: A moment of silence
Name of the Refugee: Hasina Begum
Status: Documented
Location: Kutupalong Refugee Camp
Age: 17
Project Student: Jolly Nur Haque
Institution: Department of IR, University of Dhaka

"Oh God, I must find a good interpreter today, cannot take any more chances", these were the first words that came into my mind this morning. Last day the trip to Nayapara camp was an interesting one but it was not very helpful for my case study! I totally missed so many interesting points just because I did not have a good interpreter with me! How could I be so foolish? Well, today I really got to the point. This project is so important to me not only because of the tours, travels and fun but also because for the first time in my life I got the chance to face those fears, those moments, those memories which I could never even think of. This experience has taught me many things. Any way, why am I writing all these stuff, I am supposed to write "her" story, the 17 year girl who was gang raped when she was only 15. Was that shocking for me? No, I do not think so. Because I have read so many cases with so many stories, so what was the difference? Yes, it was different. Reading something and knowing every detail from the victim, her memories, her feelings, her silence; everything was completely different. Her words made me realise, what pain is all about. I felt like I was there and I could do nothing. This was the only story which healed me. And I felt that I should write about it, may be I cannot express those feelings through my writing but yet I want to try, at least I want to let others know her story. Yes, may be it is not an extraordinary story, but it is a story of a Rohingya girl who taught me how to be strong.

Her name is Hasina Begum. When I got there, I was very confused. At first I did not know where to start from. There were so many houses and so many Rohingyas wanted to talk to me. But I was in search of something different and most of all I was in search of a good interpreter. When I was just walking around and thinking of what to do, I suddenly heard a boy of age about 17/18 passing by me and singing a Hindi movie song. I turned around and felt very amazed that even in refugee camps they listen to movie songs! I called him and asked him whether he is a Rohingya or not. At first he got suspicious. What would I ask, he started to inquire. Who was I, where did I come from, why was I here etc. I replied to all his questions. I soon convinced him to help me. When I talked to him I came to know that he is quite good at speaking my language and also that of the Rohingya because he had finished 8th grade of schooling. I felt relieved that I got my interpreter (by the way, his name was Jubayer). I asked him to take me to a house where I can find someone with an exceptional experience. Jubayer was confused but then I made myself clear; I wanted someone who could give me a story that was not only about what he/she wanted. I wanted a life story. He thought for a moment and said that he knew a girl, she was gang raped and she fought for justice. I got interested and insisted him to take me there. He agreed.

Jubayer took me to Hasina's house. Well, I must say it was quite a big house compared to the others I saw at Nayapara camp. Jubayer knocked the door and after few minutes a skinny girl opened it. She looked disturbed yet curious about my presence. But this experience was a little different for me because ever since I visited Nayapara camp, yesterday and today, I found that most of the Rohingyas were very much interested to talk to us. This was the first time I got someone who was disturbed and did not want to cooperate that much. At first I couldn't understand that she was feeling uneasy with me. Then by looking at her I realised that for some reason she was angry at me. She was standing by the door as if she wanted me to get out of her house. But I was desperate! So I requested her to talk to me and to share her story with me. She said straightly that she did not want to talk to me about that incident. I got confused and stood there like a fool. Then after a few minutes she asked me to come into her house and gave me a wooden seat. But I sat on the floor with her and I said nothing. She was staring at me for some time and then she asked that why I need to hear her story. I replied that I want to know, how she managed to get out of the trauma she faced and how she fought for justice. I added that if she did not want me to publicise her story then I won't. She thought for some time and then agreed to share her story with me. By the time we were talking, 2/3 boys came and stood by her door. Hasina and I both were very disturbed by them and she asked me to tell them to leave otherwise she won't talk to me. I had to be harsh and asked them to leave. They left. And I felt how humiliating Hasina's life was! Human beings, no matter whether they are Bangladeshis or Rohingyas, all take advantage of others and make fun of other's lives.

Hasina came to Bangladesh with her mother and sister when she was very young. Her age was about 3 or 4 years then. So her life started here in this camp. At first they stayed at Duapalong camp and then they were transferred to Kutupalong camp under the supervision of UNHCR and they got registered then. When she came to Kutupalong camp she was 7 years old. Her father came to Bangladesh long before they arrived. But he was forcefully repatriated to Myanmar. Hasina had a good life with her mother (Johora) and elder sister (Tasmina) in the camp till the incident happened to her.

Hasina was raped in 2006 when she was only 15. A woman named Anu who married a local man called her and convinced her to go to a marriage ceremony in a nearby village of the camp with her. Hasina knew Anu from the past. And as life is very restricted in the camp, when she heard about a marriage ceremony she got excited and agreed to go with Anu. They went out from the camp in the morning and after some time Hasina realised that they were not going to the place they were supposed to go. She asked Anu where they were going but she did not reply. When it was almost noon Hasina saw that Anu was talking to three boys and she took 10 taka from each of the boys and left Hasina alone with them. Hasina was extremely confused about what was happening. Then suddenly those boys put a jute bag on her head and forcefully took her to a jungle. There they brutally raped her and they even tortured her so much that she lost two teeth. When she regained consciousness it was already 8 o' clock at night. Those boys (Jan-e-alam, Shahid and Mojammel) gave her 120 taka and sent her to the camp by a rickshaw. When she got back to the camp she was terribly sick and so weak that she could not walk. People helped her to get back to her room and she fell unconscious when she saw her mother.

I asked her, how you feel when you remember those moments. She laughed and replied, "I have nothing to say. I was only 15 and I did not know what relation a girl and a boy could have. They treated me as if I was not a human being. Actually I do not know how I should answer." I felt ashamed and I realised my mistake. I asked her about her experience during the trial at the court. She said she had to live in prison for 15 days because at first police and others thought that she was lying. The doctor who examined her gave a false report about her condition and he said that she was not raped at all. Then it was discovered that Anu's husband bribed the doctor to prove that his wife is innocent. When Hasina told me that she had to live in prison she had tears in her eyes and said that "Your (Bangladeshi) police did not believe me because I am a Rohingya, could they disbelieve me if I was a Bengali?" How could I make her believe that Bengali girls are as helpless as Rohingya girls, may be they are more helpless than her because many of the raped girls could never even file a case against the criminals. Anyway, after a long conversation I asked her whether she wanted to leave this country or not. Or was she interested to go back to Myanmar? When I asked her these questions she became furious. She stood up angrily and asked me, "Why? Why should I go back to Myanmar? They tortured my father so we came here. Now you people tortured me so you want me to go back? Why should I go back? Yes, I was not born in this country but I have known that this place to be my home. I will never go back to Myanmar." I asked her whether she wanted to go to a developed country. She smiled and said if you send me with my mother and if you can give me peace then I will move to anywhere in this world. For the record I should also mention that Hasina got justice from the court and those three boys are still in prison. Anu was also sent to prison for 7 months but she was bailed by Hasina because Anu has three children and Hasina did not want those children to suffer for their mother's faults.

Case No: 05

Case Title: I wish to die on my motherland
Name of the Refugee: Nabinshona
Status: Documented
Location: Kutupalong Refugee Camp
Age: 45
Project Student: Shagufta Mahjabin
Institution: Department of IR, University of Dhaka

"I cannot remember my childhood very much. I can only recall the excitement of Eid. My father used to go on visits with all of his sons and daughters. Only twice a year on both the Eids we had this occasion." Nabinshona took a break, after saying this. More or less 45 years of age, dark black skin with bright gleaming eyes.

"Many Buddhist families lived all around our village. We had a great relation at first. They did not have conflict with us that much. Buddhist and Muslim, we lived in our own ways. But things started to change slowly. The Buddhist did not directly afflict the Muslim families, but there was a fear lurking in the atmosphere. Like the dynamite was ready, waiting for the slightest touch of fire."

"We grew up in that fearful environment. We were three sisters and a brother. When we reached the suitable age, our parents arranged for our marriages. Though our native village was at Mangdaw, my father married us off in Rathidang in a Muslim family. My husband was a fisherman living in a village named Dhunchi. We were living happily and I was the mother of five kids."

"We could not live there any longer and had to leave before my sixth child was born. All of a sudden the NASAKA troops attacked our village. They burnt down our house and took me, my husband and my mother-in-law, who was living with us, to a camp. They compelled my husband to work and immensely tortured my mother-in-law and me. I was five month's pregnant at that time, I did not expect such brutality. The unborn child inside of me was still alive. The NASAKA then let us go on condition that we had to leave the village. We had no alternative but to flee."

"Mother-in-law advised us to escape to Bangladesh, as many of us were doing so. Everyone thought it was a Muslim nation; maybe they would give us shelter. So we came here with my own parents and my brother and sisters. But we lost my younger sister during the journey. I do not know where she is now—alive or dead. Whenever someone comes from Burma, I ask about her, but still no sign of her. I have not seen her for 17 years. When we first came to this land we were in a refugee camp at Balukhali. There were hundreds of refugees like us there. After living there for two years, the people from the UNHCR took us to Goondoong camp. Couple of months later, Bangladeshi Government was eager to send us back to Burma, but they could not. Then we were transferred to another camp at Moshengdi where we lived for a month. Again we were about to be sent back to Burma but people from the UNCHR protested, we were saved once more. From there, we finally moved here at Kutupalang camp."

"I am living here for quite a long time. I have brought up my children here and married off my daughters. I have sent all of my kids to the camp school. My eldest son is now the teacher in the school of the camp. I have always regretted not having a chance to study in Burma. I have always wanted my kids to be educated and learned person. My husband works here inside the camp; he makes stoves and earns about Taka 700 every month. I am a member of the Mosque Committee here. There are consulates here for the arguments and wrangles inside the camp. Clashes are usual, when so many people are living together. Along with others I solve and reconcile the conflicts among the camp dwellers. Today I went with an application to the CIC office. My house is too small to live. I requested for a larger house. There is no room in the house but there is a partition inside. It does not work. My daughter and son-in-law live with me. We do not have any privacy. So I need a large house immediately."

"Once we had a terrible time here because of the oppressive Majhis. They tortured us, but now things are much better. The Majhi system has been abolished for about two years. After coming here I was locked up twice, once in 1997 and then in 2003 for the second time. I am not a criminal—I just sold my ration at an outside market. What else I could do? I do not feel guilty at all. Look at me, I do not want to wear these torn clothes, we get clothes two times in a year from the camp office, but that does not fulfill the demand. You need money even to buy clothes. And you need money for everything. I seriously needed the money and I managed it by selling my ration. They put me in jail just for that, though I was out within three months both times. I can still get sent behind bars at any time again. I am always living in fear. I was lucky enough to be out so soon. Some are rotting there since 1997. Who knows when they will be out?"

"Bangladeshis here point us out as Rohingyas. I do not want to be known as a Rohingya. I was born in Burma; I grew up in Burma's sun, air and water. The tyrannical Government made me and my family to move here. But is the government here in Bangladesh less suppressive on us? They try to push us back again and again. Returning to Burma means confirmed suicide. The NASAKA will kill us even before we enter. They have imprisoned Suchi as well. We will return only after Suchi is freed, and Burma will have its good days back again. I often become nostalgic. The soil of Burma is really productive. It produces crops all the year round. The field here grows a single crop but it's not like that in Burma; it harvests gold there. The clear water of the rivers has shining sands beneath. Burma is beautiful. I know I will not have the chance to live their still I long to go back there. The situation there is still unchanged. Even now people with families are coming here only to save their lives."

"There are families here in Kutupalang who have fled from Burma just a few days back. They live on the ridges of the hills at the outskirt of the camp. They are living here in worse situations. They are the poorest of the poor. They make houses with bamboos and 12 to 15 people, sometimes even more than that, live together in such a small house— these bamboo houses blow away in every storm or the Bengalis here crush them in the darkness of nights. At sunrise we see piles of wood where the house stood last night. This happens often. They are undocumented and live in continuous fear. If the camp officers catch them they will drive them away for certain. The newcomers are really helpless. They have no ration and it's hard to manage a work. They beg and seek food inside the camp—they live in real misery. Among them the girls are the most vulnerable. Bengalis irritate them, tease them and sometimes their behaviour is even worse. Sometimes these Bengalis come here in groups and destroy whatever they see in their way. They tease them to return to Burma, but do they know what the situation in Burma is? Do they know how it feels to live in fear? I wish they could understand."

"These undocumented newcomers have the most recent news of Burma. A few days back Habiba Khatun came here. The NASAKA army blindfolded her husband and two of her sons and killed them. They have snatched her daughter and taken her to the camp. She is still trying to contact her daughter. Habiba only cries. But crying does not help. She will at least survive here. So many people like her are coming. Many of them are the relatives of the documented refugees living inside the camp. Almorejaan came here about three or four months back. She has her relatives living here as documented refugees. So she started to live with them. There are so many people like her. You know when I meet these people who came a few days ago from Burma, I become nostalgic and remember the days of Burma. How we used to live there, what the present situation is, Burma's soil, the beauty of Burma all attracts me like a home calling me from far behind."

"We have to suffer in Burma only because we are Muslims. Who can be happy leaving their own land? No one. Your own land is half of your faith. And they did not let us live there. The government here tries to thrust us back every now and then. It's a strange situation. I do not know where I will be living in future but I do not want to live here. I want to live on my native soil.

I want to live where I was born. If I can die in peace there, I won't regret a thing. Today everybody in the camp knows me, respects me, still I do not want to live here. The pain I had here makes me wish for death. Looking at the faces of my children I breathe, and cherish a dream to return to my country some day. Who does not want their own land, farm, and house? Even if I cannot get those things back, I want to have my last resting place there, I want to return to my loving Burma."

Case No: 06

Case Title: Irony of fate
Name of the Refugee: Khairul Amin
Status: Undocumented
Location: Kutupalong Refugee Camp
Age: 32
Project Student: Meherunnessa
Institution: Department of IR, University of Dhaka

> "I am a doctor. The residents of this camp come to me to get medical assistance. I provide them medical assistance for a small amount of money. We are closely linked to each other. We do not quarrel with one another. I am so happy to be here. I am sure that I am in a much better position than my family members and my relatives are, in Burma. I do not have any complaint against the Bangladesh government; I just want to express some of my desires and want to go back to my own country; because a life of a refugee is not a life of a human being."
>
> *Khairul*
> *(An undocumented Rohingya refugee living inside the Kutupalong Camp).*

His name is Khairul. He has his wife Zamila, a son and a daughter in his family. They are four in number. His children are not adults. They are minor. The son is three years old and the daughter is less than one year old. They live in the western side of the Kutupalong Camp. That is a very beautiful area, beautiful in the sense that it is full of natural beauty, since it is a hilly area. They live just under the hill. This type of area looks very beautiful to people who live in the town. But the people who live in hilly areas understands how such living could be painful as well.

Khairul is an unregistered Rohingya refugee in Bangladesh. He came from Raimongkhali, Burma in 1991. When I asked him why he came here, he answered they were not happy in Burma. They were been tortured their, physically and mentally. When he came here, he was a school going boy. At that time, the younger generation in Burma was tortured more than the other age group. The police arrested the younger Muslims without any reasons and put them in jail, making them victims of false cases. The only reason was that they were Rohingyas, they were Muslims. The Burmese government never accepted them as citizens. To get relief from the oppressive government, people like Khairul came to Bangladesh. They crossed the border and came here and since then took the identity of a refugee.

Khairul was not an unregistered refugee before, like he is now. He took the unregistered refugee identity since 1996. Before 1996, he was a documented refugee in Bangladesh. When he came here, he did not have his family with him. All the members of his family; his parents and brothers and sisters are still in Burma. He took shelter in the Musoni Camp when he came here in 1992. That camp was situated in Noyapara, Ukhiya. At that time, as he was a registered refugee, he got assistance from the camp. But now as he is an unregistered refugee, the camp is not bound to give him assistance though he lives inside the Kutupalong camp. So he and his family do not have the right to claim assistance from the camp authority. They can only get assistance if the camp authority wants to give otherwise he has nothing.

Khairul explained how he became an unregistered refugee. The service of the camp (Musoni, Noyapara) was not good. Moreover, the Bangladesh government did not include them in the voter list that time (1996). So he fled from the camp and started to live outside the camp. At that time he used to live on the alluvial land situated on the western side of the Chittagong Airport. He started to seek job for his livelihood. He used to work in different shops at different times. In 2004, he got married with Zamila Bibi. She was also an unregistered refugee. Both of them lived on that alluvial land. They had passed their lives in that area till January, 2006. In 2007, they came to Kutupalong Camp and started to live as unregistered refugees. After coming here he left his fish business. Then he took training from "Human Resource Development Training Organisation; L.M.A.F". This training was on providing medical assistance. He introduced himself as a doctor. Now he practices his profession on the refugees inside the camp. As medical assistance provided by the UNHCR is not enough for the camp, people living around him often come to him and take assistance for a small amount of payment. I was amazed to hear this and got interested to know his educational background. Then he explained to me that he was a class eight student when he came here. After coming here he took primary education again. So it was quite easy for him to take training from the L.M.A.F. He could not complete the course because of lack of financial support. It was a 6 months course but he completed only 4 months. He had to pay 1000 taka only to complete the 4 months of his training. He was not able to tell me about the whole system of his training. He only said that he took training and now he is a doctor.

The condition of the cottage where Khairul and his family live is not so good and the location is totally unfavourable, especially in the rainy season. The cottage was made of soil. So in the rainy season they suffer more. In fact, one cannot imagine how much they suffer in the time of natural disasters. But in spite of these problems they try to keep their cottage neat and clean. When

I was talking to him he wore a t-shirt. His wife and his children were well dressed up too and they were also looking good. His wife did not talk to me. She felt shy. She just looked at me and listened to whatever I said.

Though Khairul had no complaint against the government of Bangladesh and the international community like the UNHCR, he did have some issues to raise. He said that they cannot eat properly, they cannot move freely, they cannot entertain themselves, they cannot enjoy their life, and the biggest problem for them is that they have no permanent job. They are just living a life, going with the motion, nothing more than that. He wanted a solution, though he knew that the solution would not come easily. He expressed that since they were undocumented refugees they did not have the chance to resettle themselves in another country. As a whole he expressed that the life of an undocumented refugee can be considered as a life in hell. When I asked him whether he wants to go back to his country he answered: "If the Myanmar government accepts their demands then he would go back to their own country; they must be accepted as citizens of Myanmar; democracy must be established in Myanmar; basic rights must be fulfilled; false cases against innocent people must be withdrawn; they must not be harassed for practicing Islam". He promised that if the government fulfills these demands then they will go back to their country.

Case No: 7

Case Title: Denial from denied
Name of the Refugee: Kashem
Status: Undocumented
Location: Taal
Age: 45
Project Student: A.S.M. Tarek Hassan Semul
Institution: Department of IR, University of Dhaka

> But are we not all refugees from something?....I was learning that human history is always a story of someone's diaspora: a struggle between those who repel, expel or curtail—possess, divide and rule—and those who keep the flame alive from night to night, mouth to mouth, enlarging the world with each flick of a tongue.
>
> *Romesh Gunesekera*[1]

Her name was Khadiza, age would be around mid-thirties. I requested her to take me to her home so that we can speak freely. The camp was just beside the slope of the highway in the bank of Naaf. Due to heavy rainfall the whole camp, which is no different from the slum of Dhaka, was muddy. Houses were made of bamboo, with plastic sheets as roofs; so small that I was wondering how so many people can live there. Smoke was emanating from the stoves. Curious faces were peeking out of the houses. When we reached Khadiza's house, I told myself, "not again" as I had to crawl with my six feet body through a two and half feet door. When I started talking to Khadiza, I discovered my limitation with the Chittagonian dialect. I couldn't understand what she was telling me, although she seemed to understand me pretty well. Lots of other people were trying to enter Khadiza's house and one of them was Mohammad Kashem. Khadiza seemed to be alright with Kashem getting in while she disallowed the others. Out of nowhere I discovered that Kashem was helping me out with the language problem as it turned out that he spoke fluent Bengali. Most interestingly he was trying to use English and speak Bengali in quite a good accent. It was not one or two English words that he was trying to put in, rather he was using grammatically correct English sentences during the conversation which made me far more curious to know him. Kashem did not have any difference in his appearance than any other ordinary Rohingya Muslim guy, but there was something in his personality which attracted me. He was wearing a white full sleeve shirt and a lungi, his face was

1 Romesh Gunesekera, *Reef* (London:Granta,1978) p.174.

covered with a beard. He was lean and small in stature with bright eyes which showed his intelligence. Kashem told me that he was 45 years old and came to Bangladesh in 2002. Before he came here with his wife and daughter, he was a teacher of a non-formal educational school run by WFP (World Food Program) in his village, Ulapi in Akyab in Myanmar. He passed high school from a non-government school in Myanmar and could not continue his studies, as studying for the Rohingyas is not easy in Myanmar due to government restrictions. Kashem told me, "Government of Myanmar hates us and always tries to ignite conflicts between the Rakhine[2] and the Rohingyas and we are always discriminated. They always hated educated Rohingyas, as they can educate others and organise movement against their discrimination, so they hated me."

In December 1999, a strike was called by the Rakhines against the poverty and discrimination the Rohingya people were facing from the Government of Myanmar. Kasem told me that this kind of strike is nothing new in Myanmar and he was accused by the government of provoking the strike. The Government wanted to nail him down and filed a false case of corruption against him. The Government also brought another charge for not taking permission from the government before his marriage, as it is a compulsory for the Rohingyas to seek permission before getting married. On these two charges he was sent to the prison. When Kashem was telling me about his experience in the prison, it reminded me of some of the stories of torture by the Pakistani occupational forces on the innocent Bengalis during the liberation war of Bangladesh in 1971:

> "In the prison they wanted to make me suffer so much that I would testify against myself and they can put me on trial. They tied my hands and legs with tree logs, and then they hammered a nail through my arm into the log. When I cried out in pain they poured hot water in my nose and mouth so that I cannot shout. Sometimes they just used to kick my chest with their boots."

Tortured Kashem accepted all the charges against him, he thought this would give him a respite, but in return his nails were torn apart from his fingers. With severe physical injuries he was left behind outside his home. He still wonders why they left him alive. In this condition he knew that his family might be the next target of the government and with such severe injuries he cannot go to the hospital because he might get arrested again. After some local treatment and several days later he and his wife decided to escape to Bangladesh. Kashem left his loved home, his land, property, his students and school, everything he had in his whole life to save the lives of his beloved

---

[2] The Arakan State of Myanmar, bordering Bangladesh, is mostly inhabited by two ethnic communities - the Rakhine Buddhist and the Rohingya Muslims. The Rakhine Buddhists are close to the Burmese in religion and language. The Rohingya Muslims are ethnically and religiously related to the people from the region of Chittagong in south-eastern Bangladesh.

daughter and wife. One night, three of them started their journey to the unknown. With injuries that had not healed yet, Kashem, his wife and daughter walked twelve hours non-stop to a nearby town. After reaching the city in the morning, they had to hide in the woods till dusk. At dusk he met a man in the city who helped them cross a road to get to the mountain. After three hours of walking in the mountain Kashem reached the shore and took a boat to cross the river Naaf. That boat was full of other refugees who were also escaping like them from their own country. In that whole journey Kashem could not provide any food to his family. After reaching Bangladesh he felt relieved as he no longer had to worry about his wife's and daughter's safety and at the same time felt bad about his parents and relatives he left behind. At first he did not live at Taal, he went to Teknaf, there he pulled a rickshaw and worked as a day labour to run his family. After three years of living in Teknaf he came to Taal. When I asked Kashem what he does now for a living he told me that he teaches Rohingya children. His answer surprised me. In the living condition of Taal it is unimaginable that Rohingya refugees are trying to get their children educated in whatever form it may be. Their survival is almost a surprise, because they do not get adequate help from the government of Bangladesh or the UNHCR what so ever. Only some NGOs are trying to provide some assistance in the health sector. These refugees are just surviving, and despite all these uncertainties with their future and their miserable present, they refuse to give up. This fact was an eye opener for me as it revealed the other part of human nature and the relentless endeavour to get rid off this despondent condition, which really excels in worse conditions. Kashem told me that he now has 12 to 15 students; he goes to his students' homes to teach them. He earns 200 hundred taka per month but that is nothing to run his family. The people of the Taal respect him and they try to help him in whatever way they can. When I tried to find out the reason behind this help I found another wonderful example of human spirit and its triumph. Kashem told me that he along with another educated Rohingya young man, whom he referred to as his "partner", started an informal school for the kids in 2008 and they got massive response from the parents as they had one hundred and eighty students in their school. When Kashem was telling me the story, he told me that they also maintained a register book to put up the name of their students and they used to take a daily roll call. Unfortunately after two months of running the school they had to shut it down. As they started the school in an abandoned house of another Rohingya female who left for Cox's Bazar; she came back and complained to the majhi[3] and claimed her place back, so they had to give back the place. Thus the school has stopped, but Kashem did not. He continued to give his teachings to the new generation of Rohingyas. He

3 A leader among the Rohingya refugees who used to co-operate with the government and UNHCR. After many controversies and complain majhi system no longer exist in Kutupalong and Nayapara refugee camps.

believes that education is the key for the freedom of his people. He was telling me that if he can provide education to the Rohingya children then they would know their rights and only then they can fight for it. He also believes that if the government changes in Myanmar; if their great leader Aung Sun Syu Ki can free herself then peace will return to his country. He dreams one day he will return to his country and will go fishing in his dearest river Kaladan which he misses most after his mother. He does not know where his mother and father are. He does not know if they are dead or alive, he can only feel that they are waiting for him to return somewhere over the river Naaf.

When I was leaving Kashem was telling me that he has been waiting to be shifted to the newly built camp at Leda and now for him the most important thing is to get registered as a refugee with the UNHCR and Bangladesh Government. He was also telling me about another dream: if he could get help from a NGO to build a school then with his "partner" he would again start the school. At twilight I left Kashem and his dreams behind, but what I took from him is the refusal to give up.

Case No: 8

Case Title: We pass our days crying
Name of the Refugee: Rashid
Location: Kutupalong
Age: 43
Project Student: Shaon Shyla
Institution: Department of IR, University of Dhaka

"What comes to our mind when we think about a home, 'our sweet home,' definitely not that of a house which consists of 3`/2` door without windows? The house that I live in is almost like that. I remember the house where I was born which only brought grievances. Now I am in a place that is a long lane that has no turning. Now I fear that I shall die here. I often wonder how I am living here. It grieves me to know that there is no hope for democracy in my country. I do not want to understand democracy which is all about hope. A rose by any other name would smell as sweet. I want to know how far it is from today. Can you guess what I want? It is nothing but peace. The reason why I want it is crystal clear. The time of its arrival cannot be guessed. The military regime in Myanmar seems to be going on for eternity. Before I die, I intend to go to my country. Can a man live when his soul is dead?"

These words are not mine, but of a 43 year old Rashid, an inhabitant of the village named Mujai at Rashidong Thana in Akyab in Myanmar. Rashid is now living in Kutapalong refugee camp.

"I was born in an independent country. I used to dream to do something for the country. Suddenly my dreams shattered when Buddhist Rakhaines became reckless. It is a matter of no importance to them that this is our forefathers' land. In my own country there is no place for me. Nobody can avoid an inevitable event. That's why today I am here but I am not vindictive. I want only peace. There was peace and perfect amity in my country but now there is communal violence and social anarchy. The military regime has taken the whole country to the brink of devastation and has turned the land into a bloodbath. Now in Myanmar the voice of peace and communal harmony is a far cry."

Rashid fled from Myanmar along with his four family members in 1992. At that time he was prevented by the BDR in the border area but later he made his way through by giving bribe. Their life was in a state of insecurity because of the Moghs. He told me, "We were all under threat".

Back home he was a fisherman and used to catch fish in the *Ondying River*. Even now he becomes nostalgic. Wherever he goes he hears the rippling sound of the river. His eyes were shining when he was talking to me about all his catches. He told me, "Even now my heart leaps when I hold a big fish."

A huge amount of land belonging to his family was grabbed by the Rakhaines. There was one Muslim 'para' where they lived surrounded by twenty Mogh 'paras.' Their freedom of movement was severely restricted. He noticed many of them were subjected to various forms of extortion and arbitrary taxation, land confiscation, forced eviction and destruction of houses at the hands of the Buddhist Rakhaines. Rohingyas continue to be used as forced labourers in building roads and at the military camps. Their own house was set on fire by angry crowds allegedly instigated by the Buddhist monks. Rashid instantly turned pale remembering that incident. He told me that not more than five people can pray together even in the privacy of their homes. In Myanmar there is no freedom for anyone but for the Muslims it is even worse. Actually in the Arakan, violence against the Rohingyas is a way of life despite the fact that the Rohingyas are one of the largest ethno-religious minority groups in Myanmar. The military government still does not recognise the Rohingyas as a distinct ethnic group.

At the end of our conversation, Rashid started humming a Rohang song:

"Ara khandi khandi zibon khataisi mog bormar vitor
Tai alom sikhi na phorilam mog bormar boi
Moger phua dos chelasa the dhoctori kore
Musolmaner phua bhas kori phane khili beche."

[We pass our days crying in Myanmar
And so we hardly have time to learn and teach.
Children of Moghs become doctors
While Muslim children pass their days doing menial jobs].

Case No: 9

Case Title: "I have nothing else to do!"
Name of the Refugee: Khodeja
Status: Documented
Location: Nayapara
Age: 26
Project Student: Sheikh Shams Morsalin
Institution: Department of IR, University of Dhaka

It was raining quite heavily. The mud was almost up to the knee, but still I went through the narrow lane of the camp. I kept on walking. Hundreds of eyes were staring through the fences, asking—'who is this man?' I could hear their voices. I still went on and found the place where the Rohingyas live.

Khodeja's husband was not at home. She was breastfeeding her 11-month old son, the youngest one in the family. The number of children she had may sound quite incredible, but compared to other camp families, it was 'average'. Among her seven children, the 12-year-old, who was the eldest and also the smarter, received me cordially. She asked me to come in and sit down on an easy-chair, which was in fact the only furniture in the whole room. The 10 x 6 feet room was pretty neat and clean. I was in fact the dirtiest person with mud all over my body.

The first thing Khodeja told me was, "My husband is outside". I said, "I'm here to listen to you, not your husband". She smiled. Who knows whether she understood my language? The eldest girl noticed that her mother was not getting my dialect. She smartly started to play the role of an interpreter.

"How are you doing here?" I expected a bundle of complaints and allegations about the camp life from Khodeja. But surprisingly she said, "We are fine". "How come you are fine here?" I pointed out their house, their health, education, rationing and so on. She casually replied, "These are natural things", and added "everybody faces some difficulties in their lives". Her words sounded like she was very satisfied with her limited means.

Khodeja could not recall, when, how and why she came to Bangladesh. She only remembers that she came here some time in 1991-92 with her parents. Later she came to know from them that there was no peace in Burma. She also heard many other things from her neighbours about Burma, but she had little interest in those stories. "If conditions get better, will you return to Burma?" Khodeja quickly replied, "I do not know, whatever my husband says."

Being illiterate Khodeja spends most of her time at home. She married at the age of 13 and after that all she had done was produce children. Khodeja herself had no future plan at all; surprisingly she had no future plans for even her children. But the good thing was that five of her children were studying at the camp primary school. "Why did you decide to have so many children?" She blushed and said: "I have nothing else to do!"

Case No: 10

Case Title: Waiting for Suu Kyi
Name of the Refugee: Zakaria
Status: Undocumented
Location: Kutupalong
Age: 40
Project Student: A.S.M. Tarek Hassan Semul
Institution: Department of IR, University of Dhaka

I met Zakaria in the Kutupalong camp. He was wearing an off colour blue full sleeve shirt and a *lungi*. It was hard to tell which one was the real colour of the shirt, blue or white. Zakaria was tall, dark and middle aged with a small beard on his chin. He was carrying a folded grocery bag and an almost broken black umbrella in his hand. I asked him his name and he told me that his name is Zakaria and that his house is not far away. When I reached his home I literally crawled through the door to enter the house. After getting in it took me some time to see anything inside. The house was completely dark because firewood was being used for cooking inside the house. The fume made it dark. The floor was muddy because of the rain water. Two kids were sleeping on the muddy floor; one had no clothes on. Their mother for no reason started slapping them to wake them up. My request couldn't stop her from making room for us to sit. The house consisted of only one room, in length twelve feet and in width eight feet. Zakaria and his wife were very anxious with my sitting arrangement. I assured them that I am fine sitting on the floor.

I asked Zakaria if he would introduce his family members. Zakaria introduced his wife first. Her name was Laila. She was around 30 years, but she looked much older than her actual age. Poverty and the environment of the refugee camp made her so, I guessed. Giving birth to a lot of kids, malnutrition and the struggle for survival may have also contributed to Laila's ill health. She was wearing the traditional blouse, skirt and scarf. Her eyes were full of sadness and in a way reflecting the stress she was going through with her family. She was always trying to participate in the conversation in her own way along with her husband. But Zakaria was relentless in avoiding her, only when I was interrupting and giving her the attention, he understood that I am equally interested to listen to them both. Zakaria and Laila had six children; two of them died early, so they are now a six-member family. The age of the children ranged from three to twelve years, two girls and two boys. Malnutrition has taken its toll on the health of the children too. Their bellies looked fat but the bones in their bodies could easily be seen. I asked Zakaria to say something about their home in Myanmar and why they came to Bangladesh.

Zakaria used to live in the Koansimung village, Thana: Mongdu in the Akyab district of Myanmar. He had some cultivation land and a home there. He had to give away eighty percent of his harvest to the Myanmar government. There was very little left for him to feed his family. Like all other Muslim Rohingya males he was also made to do forced labour for the Myanmar army. He had to give his labour for the construction of roads so that the army could move easily; he also had to work as a carrier of army supplies and sometimes he gave sentry duty on behalf of the army to prevent any kind of insurgent activity. Most of his time went away for these unpaid jobs for the government so he had little time for work to feed his family. At that time he had six children and an eight-member family to feed. If someone denied giving free labour, they faced severe torture at the hands of the army, for instance, they were forced to lie down on a nailed wooden bed, hot water would be poured down their noses, they would be beaten up by steel rods, and guns would be banged on their heads. The Army and the NASAKA[1] sometimes just shot them; it really all depended on their will.

While Zakaria was explaining these horrific incidents, Laila was telling me how helpless she was when her husband was taken away for forced labour. There was no one to earn or to feed her children. Sometimes they were starving for a week and it was unbearable for her. When she was telling me these events her two hands were on her cheek and it seemed like those horrific memories kept coming back to her and she was just talking as a reflexive action induced by her husband's stories.

So under these circumstances Zakaria and Laila decided to flee to Bangladesh. Their decision was influenced by another incident which happened with their neighbour. The male member of that neighbouring family was shot dead by the army when working as a carrier for the army. The crime was simple, that man accidentally dropped the heavy supply from his head. So this event affirmed their decision that their lives are no more secure in Myanmar. At the same time many families were also escaping Myanmar and going to Bangladesh. So they thought in a Muslim country like Bangladesh they would have some place to live. One night in 1991[2] Zakaria and his family started towards the border on foot. The destination they had to reach was the bank of the river Naaf. They walked through the woods all night and hid in the hills during the day. After almost 48 hours of walking with their lives at risk, with almost no food and their six children they crossed the mountain at night and reached the bank of the river at twilight. They crossed the sea by boat with some other families and reached Bangladesh. They first came into the Marrissha camp. During their stay at the camp they were helped by the

1 The border security force of Myanmar.

2 By March–April 1991, the second major influx of Rohingya refugees started.

Red Cross. In that time they were enlisted by the UNHCR and the Bangladesh government as registered refugees recognised by the Bangladesh government. But in 1992 four refugees were killed by the police and the BDR in the Marrissha camp. From the camp authority, there was pressure on many other families including Zakaria's family for repatriation to Myanmar. They were told by the GoB that Myanmar is safe now for the Muslim Rohingya, so they should leave Bangladesh. There was also a fear that they might also be shot dead if they did not go. When they asked the UNHCR for their security they also encouraged them to go to Myanmar as UNHCR is not in a position to ensure their security in Bangladesh. Zakaria and Laila was also induced by the fact that they would get one *sari*, one *lungi*, half kilogram of *chira*[3], one kilogram of *gur* (molasses), one quilt and a sack of rice. So one day in the year 1992, with all these aid they decided to go back to Myanmar as it is no longer safe in Bangladesh as well. After going back to Myanmar it was no less of a torture, coming mainly from the Myanmar government. It was more severe for Zakaria's family as he had to work as day labourer for the army and at night he had to give sentry duty. So there was no time for him to earn and he again decided to escape as he heard many families are again fleeing to Bangladesh. So they fled to Bangladesh again in 1995. But they did not know that they will no longer be considered as registered refugees rather they would have a unique status of unregistered Rohingya refugees.[4]

In the second term in Bangladesh Zakaria and Laila kept shifting their home from one place to another to be able to feed their children. They also lived in a Bengali village, hiding their refugee identity. When their identity was discovered they were compelled to come back into the Kutupalong camp albeit as unregistered refugees. At this point, Laila brought their previous registration card given by the UNHCR and tried to seek my support, if I could enlist their names as 'registered' refugees. For them to enlist their names as registered refugees is the only objective of their life. Some will wonder why this is so important. That's because in a way it is a fine line between life and death to them. Those who are registered refugees are far better off than the unregistered. Registered get ration from the UNHCR regularly, they also get educational opportunities for their children; they have access to vocational training, library, community centre, health centre and so forth. But none of these facilities are available for the unregistered. Hearing all these from Zakaria and Laila I realised discrimination can exist even among the refugees. Zakaria was explaining to me that his family is solely dependent from his earnings as a day labour. Someday when he gets work his family can have food once as his earning is not more than 50 to 80 taka. Severe competition in the local job market for these kinds of jobs makes it really difficult for him to

3 Dried rice.

4 The GoB and the UNHCR closed the camps to additional Rohingya arrivals. Registration of the Rohingya refugees was completed by September 1992.

earn. The day when I was taking their interview, Zakaria told me he couldn't find any work for the last three days and his children and his wife did not have any food for the whole day. At that point of time I thought, I could help them, I have enough money to give them which would be enough to feed his family at least for two days. Then again I thought this generosity from my part would not solve the problem. Hundreds of other families are living the same life as Zakaria's. Besides Zakaria did not ask for money from me, he just wanted to say his story so I again concentrated on their story. Just before we came here, we visited schools for the kids of the camp and came to learn that they only get their primary education there. After that, for the kids it's over, they cannot dream of becoming a doctor or a teacher or anything else. But it cannot stop them from dreaming. Some of them told me they want to be a teacher, some engineer, so I was interested to know about the education of Zakaria and Laila's kids. They told me, as they are unregistered refugees their children have no access to the schools of the camp and I realised the harsh reality that these kids do not have the right to even dream. Laila was telling me that she tried to send them to school but they were sent back from the school so these kids were facing such discrimination from childhood, if some can call this a childhood. By looking at their eyes I do not know why, I felt ashamed and guilty for somehow taking away their childhood.

One of my objectives was to explore if the refugees are traumatised by the memories of home or is it worse here. I probably invaded their privacy unknowingly when I asked them about the death of their two children. At first, listening to my question both of them became silent for a while. I was trying to understand what was happening by keeping my eyes on Laila. I discovered tears rolling down her cheeks, her voice was getting muffled. She then told me how their two children died. The name of her eldest daughter was Rashida; she was married off at the camp when they came here for the second time. During the delivery of her first child, Rashida died in 2002. Zakaria was sobbing with his hand on his head and telling me that as they are unregistered refugees they couldn't take her to the health clinic, they did not have any money to take her to Cox's Bazar for better treatment. If they would have enough money it would be possible to save her. Then they told me about the other child, who died from jaundice. His name was Hossain and he was one and half years of age when he died. Local doctor told them it would take about 5000 taka to save their son's life. Zakaria was weeping and telling me that he couldn't manage even 100 taka to save his son. Then there was a pause, a dead silence. After a few moments, Laila broke the silence by telling me that if Suu Kyi was in power none of this would happen and then continued saying: "one day she will come and we'll all return home."

Case No: 11

Case Title: Better to kill us all by bombing!
Name of the Refugee: Ali
Status: Undocumented
Location: Near Kutupalong Refugee Camp
Age: 29
Project Student: Md Zafar Imam
Institution: Department of IR, University of Chittagong

I was a boy of ten or eleven. Still now I cherish those days in my heart which were full of happiness, especially in the harvesting season when we used to produce golden paddy. Every individual of our family worked together in the field enjoying thrashing and collecting paddy. After days of hard work in the field we used to become ecstatic to see the field full of golden coloured paddy. We started cutting paddy with great zeal and enthusiasm. After thrashing and finishing all other associated works we stored paddy in the granary. We also used to produce different types of vegetables including pumpkin, cucumber, turnip etc .We were passing our days with happiness. Those days were dreamlike. But this happiness diminished quickly as the racial persecution became severe.

In the mean time, my brother's father-in-law and his family decided to leave Burma because of persecution and insecurity. My elder brother also decided to leave Burma along with his father-in-law. After my brother left our family became vulnerable. We faced many problems including financial constraints. We were fined excessively by the oppressive government .The figure was unbelievable, it was 1 million taka. The consequence of my brother leaving without authorisation proved fatal for us. As we failed to pay the fine it became inevitable that we would be arrested and tortured. We were already threatened several times by the government militia forces. Panic seized on us. We left our home and found ourselves in an unfamiliar region. We hid ourselves for several months in that hostile territory. We heard that they burnt down our houses and ruthlessly demolished our properties. They began looking for us. We kept moving because it was not safe for us to stay in a place for long. We were terrified and ran like dog in fear of death. It was unbearable. At last seeing no hope of survival we decided to leave our motherland.

One dark night we started from Tomru (Burma) through dense forest land. We walked all night through the forest without stopping as we were afraid of being caught. It was morning when we reached a little village situated at the edge of Burma-Bangladesh border. We were all exhausted specially the women and children. The same night we ventured to cross the Burma- Bangladesh border. It was a daunting task on the part of us. There was always the possibility of getting killed while crossing the border. But we had no other alternative. If we stayed there (Burma) we would have to embrace painful death. Once we crossed the border we could at least survive. Fortunately we crossed the border without any hazards as we were led by some smugglers. We paid them for their service. After reaching Teknaaf I sold my wrist-watch in order to gain some money. Then I started for Lama where my elder brother had been living since 1991. Rest of my family member joined with my sister's family. My sister and her husband had come to Bangladesh a few years back. My sister and her husband left Burma because they were also in similar position.

After one year of my arrival in Bangladesh, I returned Burma through repatriation program. After returning Burma I stayed there about three years. Then I started a business of dry fish. That time my whole family was depended on my income. But most of the time military government forced me to work for them without wages. As a result my family suffered a lot. Sometimes they had to starve for days. Besides, I was not fed properly during forced labour. In the mean time our family had arranged marriage of my younger sister. It was compulsory in Burma to have permission for marriage. But for getting permission one had to bribe the authority even though it was not easy to get the expected permission. To avoid the hazard and save little money we simply shun the path of seeking permission. But the authority was informed by a spy. As a result the authority had imposed a fine amounting to 25 thousands taka for arranging marriage without permission. To avoid persecution we decided to leave Burma again .We set for Bangladesh on 3rd November 1995. No sooner had we reached the border than the NASAKA spotted us and fired at us. We ran for our life. But we had to suffer heavy loss as my younger brother was shot dead and my younger sister was caught by them .To date, we have no information what had happened to my ill-fated sister. We feared the worst as the NASAKA was notoriously known for their treatment of detainees.

In 1995 I came to Ukhiya and started to live here by renting a home from a local member named Bokther. I had to pay him 200 taka rent per month. I married three years ago. My wife's name is Sabekun Nahar. She was about twenty years then. She came to Bangladesh in 2003 along with her family in order to cure her illness. They were permitted to stay one month in Bangladesh. But they failed to return Burma within one month. So they did not return. After my marriage we started to live together in the same village. One day I was not home, the son of Bokther tried to abuse my wife. Fortunately she managed to save herself from being raped. Because of insecurity we came to Bangladesh. But the irony is that we are also not safe here. I tried to file a case against him. But local police did not take it. I did not get justice anywhere. So

I decided to leave the village. After leaving the village I came to Kutupalong refugee camp and started to live in the camp by renting a room from Rahim majhee. I had to pay Taka 300 as rent. But it was impossible for me to pay Taka 300 as rent. Besides police allow outside people to come and stay in the camp on a temporary basis in exchange of money. Camp authorities send people to jail whenever they suspect them of being outsiders. That is why we left the camp and came here (a place near Kutupalong refugee camp).Here I am suffering from various problems. There is no available source of pure drinking water, no latrine, etc. As an undocumented refugee I do not get ration. So we have to starve when I do not get work. Besides here we live in insecurity. A few days ago my wife was harassed by a documented woman, when she went to bring water from the tube-well of the camp. I complained to the majhee against the woman. But the majhee did not listen.

Even now I want to go back to Burma, provided a democratic government comes to power and abolish all the discriminatory laws against the Muslims. But at present it is important that the Bangladesh government takes immediate steps to mitigate our inhuman living conditions. We do not want to live like animals. Let us be documented in priority basis. If the government does not do this it will be better to kill us all by bombing!

Case No: 12

Case Title: Living like insects
Name of the Refugee: Hossain
Status: Documented
Location: Nayapara Refugee Camp
Age: 41
Project Student: Mohd. Amirul Islam
Institution: Department of IR, University of Dhaka

> *When I wake up in the morning and see the sun, I wish I could see the sun in my own country. I wish I could step down from my bed in my own land.*

My grandmother named me Hossain when I was born in 1977 in Arakan, Myanmar. I have seven brothers and two sisters. I was studying in class four in 1991. Between my village and my school, there was a Buddhist village. The Buddhist Mogh children always used to tease me and my schoolmates while passing through their village. They used to slap and beat us whenever we reciprocated their teasing. The chairman, member and other village officials were usually Buddhist Moghs. Due to this reason, we could not get justice from them when we complained about the Mogh children.

One evening at 4, I was coming back from school. When I was passing through their village, two Mogh children started teasing me. One of them called me, "you son of a bitch, come here and suck my foot." Hearing that, I just couldn't control myself and I ran to him and slapped him! As it was their village, 5 or 6 children came out of their home and started beating me up badly. It became tough for me to escape that place. An older, maybe 72 years old Mogh women came out and rescued me. I came back home and called all my family members to tell them what happened. I told them that we should leave Myanmar. I argued that I have no freedom, no right to move, no right to learn in the place that I was born! And if they do not, I'll leave alone. My father and one of my elder brothers told me to calm down and they went to the Mogh chairman of that Buddhist village to complain. But the Mogh chairman along with a member locked up my father and brother for three hours on charges that they had gone there to complain. Once my father and brother came back home, they decided to leave Myanmar as soon as possible. Five days later, my father and my uncle along with four other people of our village (who were kind of intellectuals among us) were arrested on the charge of smuggling; which was absolutely false. My uncle was accused of committing rape (!). The military authority of Myanmar told them to leave Myanmar and go to their original land which is Bangladesh. There is no place for Muslims in Myanmar, they said. After six days, all the villagers along with rest of my family members went to the military camp and begged the camp leader to release those who were arrested and we also decided that we'll leave the village as soon as possible. After making the commitment, the military authority released all of them.

By the end of 1991, we sold all our lands and houses. One night in early 1992 my family along with 26 other families of our village gathered in the Makundia border of Myanmar. We stayed there for one day. The interesting thing was that the authority at the Myanmar border did not bother or resist us while we crossed the border as they also wanted us to leave Myanmar. The next day we hired a boat (which was owned by a Buddhist) to cross the border. Bangladeshi border forces also did not resist us to cross the border. Finally we reached Shahpur Deep which is located at the end of Teknaf in Bangladesh. Then we hired a mini-bus to reach Dumdum Miah refugee camp. There we found many other refugees who had arrived earlier. After reporting to the Upazilla Nirbahi Officer (UNO), the latter made a list and provided us with a white identity card. The UNO showed very friendly attitude towards us. However, there were no ready made shelters at Dumdum Miah camp.

I got admission to Teknaf Jamia Madrasa. I revealed my identity as a refugee there. The Madrasa authority was least bothered about my nationality. They were very friendly. As a Muslim, they got me admitted there. I bore my educational expenses by selling my ration. In the Dumdum Miah camp, a person got 3kg rice, 250g split peas, 250g sugar, 250g salt and other essential things per week as ration. As I had 11 family members, I sold my portion of ration to some selected refugees inside the camp. They had connection with the Bengalis outside the camp and sold them a part of the ration at a little higher price. We stayed there for several years. Then the Government of Bangladesh (GoB) told us to leave the country. But we argued that we won't be able to return to Myanmar until the situation becomes favourable there. And then some of us were brought to the Nayapara Refugee Camp in 1996 and some were forced to go back to Myanmar. Interestingly, when we first came to Bangladesh government officials were very friendly, but gradually they became hostile.

Nayapara Camp was regarded as a "Punishment Camp". Refugees who refused to return to Myanmar were brought into this camp and punished. It was assumed by the authority that refugees will go back to Myanmar as they will be unable to tolerate the punishment. For instance, the camp authority dug a figure like "8" on the open field and told us to look at the sun and walk on the figure until we agreed to return to Myanmar. Those who couldn't bear this punishment agreed to go back to Myanmar.

On 20 July 1997 the remaining refugees at the camp, including myself, decided to revolt. But we decided to keep our protest non-violent. After discussing with all other refugees inside the camp, we decided to go for a hunger strike. We assumed that many high officials and international bodies will come to us to find out the reason for our 'non-violent' action. For several weeks we refused to receive any ration. We ate tree leaves, bananas and the like from the jungle. We sealed the camp to resist the local authority to enter the camp. Finally after 22 weeks many high level officials from the GoB and international bodies, including five high officials from Geneva, came to see us. We then submitted our demands to them which included:

1. We won't return to Myanmar until our problems are resolved there;
2. We have to be recognised as full citizens of Myanmar;
3. We need compensation for our lands and houses which we lost in Myanmar; and
4. We want Aung San Suu Kyi to be free.

The visiting officials assured us that they will fulfill our demands. But we asserted that their assurance has to be written. Unfortunately, they left us by saying that they will come back soon. Few days later some of them came back and requested us to receive the rations. But we kept on pressing for a written commitment. After 52 weeks, suddenly the police, the BDR, along with other security forces and local people, entered the camp and started firing at the refugees. They became very aggressive. All the male refugees left the place and hid in the hills and jungles. Only female refugees remained in the camp. Few days later, some men returned to the camp and were captured by the authority. The latter forced those refugees to take the rations. But surprisingly the camp authority did not provide us the rations that we refused to take for 52 weeks! However, after staying outside for several months, almost all the male refugees returned to the camp. Some also went back to Myanmar. I came back to the camp after three months.

In 2000 it was declared that forceful repatriation will not take place anymore. By 2005, a complete family profile was created. In 2006 we became entitled to receive various facilities from many non-governmental organisations. Resettlement process had started. But here I want to assert that if international communities implement our four demands then we do not need to be resettled, we'll be ready to go back to Myanmar. Who wants to live outside their home country forcefully? We have our sisters, brothers, sons, daughters and other near and dear ones who cannot see their future. How can we live in a situation like this? We cannot live here and we cannot even go there. What should we do? Live like insects? You tell me....

Case No: 13

Case Title: Son of the Soil
Name of the Refugee: Kalam
Status: Undocumented
Location: Chittagong
Age: 61
Project Student: Ashraful Azad
Institution: Department of IR, University of Chittagong

I was surprised after I heard about him. In spite of being a refugee, he became a high class industrialist in Bangladesh. None but he knows how challenging the path was. He is a very busy person, and often goes abroad. When I heard that he was coming to Chittagong for two days, I made an appointment with him.

We reached his residence sometime in the afternoon. It was a two storied building with high boundary walls. In front of the building there was an open lawn, covered with bricks. We were welcomed by Mohammed Ali. He is also a Rohingya and the General Secretary of Arakan Historical Society (AHS). We were seated in a small living room. After a while, Kalam entered the room. He wore a full sleeve shirt and a lungi. He was not more than 5′ in height and had a bearded face. Coming to us, he said that he is sorry for being late and would speak to us after the Asar prayer. After five minutes we were led to another room, more spacious and well furnished.

Kalam reappeared with his colleagues after the prayer and started talking to us spontaneously. He said, "You are students of university, but you know nothing about the Rohingyas, and that is our main problem." He then took a few seconds break and said, "One District Commissioner said that all the Rohingyas are illegal migrants, even those who came 100 years ago. These words are more repressive than the torture of Myanmar government. Rohingyas are being repressed for their Bengali identity. If Bengalis use such kind of words, where shall we go?" He continued: "You got your motherland readymade. You won't understand our feelings and sorrows. Nothing is greater than the land where one is born and grows up." At that time, two cats were roaming around. Pointing to them, he said, "These cats were born under my *almirah*. They don't want to leave this house. It you take them anywhere, they will come back here somehow or other. We are just like them. We also want to go back to our birthplace."

He said somewhat angrily, "Have we come out of the Bay of Bengal or dropped from the sky? Everyone has some soil, we too have. Please show us where our soil is, we'll go there." He added, "Actually there is no difference between the people of Chittagong and the Rohingyas of Arakan. We are all of the same origin. This artificial division was made by the British conspirators. After independence of Bangladesh, our leaders went to Sheikh Mujib. He said that the area where the Bengalis live is a part of Bangladesh. If he had been alive, our problem would have been resolved."

Then I asked him about his personal life and childhood. He said, "I was born in Maungdaw in 1947. We were seven brothers and six sisters. Our family migrated to East Pakistan in 1948. We again went back 6 months later. I started my education in Urdu medium in Maungdaw. I studied up to class eight".

"Only up to class eight, why?" I asked him.

"Actually I passed my childhood in many places. I grew up in Maungdaw, Teknaf, Chittagong, Karachi, Mecca, Medina, and in other towns", he replied.

He then said, "In the 60s, our family migrated to the Middle East. In 1962, when we boarded the ship bound for Saudi Arabia, we had a huge amount of money. Even I myself carried 6 lakh taka in my belt. At that time, anyone could get 'American citizenship' spending Tk. 50,000. We could have gone there. But no Rohingyas wanted to go to the USA. Rather they preferred to go to the holy lands like Mecca, Medina and Arab countries since we are Muslims. We lost our country but not our religion. In fact, before 1985, no Rohingyas went to Christian countries only for livelihood." He continued, "At present all of my five brothers and five sisters are established in Dubai. When we went there, Arab countries were not rich. We only went for the sake of our religion. Ninety per cent of the infrastructure in Mecca-Medina was done by the Rohingyas. But in documents, all are owned by Saudi citizens."

He also said, "In 1968, I went to Saudi Arabia again. Then I saw the 'Zamindars' of Maungdaw were working as hawkers in the streets of Mecca. At that time, I was offered Saudi nationality. But I didn't accept it. I came back as I wanted to do something for the Rohingyas."

"Now I have properties of several hundred crores (several billion) taka. If I am assured to live safely in my country, I will go there with a briefcase leaving everything here."

Then I asked him about the illegal Rohingyas who are living in the Middle East with Bangladeshi passport. He answered, "In the Middle East, Rohingyas get work permit as Burmese Muslims. But they don't have any passport as they do not belong to any state. So, they buy passport from Bangladeshi and Pakistani embassies. Taking the chance of the situation, embassy officials are taking 10,000 riyal per passport via brokers whereas it usually costs only 500 riyal. We don't know what the Rohingyas say about this problem. They have no platform to speak."

Finally I asked him what his opinion about the Bangladeshi people was. He took a few seconds to think and started cautiously, "We are suffering too much because (according to Burmese govt.) we are Bengalis. The Moghs who went to Burma in 1947 became Burmese as they are Buddhists. But we couldn't as we are Muslims. When we came to Bangladesh, we weren't recognised as Bangladeshis," he carried on, "If Arakan and Bangladesh were one; there would have been no scarcity in this region. Arakan is a highly resourceful place. Twenty per cent of the land of Arakan is left uncultivated for want of labourers. When I last went there in 1963, I saw the labourers from Chittagong working in the fields there. Arakan has a huge natural lake that can supply power for the whole of Bangladesh if power plants could be established. Arakan has more gases than Bangladesh. The British divided us so that we can't be on our own."

Case No: 14

Case Title: Dream Versus Sufferings: A Tale of A Woman
Name of the Refugee: Sabura
Status: Documented
Location: Kutupalong Refugee Camp
Age: 35
Project Student: Fatema Hossain Urmi
Institution: Department of IR, University of Chittagong

I saw two veiled women standing in front of the Camp-in-Charge's Office. I approached them to draw their attention. They responded with a cooperating gesture. I very politely asked them, "Can I talk to you?" One of them (later I came to know that her name was Sabura) opened the veil on her face and smilingly replied "yes, you can talk." I was encouraged by the polite response and quickly asked her, "Why did you come to the Camp-in Charge's-Office in this heavy rainfall?" Sabura told that her daughter gave birth to a child but the child's name was misspelled in the ration card issued by the Camp-in Charge. For this reason, she came to correct the spelling. I was surprised because the lady looks much younger and she already has a grand child! With a little hesitation I asked Sabura if she would take me to her home. She happily agreed but was worried at the same time. She got worried because it was raining and the roads leading to her house was full of mud. She wondered if I would be able to walk on this muddy path. I assured her that I would not mind walking with her on this muddy path.

I had to cross three drains full of dirty water. The muddy path was so slippery that I slipped and fell down twice. She picked me up from the ground. When I arrived at her residence I found myself completely wet with mud and dirt. Her home is pretty good. It is made with C.I. sheet and looks clean and tidy. I saw three of her daughters sitting inside the small house. When asked Sabura said, she has four daughters and one son. Her husband is sick and stays at home. I found her daughter sitting by her father with the new born baby in her lap.

Sabura came to Bangladesh with her mother in 1992 when she was only 18 years old. Her home was at Sitapurikha village under Busidong district in Myanmar. She was accompanied by her mother and brother. Sabura became deeply emotional when talking about her brother. Her brother was a young boy of 20, full of youthful vigor and spirited life. But then everything was not pleasant. Very often they were tortured by Nasaka members in Myanmar.

They didn't have any land of their own although they had few cows. They had to pay tax once the cows gave birth to calves. This taxation was not imposed on other Myanmar citizens except the Rohingya people, which is really cruel. The family, despite heavy torture and exploitation, stayed there mainly for the sake of their native land inherited from their ancestors. But one day her brother was picked up for forced labour. This inhuman forced labour was mandated for the Rohingya people only who incidentally are not paid for such labour. He was ordered to shift goods from one truck to another truck. One day he fell down on the ground as the load was beyond his capacity. Only for this reason, the brute Nasaka members shot him dead and dumped him on the road side. Nasaka members did not inform this to the family. For fear of torture the family members also did not contact the Nasaka members for the dead body.

Getting tremendously scared the family planned to cross into Bangladesh leaving behind their favourite native land. This tragic incident still haunts Sabura. They cannot exactly remember how long it took them to arrive at the border. May be they had walked for two or three consecutive days and nights at a stretch. After arriving at the bank of Naaf River they took a boat and crossed into Bangladesh. According to Sabura, at least 500 Rohingyas crossed the river and entered Bangladesh on that night.

Sabura at first moved to Teknaf with her mother and started working as a maid in the house of solvent family. Afterwards they moved to Kutupalong Camp. She got married during her stay in the camp. Few days later her mother died. Sabura eventually became mother of five children. She stayed home caring for the children while surviving with the supplied ration. I saw a fishing net hanging on the wall and asked her if she had bought it. She smilingly replied that she made it on her own. It costs Taka 250 to make a fishing net but she can sell it at Taka 500. Not a bad investment of money and labour!

She again comes back to her story. With great dreams she let her elder daughter marry a boy at the Refugee Camp. Her daughter was only 14 years old then. The bridegroom however disappeared soon after the wedding and no one could find out his whereabouts. Someone said he is imprisoned in Cox's Bazaar jail while others said he left for Saudi Arabia. Even his parents do not know his whereabouts. Few days ago she gave birth to a child. I looked at the daughter but she seems to be least interested in whatever her mother was saying. She simply had a vacant look. Sabura could not help shedding tears while talking about her daughter. Her other two daughters and also the son are studying in the school. I came to know that the school here is free up to class five. Students however can continue their studies after that but they have to pay fees. Sabura wants her son to study up to class X. And on completion of class X she wants to send her son abroad for further studies with the support of the UNHCR. Sabura thinks that her sufferings would end the day her son becomes fully established in life.

It was time to end the conversation and return back to my hotel, but Sabura stopped me as I started to move out: "You came from a distant land and you are working so hard, I will be happy if you have some snacks at my place," she said. Her motherly expression made me stop. I said I will only take a betel leaf, which I saw in her hand. She smilingly gave me the betel leaf and felt satisfied.

Case No: 15

Case Title: We Stay By Crying
Name of the Refugee: Rashid Ahmed
Status: Documented
Location: Kutupalong Refugee Camp
Age: 43
Project Student: Shaon Shyla
Institution: Department of IR, University of Dhaka

What comes to our mind when we think about a home, "our sweet home", definitely not that of a house which consists of 3`/2` door without windows. The house that I live in is almost like that. I remember the house where I was born which only brought grievances. Now I am in a place that is a long lane that has no turning. Now I fear that I shall die here. I often wonder how I am living here. It grieves me to know that there is no hope for democracy in my country. I do not want to understand democracy which is all about hope. A rose by any other name would smell as sweet. I want to know how far it is from today. Can you guess what I want? It is nothing but peace. The reason why I want it is crystal clear. The time of its arrival cannot be guessed. The military regime in Myanmar seems to be going on for eternity. Before I die, I intend to go to my country. Can a man live when his soul is dead? I do think that he will die. Whether we can return back to a peaceful Myanmar seems uncertain. I do not know when I shall return. All of us are keen that peace will be established. In Myanmar I was not able to do whatever I want or think right. I cannot express how depressed I am. No one can say how this will end. I think I'm safe in Bangladesh.

These words are not mine, but of a 43 year old Rashid Ahmed, an inhabitant of the village named Mujai at Rashidong thana in Akiab, resembling 27,000 Rohingya refugees who are living under protection at the southern part of the Bangladesh, whose MRC number is 48915, present resident of the Kutupalong camp .

I was born in an independent country. I had a dream to do something for my country. Suddenly my dreams stumbled when Buddhist Rakhaines (Maghs) became reckless. It is a matter of no importance to them that this is our forefathers' land. In my own country there is no place for me. Since birth the country that was mine, I had been banished from that which is truly very incredible to me. Nobody can avoid an inevitable event. That's why today I am here but I am not vindictive; one who wants revenge. I want only peace. Where we had once been living in peace and perfect amity now have to witness many often recurrent phenomenon of communal violence, social anarchy. The military regime has taken the whole country to the brink of devastation and has turned the land into a blood- bath. Now in Myanmar the voice of peace and communal harmony is a far cry.

He fled from Myanmar along with his four family members in 1992. At that time he was prevented by BDR in the border of Bangladesh and at last they were convinced through bribe. Because of Maghs, their life security was absent. He told me, "We were all under threat".

When I was talking to him he was very attentive. He was answering me whenever I asked any sort of question. According to my observation he had a good personality. Without a doubt this man is laconic.

He was a fisherman and he used to catch fish in a river called 'Ondying'. Still now he becomes nostalgic, an abstract sadness lies within him. Wherever he goes, he hears the rippling sound of the Ondying, because this river is very close to his heart. His eyes were shining when he was talking about his twelve big snares. He told me," Even now my heart leaps when I behold a snare". He became very emotional.

A huge amount of land of his family was grabbed by Rakhaines. There was one Muslim 'Para' where they lived surrounded by twenty Maghs' 'Para'. Their freedom of movement was severely restricted. He noticed many of them were subjected to various forms of extortion and arbitrary taxation, land confiscation, forced eviction and house destruction by Buddhist Rakhaines. Rohingyas continue to be used as forced labourers on roads and at military camps.

Their own house was set on fire by angry crowds allegedly whipped up by Buddhist monks. In the blink of an eye he turned very pale remembering that incident. He told me that not more than five people can pray together even in the privacy of their own homes. He said in Myanmar there is no freedom for anyone but for Muslims it's even worse. Actually in Arakan, violence against Rohingyas is a way of life despite the fact that the Rohingyas belong to Myanmar's largest ethno-religious minority groups. The military government still does not recognise the Rohingyas as a distinct ethnic group.

He asked me about Aung Sun Suki as if I do not know about her which proves his political consciousness. When I asked him about any happy, delightful memory; he fumed by questioning me, that an adolescent boy who was a witness of a horrible killing of his own community, of using Rohingyas as a shield against the opposition party by Myanmar government to protect themselves from shooting in" Khaichampre" , how dare I ask him about any joyful memory. He answered in a very rude manner and at that time he seemed to be a man with plenty of impudence.

Though it is strange but true that being a Rohingya he is not grieved, rather he feels proud to be an Arakanese Rohingya Muslim. This is very interesting. He feels proud about his ethnic identity marker. He has chosen his regional identity first, then his ethnic identity and lastly he placed his religious identity instead of Burmese identity.

Though maybe because of this shelter in Bangladesh, local Bengali people give names to the Rohingyas like Rashid Ahmed as" Bormaiya refugee". According to him they do it to humiliate Rohingyas. They abhor Rohingyas. For this reason he does not like local Bengali people. A belief which is generally held is not necessarily one which is true. This is why at the same time he also mentioned that it's not true that all Bengalis are bad. Most of the Bengalis dislike Rohingyas. When they go outside the camp they become victims of assault. There are incidents of physical abuse and threats by local Bengalis where they get support from the camp police and other forms of abuse, such as hitting the sole of the feet is included too.

But still there remains a big question – Will he never return back to his motherland?

The answer is like–

We want citizenship
We want human rights
We want democracy
We want compensation from government
We do not want to live a life of slavery
And last but not the least, peace in Myanmar is badly needed.

If all these requirements are fulfilled then I will return back home. Security must be ensured in Myanmar. Otherwise I would rather face many problems and struggle at a refugee camp instead of returning.

To express his feeling regarding oppression and persecution of Burmese government he started humming a Rohang song which is as follows:

"Ara khandi khandi zibon khataisi mog bormar vitor
Tai alom sikhi na phorilam mog bormar boi
Moger phua dos chelasa the dhoctori kore
Musolmaner phua bphas kori phane khili beche."

That means–

"We stay Myanmar by crying
Because impossible by us to learn and teach,
Education provided by government
If we win master degree impossible by us to get a job."

Bibliography

Books and Reports

Ahmed, Imtiaz, "Environmental Refugees and Environmental Distress Migration as a Security Challenge for India and Bangladesh," in: Brauch, Hans Günter; Grin, John; Mesjasz, Czeslaw; Krummenacher, Heinz; Chadha Behera, Navnita; Chourou, Béchir; Oswald Spring, Ursula; Kameri-Mbote, Patricia (Eds.): *Facing Global Environmental Change: Environmental, Human, Energy, Food, Health and Water Security Concepts*. Hexagon Series on Human and Environmental Security and Peace, vol. 4 (Berlin-Heidelberg-New York-Hong Kong-London-Milan-Paris-Tokyo: Springer-Verlag, 2009).

Ahmed, Imtiaz, "Refugees," in Vinay Lal and Ashis Nandy, eds., *The Future of Knowledge & Culture: A Dictionary for the 21st Century* (London and New Delhi: Penguin, Viking, 2005).

Ahmed, Imtiaz, "Globalisation, Low Intensity Conflict and Protracted Statelessness/ Refugeehood: The Plight of the Rohingyas", in John Tirman ed. *The Maze of Fear,* (N.Y: The Newpress, 2004).

Ahmed, Imtiaz, "Beyond Policing Refugees: Non-governmental Initiatives and Actions," *South Asian Refugee Watch*, Colombo and Dhaka, Vol. 1, No. 1 July 1999.

Ahmed, Imtiaz, "Limits of Civil Society: Rohingya Refugees, Locals and the Passage to Unsettlement," *South Asian Refugee Watch*, Colombo and Dhaka, Vol. 1, No. 1 July 1999.

Ahmed, Imtiaz, "Refugees and Security: The Experience of Bangladesh," in S.D. Muni and Lok Raj Baral (eds.), *Refugees and Regional Security in South Asia* (New Delhi, India: Konarak Publishers, 1996).

Ayoob, Mohammed, "The Third World Security Predicament: State Making, Regional Conflict and the International System", (London: Lynne Rienner, 1995).

Barnes, C., "Weaving the Web: Civil Society Roles in Working with Conflict and Building Peace" in Van Tongeren, P. ed. *People Building Peace II Successful Stories of Civil Society* (Boulder and London: Lynne Rienner, 2005).

Baumann, G., "Contesting Culture: Discourses of Identity in Multi-Ethnic London", (Cambridge: Cambridge University Press, 1996).

Burma Centre, "Between the Crocodile and the Snake", (Netherlands: Burma Centre, May 2003).

Burma Country Brief, "Drug Intelligence Brief", (Washington DC: Burma Country Brief, May 2002).

Becker, Gay and Others, "Memory, Trauma, and Embodied Distress: The Management of Disruption in the Stories of Cambodians in Exile", (Ethos, 2000).

Berkowitz, Morton, and Bock, P.G., "National Security" in David Sills ed. *International Encyclopedia of the Social Sciences*, (New York: Macmillan, 1968).

Brah, A., "Cartographies of Diaspora: Contesting Identities", (London and New York: Routledge, 1996).

Brass A., Paul, "Elite Competition and Nation-Formation", in Hutchinson John and Smith D. Anthony eds. *Nationalism*, (UK: Oxford University Press, 1994).

Burma Centre Netherlands, "Report of the Fact-finding Mission - April/May 2003", (Amsterdam: Burma Centre Netherlands, 2003).

Buzan, Barry, "People, States and Fear: An Agenda for International Security Studies in the Post-Cold War Era", (London: Harvester Wheatsheaf, 1991).

Concern, "DRAFT Nutrition survey in Kutupalong and Nayapara camps among the Rohingya Refugees", (Concern, November 2001).

Cummings, Joe and Wheeler, Tony, "Myanmar: A Lonely Planet Travel Survival Kit", (Hawthorn, Victoria: Lonely Planet Publications, 1996).

Das, Uttam Kumar, "Legal Dimension of Rohingya Refugee Issues: A Perspective from Bangladesh", *Draft Report*, (Dhaka: IOM—MRF).

D'Souza, Borther Jarlath, "Rohingyas: A Case for Human Rights Violation", (Dhaka: SHETU, 1992).

Eade, J., "Living the Global City: Globalisation as a Local Process", (London: Routledge, 1997).

Eade, J., "The search for wholeness: The construction of national and Islamic Identities among British Bangladeshis" in A.J Kershen ed. *A Question of Identity*, (UK: Ashgate Publishing, 1998).

Enloe, Cynthia, "Bananas, Beaches and Bases", (London: Pandora, 1993).

Feeny, Thomas, "Rohingya Refugee Children in Cox's Bazar, Bangladesh", (2001).

Fischer, M., "Civil Society in Conflict Transformation: Ambivalence, Potentials and Challenge", (Berlin: Berghof Research Centre for Constructive Conflict Management, 2006).

Gain, Philip, "Rohingyas: Who Really is their Friends", (Dhaka: SHETU, 1992).

Gardner, K., "Identity, age and masculinity amongst Bengali elders in East London", in A.J Kershen ed. *A Question of Identity*, (UK: Ashgate Publishing Ltd., 1998).

Geertz, Clifford, "The Interpretation of Cultures", (London: Fontana, 1973).

Gilroy, P., "Diaspora and the detours of identity", in K. Woodward ed. *Identity and Difference: Culture, Media and Identities*, (London: Sage, 1997).

Gingrich, A., "Conceptualising identities: Anthropological Alternatives to Essentializing difference and Moralizing about Othering", in *Grammars of Identity/Alterity: A Structural Approach*, (London and New York: Berghahn Books, 2004).

Goldstein, Jashua S, "International Relations", (Singapore: Pearson Education, 2004).

Hall, D.G.E, "A History of Southeast Asia", (London: Macmillan, 1940).

Hall, S., "New Ethnicities" in J. Donald and A. Rattansi eds. *Race, Culture and Difference*, (London: Sage, 1996).

Hauchler, Ingomar and Kennedy, Paul M., "Global Trends", (New York: Continuum Publishers, 1994).

Htut, Zaw Min, "Human Rights Abuses and Discrimination on Rohingyas", (Japan: BRAJ).

Iftekharuzzaman, "Bangladesh: A Weak State and Power", in Muthiah Alagappa ed. *Asian Security Practice: Material and Ideational Influences,* (London: Stanford University Press, 1998).

Jervis, Robert, "Perception and Misperception in International Politics", (Princeton: Princeton University Press, 1976).

Jilani, AFK, "Human Rights Violation in Arakan".

Karim, Abdul, "The Rohingyas: A Short Account of their History and Culture", (Chittagong: Arakan Historical Society, 2000).

Kershen, A.J., "A Question of Identity", (UK: Ashgate Publishing Ltd., 1998).

Lewa, Cgris, "IDP's In Burma", in C. R. Abrar and M P Lama eds. *Displacement within Borders: The IDP's of Bangladesh and the Region,* (Dhaka: RMMRU, 2003).

Lintner, Bertil, "Burma in Revolt: Opium and Insurgency since 1948", (Chiang Mai: Silkworm Books, 1999).

Massey, D., "Space, Place, and Gender", (Minneapolis: University of Minnesota Press, 1994).

Maung, S.L., "Burma: Nationalism and Ideology", (Dhaka: UPL, 1989).

May, S., "Language and Minority Rights: Ethnicity, Nationalism and the Politics of Language", (Edinburgh: Pearson Education Ltd., 2001).

Medicines Sans Frontiers, "10 years for the Rohingya Refugees in Bangladesh: Past, Present and Future", (Holland: Medicines Sans Frontiers, 2002).

Miall, H., Ramsbotham, O. and Wodhouse, T., "Contemporary Conflict Resolution", (Cambridge: Polity, 1999).

Nicolaus, P., "A Brief Account on the History of the Muslim Population in Arakan", (Mimeo, 1995).

Rashid, Syeda Rozana, "A Comparative Study on Vulnerability and Coping Mechanism Between Rohingya Refugee and Chakma IDP Women", (Dhaka: BFF, 2005).

Razzak, Abdur & Haque, "Mahfuzul, A Tale of Refugees: Rohingyas in Bangladesh", (Dhaka: The Centre for Human Rights,1995).

Shew Lu, Maung, "Burma: Nationalism and Ideology", (Dhaka: University Press Limited, 1989).

Steinberg, David I., "Constitutional and Political Bases of Minority Insurrections in Burma" in Lim Joo-Jock and S. Vani eds. *Armed Separatism in Southeast Asia,* (Singapore: Institute of Southeast Asian Studies, 1984).

Tocci, Nathalie, "The European Union, Civil Society and Conflict Transformation", (MICROCON Policy Working Paper 1, 2008).

Twigger-Ross, C.L., Bonaiuto, M. & Breakwell, G., "Identity Theories and Environmental Psychology" in M. Bonnes, T. Lee & M. Bonaiuto eds. *Psychological Theories for Environmental Issues,* (Aldershot, England: Ashgate, 2003).

UNHCR, "Handbook on Voluntary Repatriation: International Protection", (Geneva: UNHCR, 1996).

WFP, "Vulnerability Survey of Refuges: September-October 1999", (WFP, 2000).

Wipperman, Tom & Haque, Mahbubul, "Between A Rock and Hard Place: The Rohingya of Bangladesh and Burma", (Dhaka: Neeti Gobeshona Kedro, 2007).

Newspapers and Journals

Mike Thomson, "The Forgotten Rohingyas", *News Today*, 14 March 2006.

Dr. Uttam Kumar Das, "Bangladesh's Obligation to refugee Protection", *The Daily Star*, 2 July 2005.

"The Blood Ties That Bind", *Newsweek*, 28 October 2002.

"Tactics Change, Smuggling Goes on", *Narinjara News*, 6 October 2002.

Udatta Bikash, "Why Bangladesh Needs Refugee Law", *The Daily Star*, 21 June 2008.

Lintner, Bertil, "Tension Mounts in Arakan State", *Defense Weekly*, 19 October 1991.

Rahman, Mohammod Asikur, "Bangladesh Foreign Policy Survey", *BIISS*, Vol. 7, No.1, (June-August, 2006).

Grosby, Steven, "The Verdict of History: The Inexpugnable Tie of Primordiality", *Ethnic and Racial Studies*, Vol. 17, No.1, (1994).

Toyota, M., "Contested Chinese Identities among Ethnic Minorities in the China, Burma and Thai Borderlands", *Ethnic and Racial Studies*, Vol. 26, No. 2, (2003).

Bloul, R., "Beyond Ethnic Identity: Resisting Exclusionary Identification", *Social Identities*, Vol. 5, No. 1, (1999).

Hauge, A. L., "Identity and Place: A Critical Comparison of three Identity Theories", *Architectural Science Review*, Vol. 50, No. 1, (2007).

Maluwa, Tiyanjana, "The Refugee Problem and the Quest for Peace and Security in Southern Africa", *International Journal of Refugee Law*, Vol. 7, No. 4, (1995).

Sakiko, Fukuda-Parr, "Gender, Globalisation and New Threats to Human Security", *Peace Review*, Vol. 16, No. 1, (March).

HRWA, "Burma: The Rohingya Muslims: Ending a Cycle of Exodus", *Human Rights Watch Asia*, Vol. 8, No. 9, (1996).

Ahmed, Imtiaz, "Small Arms & Subaltern Globalisation", *CODESRIA Bulletin*, Nos. 1 and 2, (2004).

Arakan Historical Society, "The life and living of Rohingyas: Problems and Solutions", *Arakan Historical Society Annual Magazine*, (2001-2003).

Altsean, Burma, *Report Card: Balancing Act*, March 2003.

The Daily Cox's Bazaar, 18 May, 2008.

Banglar Jamin (Cox's Bazar, Chittagong), 8 June, 2008.

The *Ajker Desh Bidesh*, 4 June, 2008.

The Monthly Rohingya Review, October 31, 2008.

The *Daily Ittefaq*, 19 November, 2004.

The *Daily Ittefaq*, 17 September, 2007.

The *Daily Prothom Alo*,22 November, 2002.

The Daily Star, June 21, 2008.

The *Dainik Bhorer kagoj*,19 January, 2000.

Internet Sources

Chan, Aye, "The Development of a Muslim Enclave in Arakan (Rakhine) State of Burma (Myanmar)", *SOAS Bulletin of Burma Research*, Vol. 3, No. 2, (Autumn 2005), Available at: http://web.soas.ac.uk/burma/3.2files/03Enclave.pdf

Siddiqui, Habib, "A Long History of Injustice Ignored: Rohingya: The Forgotten People of Our Time", sited in: http://www.islamawareness.net/Asia/Burma/ro_article003.html

Institute for Conflict Management, "South Asian Intelligence Review", Vol. 2, No. 38, (2004), Available at: http://www.unsystem.org/SCN/archives/nics01/index.htm

"Forgotten People: The Rohingyas of Burma", Available at: www.safhr.org/refugee_watch18_4.htm

Morshed, Kaiser, "Bangladesh—Burma Relations", Available at: http://www.idea.int/asia_pacific/burma/upload/chap2.pdf

Human Rights Watch, "Rohingya Refugees in Bangladesh: The Search for a Lasting Solution", Available at: http://www.hrw.org/reports/1997/bangladesh/

"The Search for Durable Solutions", Available at : http://www.hrw.org/reports/ 2000/burma/burma 005-05.htm

"29 unregistered refugees die in Leda camp in two months", 5 September 2008, Available at: www.kaladanpress.org

"Rohingya Refugees", *The Daily Star*, 11 October 2008, Available at: http://www.thedailystar.net/story.php?nid=25644

Wikipedia, "International Community", Available at: http://en.wikipedia.org/wiki/International_community

Reliefweb, "Canada is first country to resettle Rohingya refugees from Bangladesh", Available at: http://www.reliefweb.int/rw/rwb.nsf/db900SID/EGUA-72FPN6?OpenDocument

"Address to the United Nations High Commission for Refugees on World Refugee Day 2008", Available at: http://www.minister.immi.gov.au/media/speeches/2008/ce080620.htm

Arakan Rohingya National Organisation, "First batch of Rohingya refugees resettled in New Zealand", Available at: www.rohingya.org/index.php?option=com_content&task=view&id=191&Itemid=28

Human Rights Documentation Unit, "Burma Human Rights Yearbook 2006", Available at: http://www.ncgub.net/BHR Y/2006/Refugees.html

"Monitoring and Evaluating Refugee Camps in Asia", Available at: www.state.gov/g/prm/rls/65215.htm

"Rohingya Refugees", Available at: http://www.aliran.com/index.php?option=com_content&view=article&catid=34:2007&id=254:rohingya-refugees-dilemma-remains-unsolved

VOA, "ASEAN Head Says New Charter Will Put Pressure on Burma", Available at: http://www.voanews.com/english/archive/2007-07/2007-07-24-voa25.cfm?CFID=245737009&CFTOKEN=10397856

Burma Review, "ASEAN Charter and Burma's Democratic Agenda", Available at: http://burmareview.com/2007/07/29/lost-promises-of-asean-asean-charter-and-burma%E2%80%99s-democratic-agenda/

Europa, "The EU's Relation with Myanmar", Available at: http://ec.europa.eu/external_relations/myanmar/intro/index.htm

Tamen, Anais, "The European Union's sanctions related to Human rights: the case of Burma/Myanmar", Available at: http://www.burmalibrary.org/docs/Memoire-AT.htm#_Toc54419312

"EU Provides 3.9 million Euros for the Rohingya Refugees", Available at: http://www.mizzima.com/component/content/archive.html?year=2007&month=12

MSF, "10 years for the Rohingya Refugees in Bangladesh", (2002), Available at: www.doctorswithoutborders.org/publications/reports/2002/rohingya_report.pdf

WFP, "Assistance to the refugees from Myanmar", (2005), Available at: www.wfp.org/operations/current_operations/project_docs/100453.pdf

Marchetti, R. and Tocci, N., "Conflict Society and Human Rights", (2007), Available at: http://www.luiss.it/shur/wp-content/uploads/2007/10/shurwp03-07.pdf

"Seminar held in Chittagong on Rohingya refugee problem on May 19, 2008", Available at: http://www.kaladanpress.org//index.php?option=com_content&task=view&id =1335&Itemid=2

Phayre, A. P., "History of Burma", quoted in C.R. Abrar, *Repatriation of Rohingya Refugees*, (London: 1883), Available at: http://burmalibrary.org/docs/Abrar-repatriation.htm

"World Refugee Survey: Country Reports, Bangladesh", Available at: http://www.refugees.org

http://epic.org/privacy/terrorism/hr3162.html

http://www.mizzima.com/news/regional/1021-rohingyas-in-dire-straits-csw.html

http://www.satp.org/satporgtp/sair/Archives/2_38.htm

www.cidcm.umd.edu/mar/chronology.asp?groupId=77501 - 48k

http://condor.depaul.edu/~rrotenbe/aeer/aeer13_1/Olujic.html

www.burmalibrary.org/docs/HRDU2003-04/Forced%20Labours.htm

www.unhcr.org/publ/PUBL/44b5021d2.pdf

http://www.undp.org/cpr/we_do/armed_violence.shtml - 21k

Index